HOTEL/MOTEL DEVELOPMENT

ULI–the Urban Land Institute

Hotel/Motel Development

Laventhol & Horwath

Principal Authors
David E. Arnold
Daniel W. Daniele
John M. Keeling
Nancy H. Landino
Christopher E. Lee
James D. Noteware

Contributing Author
W. Paul O'Mara, ULI

ABOUT ULI– THE URBAN LAND INSTITUTE

ULI–the Urban Land Institute is an independent, nonprofit research and educational organization incorporated in 1936 to improve the quality and standards of land use and development.

The Institute is committed to conducting practical research in the various fields of real estate knowledge; identifying and interpreting land use trends in relation to the changing economic, social, and civic needs of the people; and disseminating pertinent information leading to the orderly and more efficient use and development of land.

ULI receives its financial support from membership dues, sales of publications, and contributions for research and panel services.

James A. Cloar
Executive Vice President

ULI STAFF

Frank H. Spink, Jr. . . . . Senior Director, Publications
W. Paul O'Mara . . . . Project Manager
Ann Lenney . . . . Editor
Robert L. Helms . . . . Staff Vice President, Operations
Regina P. Agricola . . . . Production Manager
Melinda A. Bremmer . . . . Art Director
M. Elizabeth Van Buskirk . . . . Artist
Christopher J. Dominiski . . . . Artist

Library of Congress Catalog No. 84-50901
ISBN 0-87420-629-4

Recommended bibliographic listing:
Laventhol & Horwath. *Hotel/Motel Development*. Washington, D.C.: ULI–the Urban Land Institute, 1984.

ULI Catalog Number HD-1

Printed in the United States of America

REVIEW COMMITTEE FOR HOTEL/MOTEL DEVELOPMENT

CONTENTS

Introduction 1

Chapter 1. Historical Perspective 3

A Singular Form of Income-Producing Property 3
Community Impact 4
General Factors Affecting Growth of the Hotel Industry 5
Profile of the Industry After World War II 7
Factors Affecting Growth and Change Since 1950 9
Diversification and Evolution of the Industry 11
The 1980s Setting 12

Chapter 2. Travel and Markets 17

Market Segmentation 18
Fluctuations in Demand 19
Supply-Induced Demand 22
A Caution 23
The Magnitude of Future Travel 24

Chapter 3. Product Response to Markets 27

Downtown Facilities 27
General Characteristics 27
Convention Hotels 28
Commercial Hotels 31
Luxury Hotels 31
Downtown Facilities in Smaller Cities 32
Resort Hotels 33
General Traits 33
Chain Resort Hotels 34
Condominium Resort Operations 35
Highway/Interstate Facilities 36
Suburban Facilities 37
Airport Hotels 37
Economy Facilities 39
All-Suite Facilities 42
Executive Conference Centers 45
Multitiered Marketing Strategies 47

Chapter 4. The Development Process 51

An Overview of the Development Process 51
Conceptualization, Planning, and Initiation 51
Feasibility Analysis 52
Commitment 53
Design and Construction 54
Management/Operation 54
Conceptualization, Planning, and Initiation 55
Feasibility Analysis 59
Assessing Market Support 59
Projecting Revenues 64
Projecting Operating Costs and Expenses 67
Preparing a Cash Flow Statement 68

Determining Preliminary Development Costs 68
Determining Preliminary Financing Structure 68
Commitment 69
Design and Construction 73
Management/Operation 76

Chapter 5. Financing in the Lodging Industry 79

Major Sources of Financing 80
Institutional Lenders 81
Institutions Acting As Intermediaries 83
Syndications 84
Developers 85
Hotel Operating Companies 85
Brokers and Mortgage Bankers Acting As Intermediaries 86
Government 86
Selecting the Proper Financing Method 88
Preparing a Loan Package 90
Criteria for Evaluating the Financing Package 91
How to Finance that Unworkable Deal 92
Savings Institution 92
Insurance Company 93
Syndication 94

Chapter 6. Trends in Hotel Development 113

Supply and Demand 113
Major Influences on Hotel Development 114
Future Trends 117
Product Diversification 117
The Increase in Franchise Opportunities 118
The Sunbelt Growth Corridor 118
The Upgrading and Diversification of Products and Services 118
Retirement Inns 120
International Hotel Development 120
Downsizing 120
The All-Suite Concept 121
Financing 121
Personalized Guest Services 122

Chapter 7. Case Studies 125

◆ Chain Luxury Hotel—Sheraton Grande—Los Angeles, CA 127
◆ Independent Luxury Hotel—The Queen Anne—San Francisco, CA 133
◆ Independent Resort Hotel—Buena Vista Palace—Walt Disney World Village, FL 139
◆ Executive Conference Center—Scanticon-Princeton—Princeton, NJ 145
◆ Suburban Company-Owned Hotel—Holiday Inn—Nashville, TN 153
◆ Suburban Franchise Hotel—Holiday Inn—Westlake, OH 157
◆ Economy Hotel—Comfort Inn—Woodbridge, VA 163
◆ Economy Hotel—Super 8 Lodge—Great Falls, MT 169
◆ Economy Hotel—Signature Inn—Castleton, IN 173
◆ All-Suite Suburban—Granada Royale Hometel—Bloomington, MN 179
◆ Multitiered Marketing Strategy—Ramada Renaissance—Atlanta, GA 183

Appendices 189

Appendix A: Selected List of Hotel Chains 191
Appendix B: Preliminary Development Commitment Agreement 192
Appendix C: Unnegotiated Management Agreement 196
Appendix D: Marriott Corporation Hotel Management Agreement 204

LIST OF FIGURES

1-1 Lodging Properties by Size Category in 1948 6
1-2 Region Identification Map 8
1-3 Lodging Properties and Rooms by Region of the Country
in 1948 8
1-4 Population Growth and Shifts 10
1-5 Interstate Highway Miles Completed 10
1-6 Vehicles Registered in the United States 10
1-7 Air Passenger Growth 10
1-8 Types of Hotels, By Selected Development Criteria 13
1-9 Lodging Properties by Size Category in 1981 14
1-10 Occupancy Trends in the U.S. Lodging Industry 14
1-11 Lodging Properties and Rooms by Region of the Country
in 1981 14
2-1 Market Segmentation 19
2-2 Typical Profiles for Selected Demand Segments of
Destination Travelers 20
2-3 Quarterly Distribution of Person-Trips, 1981 21
2-4 U.S. Nationwide Seasonal Adjustment Factors 21
3-1 Some Facilities, Amenities, and Services Available
at Major Downtown Hotels 28
3-2 Operating Statistics for Center City Properties 29
3-3 Composition of Sales for Center City Properties 29
3-4 Market Data for Center City Properties 29
3-5 Market Data for Resort Properties 34
3-6 Operating Statistics for Resort Properties 34
3-7 Composition of Sales for Resort Properties 34
3-8 Operating Statistics for Highway Properties 36
3-9 Market Data for Highway Properties 36
3-10 Composition of Sales for Highway Properties 37
3-11 Market Data for Suburban Properties 38
3-12 Operating Statistics for Suburban Properties 38
3-13 Operating Statistics for Airport Properties 39
3-14 Market Data for Airport Properties 39
3-15 Return on Total Assets Comparison 41
3-16 Market Data for Economy Properties 42
3-17 The U.S. Budget Lodging Industry Dollar, 1981 43
3-18 Profiles of Selected All-Suite Hotels in
Washington, D.C. 44

3-19 Executive Conference Centers: Percentage of Rooms
Occupied by Market Segment 47
3-20 Executive Conference Centers: Profile of a Typical
Meeting 47
3-21 Chain Multitiered Brand Marketing Strategies 48
4-1 The Hotel Development Process 52
4-2 The Five Phases of the Hotel Development Process 54
4-3 Sources of Business for the U.S. Lodging Industry
in 1981 61
4-4 Estimated Lodging Demand Base and Market Segmentation
for a Proposed 275-Room First-Class Hotel 63
4-5 Typical Number of Rooms in Specific Hotel Categories 64
4-6 Percentage of Fair Share: Summary of Penetration Rates
for a Proposed 275-Room Hotel 65
4-7 Sources and Uses of Funds: 1982 U.S. Lodging
Industry 66
4-8 General Guidelines on Range of Fixed and Variable
Expenses by Category 68
4-9 Ratios To Total Sales for the U.S. Lodging Industry,
1981 70
4-10 Statement of Projected Cash Flow From Operations, Before
Debt Service and Income Taxes, For a Proposed
200-Room Hotel 72
4-11 Typical Development Costs Per Hotel Room, 1983 73
4-12 Space Allocation Guidelines for Hotel Facilities 74
5-1 Developer Nonrecourse Mortgage 96
5-2 Developer Recourse Mortgage 98
5-3 Eleven Percent Nonrecourse Mortgage With a 50 Percent
Kicker 100
5-4 Eleven Percent Nonrecourse Mortgage With a 14.5
Percent Second Mortgage and a 50 Percent Kicker 103
5-5 Syndication With an 11 Percent Nonrecourse Mortgage
and a 50 Percent Kicker 106
5-6 Syndication With an 11 Percent Nonrecourse Mortgage,
a 14.5 Percent Second Mortgage, and a 50 Percent
Kicker 109
6-1 Average Annual Increase in Guest Rooms 115
6-2 Lodging Guest Rooms Added, 1960–1982 115

ABOUT THE AUTHORS

Laventhol & Horwath (L & H) is one of the largest diversified accounting, tax, and consulting firms in the United States. Since 1915, L & H has provided a wide range of analytical, financial, management, and operational advice and services to the lodging industry. L & H publishes an annual report on hotel operations entitled *U.S. Lodging Industry*; the 1983 report was the 51st edition.

David E. Arnold is a senior principal in the executive office of Laventhol & Horwath in Philadelphia. He is the national Management Advisory Service partner and served as L & H project manager for this publication. Arnold has 12 years of diverse experience in real estate development planning, specifically in hotel operations, marina operations, and development planning of hotels, conference and convention centers, and retail, mixed-use, office, and residential projects. He is the author of L & H's annual publication, *The Executive Conference Center: A Statistical and Financial Profile*. Arnold's education has concentrated in economics and hotel administration; he holds a B.S. from Cornell University.

Daniel W. Daniele is a manager in L & H's Chicago office with over four years of experience in performing a wide variety of services such as site selection, market analysis, and financial projections for hotels. In addition, Daniele developed and coordinated L & H's first annual *U.S. Budget Lodging Industry* study. He received his B.A. degree in hotel, restaurant, and institutional management from Michigan State University and his M.B.A. degree from the College of St. Thomas.

As partner in charge of the Houston office's consulting practice, **John M. Keeling** has provided real estate advisory services to developers, financial institutions, and government agencies in Texas and Louisiana for the past six years. Keeling is an active member of the International Council of Shopping Centers and of the Texas Hotel & Motel Association, and serves on the Construction Panel of the Houston Chamber of Commerce. Keeling received his M.B.A. from Michigan State University.

Nancy H. Landino, a manager in L & H's Washington, D.C., office, has conducted and supervised numerous feasibility and market studies for proposed lodging facilities since joining L & H in 1973. Landino has published several articles and has been a guest lecturer at a number of universities and for the Educational Institute of the American Hotel & Motel Association. Landino holds a B.A. degree from Grove City College and an M.B.A. from Florida State University.

Christopher E. Lee, a manager in the Los Angeles office of L & H, brings with him extensive experience in the planning, development, and management of a wide variety of real estate projects. Lee has published several articles, has been a keynote speaker at several conferences, and has recently served on a special governor's task force to formulate a 10-year, statewide plan for the development of California's outdoor resources. Lee received a B.S. degree from San Diego State University, an M.S. degree from San Jose State University, and a Ph.D. in management and organization development from United States International University.

As national director of L & H's Real Estate Advisory Services, **James D. Noteware** has been involved in many real estate consulting assignments. Noteware has appeared as a keynote speaker at several national real estate conferences, is the author of a major paper on construction economics, and was a contributing author to a ULI publication entitled *Large-Scale Development: Benefits, Constraints, and State and Local Policy Incentives*. Noteware received a Bachelor's degree from Stanford University and an M.B.A. degree from the Wharton School of the University of Pennsylvania.

Contributing author **W. Paul O'Mara** has been employed by the Urban Land Institute since 1974. Currently program director, he is in charge of the housing-related research for the Institute. He is the author of three books published by ULI and is working on a fourth, on rental housing. The author of numerous articles on land use planning and development, he serves as executive editor of *Urban Land* magazine. Before joining ULI, O'Mara was with the Chicago-based American Society of Planning Officials. He is a graduate of the University of Notre Dame, with an M.S. in environmental design.

FOREWORD

Innkeeping has changed dramatically since 1948, when the lodging industry consisted almost entirely of independently owned and operated properties. Hotels with fewer than 50 rooms dominated the market. At that time, the typical hotel was located in an urban setting near the railroad station and the downtown business district.

Today, the hotel industry consists of many types of hotels from coast to coast and around the world, in various sizes and shapes, ranging from 20- to 30-room inns to large convention hotels. In the last 30 years, the great majority of hotels have been developed as freestanding projects. They have, however, been developed near major downtown complexes, residential projects, shopping centers, and industrial and office parks. Recently, however, several hotels have been included as integral parts of mixed-use developments.

Except for a brief discussion of motels in the 1968 *Community Builders Handbook,* a mention of hotels in the *Downtown Development Handbook,* and several articles in *Urban Land* magazine, ULI has published relatively little on the subject of hotel development. This has probably been attributable to the special nature of hotels, which, on the one hand, are real estate in that they consist of land and bricks and mortar, but on the other hand, require an unusually high degree of specialized management expertise in order to succeed.

The idea for this book originated at the Commercial and Retail Development Council's executive group session at ULI's 1980 spring meeting in Honolulu. Don Riehl, chairman of the Council, appointed a steering committee to define the need for and the scope of a projected publication on hotel development.

Recognizing that hotel development is a highly specialized field, ULI anticipated that the steering committee, which consisted of members experienced in hotel development, would write the book, with assistance from ULI staff. When that course proved infeasible, ULI reached an agreement in 1983 with the national consulting firm of Laventhol & Horwath to prepare a manuscript on hotel development.

To enhance the timeliness and scope of this book, a review committee of ULI executive group members experienced in hotel development reviewed the manuscript before publication. While unanimity of opinion was neither sought nor obtained regarding content, the book does reflect the views of a body of experienced professionals who gave freely of their time to participate in its preparation.

In the past five years, many new concepts in the hotel industry have been developed and old ones expanded. Overnight accommodations that suit the needs of almost any type of traveler are available in almost every metropolitan area. All-suite hotels, budget hotels, rehabilitations and adaptive-use projects, condotels, and timesharing facilities exemplify the specialization that is now occurring in the hotel industry. This trend toward specialization will continue, and lodging will more and more specifically target particular market segments. Newer products will appear as markets continue to change; but the process outlined in this book should remain constant for some time.

W. Paul O'Mara
Program Director

INTRODUCTION

The authors have prepared this book in response to the dramatic changes that have occurred since the mid-1960s in the scope, purpose, and complexity of hotel development in this country. These changes occurred because of the rapid evolution of both the market's perception of its need for hotels, and the development community's attraction to the profitability of successful hotel development and ownership.

Starting from its origins as transient lodgings for railroad travelers and as focal points for downtown social activities, the hotel industry has evolved into a sophisticated web of hotel chains, specialized management, and diversified types of properties for different locations and purposes. This diversification has allowed the industry to serve all segments of the traveling public.

The hotel industry has divided itself into four primary functions: development; ownership; franchising; and management. Although the development process constitutes the main subject of this book, the authors are aware that an understanding of the various processes involved in a hotel's operation requires an appreciation of the decisions and judgments that must be made while the project remains only a concept.

Financing for the hotel industry can be more difficult than for other forms of property because of several factors:

✦ The lodging industry really comprises a series of businesses, all of which may be contained in one hotel struc-

ture. These may range from lodging and food and beverage services, to retailing and recreation.
✦ The value of the property depends upon the success of these businesses on a combined basis.
✦ The high fixed costs, high operating leverage, and volatile nature of the income stream involve a high risk/high reward situation.
✦ Management and ownership often represent separate and discrete functions.

All of these factors can usually be accommodated by a sophisticated development and management team. Proper control of the risk elements involved can yield returns that are high, relative to those of other forms of real estate investment.

Currently, the hotel industry is experimenting with new products that should accomplish wider development objectives than those accomplished by the traditional freestanding project. Hotels, accordingly, are increasingly becoming integral components of downtown redevelopment areas, resort communities, office parks, mixed-use projects, and themed attractions. Therefore, an understanding of how hotels work in the marketplace represents a requirement for the entire development community.

The book proposes to discuss the intricacies of the development process as currently practiced, and to provide a better understanding of the changes that will characterize hotel development in the future.

HISTORICAL PERSPECTIVE

CHAPTER ONE

Since World War II, a variety of terms have existed to describe a lodging property. Some definitions revolve around the location of the property, the market orientation, the number of guest rooms provided, or the building height. Others may consider the availability of parking, the types of facilities and amenities offered, the types of guests accommodated, or the prices charged for a room. The labels range from the traditional term "hotel" to more recent terms such as "motor hotel," "motel," or "motor inn." Regardless of the specific label, all hotels exist to provide away-from-home sleeping and living accommodations to transient travelers for a daily remuneration. Throughout this book, the term "hotel" is used in the generic sense to refer to all lodging properties. Readers should recognize, however, that the size of a lodging establishment and the other factors considered in labeling a property as a particular type also influence, in varying degrees, the capital cost of the development process, the duration of construction, the complexity of the deal structure, the project's impact on the community, and the level of support needed from surrounding land uses.

A SINGULAR FORM OF INCOME-PRODUCING PROPERTY

Hotels represent a distinctive type of income-producing property. Because a hotel's major revenue comes from the selling of rooms on a daily basis, a hotel is a perishable product. A room not sold one night can never be sold for that night again. No guarantee exists, either, that a hotel's guest rooms will be sold every night. Often, the number of rooms rented varies from weekdays to weekends and from season to season. In contrast to office buildings and industrial/warehouse facilities, hotels do not have tenants on long-term leases. Hotels must rely on competent management, facilities that respond to the market, a recognized reputation, capable marketing personnel, and effective marketing programs to maximize occupancy and revenue. These circumstances, among others, have resulted in the dominance of national and regional chains in the U.S. lodging industry. Chains offer advantages such as a recognizable image and identification, a central reservation system and referral network, standardization of the product at many locations, and a professional marketing and advertising department, all aimed at increasing a hotel's penetration of market demand.

Another factor that makes hotels special is their labor-intensive nature, with their emphasis on personal service. Employees must be trained, motivated, and supervised properly. Positive or negative impressions made by employees have a direct impact on a guest's perception of the facility and may very well influence whether the guest will return. A similar situation exists in any labor-intensive service industry. Two complicating concerns, however, stand out with regard to hotels. First, hotel managements must deal with an extremely high turnover of personnel. This turnover often results from operating 24 hours a day, 365 days a year, with the round-the-clock work shifts that this requires. In other cases, turnover results from a hotel's closing for certain periods of the year, or from severe fluctuations in demand. To avoid releasing or laying off trained personnel and then rehiring new personnel the next season may prove to be impossible. The second complicating issue involves the minimum-wage employees who fill many positions in a hotel.

Often, such employees have limited education or poor work habits; properly motivating and retaining them can place demands on management.

Hotels are not only labor intensive, but also capital intensive; this situation creates a challenging development and operating environment. Hotels regularly need to replace furniture, fixtures, and equipment as these become worn out or as changing public tastes dictate, in order to maintain a competitive market position.

The characteristics differentiating hotels from other properties also mean that they severely and quickly feel the impact of market forces outside management's control. Sometimes market forces can cause a significant decrease in demand. The energy crisis in the early 1970s, for instance, had a severe impact on hotels located near interstate highways. On other occasions, the lack of sufficient snowfall has hurt the occupancy and profitability of mountain ski resorts. The closing of a major company's operations, of military bases, or of other primary demand generators can cripple hotels primarily serving these demands. Changes in competitive supply represent another possibly negative market force. If one or two new hotels open, and if market demand remains insufficient to keep all hotels occupied, an existing hotel can decline in occupancy.

Market forces outside management's control can affect a hotel's expenses as well as its market demand. Rising expenses caused by inflation for such items as labor, energy, and construction will erode profit margins, if the hotel finds itself unable to raise room rates proportionally because of prevailing market conditions.

A hotel cannot operate in a vacuum. Indeed, a hotel is not only affected by forces outside the control of its management, but also affects the area in which it is located. The larger the hotel and the more revenue it creates, the greater its impact.

COMMUNITY IMPACT

The development of a hotel can make a major impression on a community's economic stability and growth; conversely, the community's stability and growth typically influence the performance of a hotel. A hotel can serve either as a positive impetus for redevelopment, or as a challenge to the community to help attract or retain new development to the hotel's locale. Hotels that depend on commercial travelers need the support of complementary developments such as office buildings, retail space, entertainment facilities, and convention centers to create room demand.

A hotel frequently functions as a major employer in a community, with a typical full-service hotel employing one staff member per room. A lodging facility also generates a substantial amount of revenue for the community by attracting dollars from travelers who live outside the market area. These travelers not only spend money in the hotel, but also make outside purchases. This results in an economic multiplier effect throughout the market area.

In addition, the development of a hotel generates tax revenues through county or municipal room and sales taxes.

Many communities have recognized the value of a hotel project in enhancing a city's tax revenues. One such project is the 19-story, 630-room Hyatt Regency hotel that forms part of the James L. Knight International Center in Miami. The center also includes a 410,000-square-foot conference center with a 5,000-square-foot auditorium; 20,000 square feet of retail; and 1,450 parking spaces. The project was completed in September 1982.

Real estate tax revenues related to the development typically increase.

Many communities recognize the value of a hotel project in enhancing the city's tax revenues and its overall image. In analyzing the potential for a new hotel, a developer should investigate the community's development position and look into projections of the economic viability and growth of the area. In some cases, a developer may need community assistance to make a hotel a reality.

GENERAL FACTORS AFFECTING THE GROWTH OF THE HOTEL INDUSTRY

The four general factors that directly influence the growth of the industry and that a developer should evaluate in relation to each project are:

◆ Continued growth in travel, by market segment for the location under review;
◆ Availability of sites for development;
◆ Availability and affordability of financing; and
◆ Availability of qualified management.

To assess the potential for continued growth in travel, consideration must be given to the two basic groups that create demand for hotel rooms:

◆ *Business/commercial travelers,* such as corporate business personnel, salespersons, convention and conference attendees, government and military employees, and airline crews.

◆ *Pleasure/noncommercial travelers,* such as tourists, vacationers, travelers for medical reasons, corporate incentive groups, students, visitors to friends and relatives, and sports and special-event spectators.

Travelers in each segment possess varying demand characteristics that influence when they travel, why they select a particular hotel, how long they stay, how much they are willing to pay for a room, and other considerations. (Fluctuations in room demand, the number of guests per room, average length of stay, facility and amenity preferences, and price sensitivity all come under discussion in Chapter Two.)

The future growth of hotels also depends on the availability of sites. The tremendous expansion of the lodging industry since World War II has occurred during a period of extraordinarily rapid economic development in the United States. New types of sites have been identified. No longer do hotels concentrate in downtown or resort areas; now they stand along the country's major highways, at airports, and in suburban settings. Most recently, "new" sites are actually "old" sites located in redeveloping areas of cities around the nation. New hotel sites will continue to become available thanks to evolving trends in business and industry, economic growth, demographic shifts, and the reuse of existing land. (Chapter Three profiles the different types of hotel products that have been developed on different types of sites.)

New commercial centers will continue to be built in the suburbs, and the lodging industry must respond to this trend. Four miles from New York City, a 350-room Loews hotel and a 23,000-square-foot conference center form an integral part of the Glenpointe MXD in Teaneck, New Jersey, and will support the 551,000 square feet of planned office space.

The availability and cost of new hotel financing have remained relatively stable, despite the fluctuations in the U.S. economy since World War II. Except during relatively short periods when interest rates and restrictive credit policies imposed tight money, the lodging industry has been an attractive investment medium so long as the risks involved were associated with compensating returns.

Before the late 1970s, hotels were financed through long-term, fixed-rate mortgages. Today, more variety in financing exists. Lenders often take an equity position, receive a variable interest rate based on a financial index, or play a participating role in the project's cash flow. (Chapter Five covers the financing of hotels.)

The fourth major factor that will influence the future growth of the hotel industry is the availability of qualified management talent. The evolution of major lodging chains over the last 35 years has provided attractive opportunities for trained professionals to enter the industry and to assume substantial management responsibility. The growing domination of the industry by lodging chains, including franchise, management, and referral organizations, should increasingly attract qualified personnel. Chains benefit from several advantages in this effort. Overall, they offer:

◆ Industry-competitive compensation packages;
◆ State-of-the-art technological equipment;
◆ Opportunities for personnel to travel;
◆ Comprehensive training programs;
◆ Relative employment security;
◆ Systemization and standardization; and
◆ The economic muscle with which to survive downturns.

Since this book emphasizes the development, not the management, of hotels, discussion of management issues must be limited. Some benefits that franchise and referral systems bring to a hotel owner, however, will be discussed where appropriate.

FIGURE 1-1

LODGING PROPERTIES BY SIZE CATEGORY IN 1948

Size Category	Number of Properties	Percent of Total	Number of Rooms	Percent of Total
Fewer than 50 rooms	46,905	84.4%	790,401	42.6%
50–99 rooms	5,268	9.5	357,819	19.3
100–299 rooms	2,862	5.2	440,679	23.8
300 rooms or more	534	.9	264,824	14.3
	55,569	100.0%	1,853,723	100.0%

Compiled by Laventhol & Horwath from various sources.

Hilton purchased the Statler hotel chain in 1954 and renamed this downtown Washington, D.C., hotel the Statler Hilton. Recently, the hotel, now called the Capital Hilton, underwent a major facelift that included the addition of a porte cochere.

PROFILE OF THE INDUSTRY AFTER WORLD WAR II

In 1948, hotels with fewer than 50 rooms dominated the industry. They represented 84.4 percent of all hotel establishments and 42.6 percent of the number of rooms available. (See Figure 1–1.) Concentrations of hotels existed in the population and trade centers of the United States. In 1950, the eight states comprising the Middle Atlantic and East North Central regions contained 40 percent of the nation's population. (See Figure 1–2.) These regions included such trade centers as New York City, Philadelphia, Cleveland, Detroit, Chicago, and Milwaukee. Twenty-six percent of the hotels, and over 36 percent of the rooms in the country, were concentrated in these two regions. (See Figure 1–3.)

The typical hotel at that time was located in an urban setting, usually in a downtown business district and often near a railroad terminal. Resorts existed, but they primarily served the wealthy. Many resorts were seasonal operations sited near a body of water or in the mountains. Such resorts catered to individuals, not to meeting groups, as became common later. Few highway properties existed, and suburban and airport properties did not yet exist at all.

In the late 1940s, the lodging industry almost entirely consisted of independently owned and operated properties. Only 4.7 percent of all hotels and 12.7 percent of all rooms belonged to a chain in 1948. The major chains of the period were Sheraton and Hilton. Both of these chains, under the leadership of their founders, Ernest Henderson and Conrad Hilton, grew by absorbing either smaller lodging chains or distressed independents.

Ernest Henderson, who built Sheraton into one of the largest hotel chains, was actually an investor rather than a hotelier. Between 1937 and 1941, he became the owner of four hotels, one of which was the Sheraton Boston Hotel, the namesake of the new chain. Henderson continued to

Built at a cost of more than $3 million by Harry Wardman in 1926, the Carlton, at 16th and K Streets in Washington, D.C., is now the Sheraton Carlton. Wardman also built the Wardman Park (now the Sheraton Washington) and the Hay-Adams hotels in Washington.

The Conrad Hilton on Michigan Avenue in Chicago.

expand by purchasing additional properties, building new ones, and acquiring Eugene Eppley's hotel chain.

Conrad Hilton, one of the best-known names in the history of the hotel industry, figured eminently during this period of time—along with Ellsworth Statler and his chain, which Hilton purchased in 1954.

Hotels operating in the late 1940s did not exhibit any standardization of product, of amenities, or of services. Rooms were typically small, and some lacked private bathrooms. Most rooms had no telephone, and hotels with swimming pools were uncommon. While larger facilities supported restaurants and bars, many smaller properties could not support them. The average room rate for the industry in 1948 was $3.75.

During the late 1940s, business travelers constituted the primary source of room demand. Hotels began to experience occupancies in excess of 80 percent as businesses expanded to supply the rebuilding of Europe after the war. At the same time, a shift occurred from wartime production to consumer and durable-goods production, to satisfy the shortages created by the war and by the expansion of the American population. The urban areas were the financial and retail centers, attracting travelers who conducted business and attended meetings. A significant amount of updating, replacing, and building of various types of new facilities proceeded, after years of neglect brought on by the war.

During the next several decades, the lodging industry would undergo dramatic change. The profile of the industry would become more diverse with regard to the types of travelers demanding services and to the types of hotel facilities that would be built in response to changing trends.

FIGURE 1-2

REGION IDENTIFICATION MAP

1. New England
2. Middle Atlantic
3. East North Central
4. West North Central
5. South Atlantic
6. East South Central
7. West South Central
8. Mountain
9. Pacific

FIGURE 1-3

LODGING PROPERTIES AND ROOMS BY REGION OF THE COUNTRY IN 1948

Region of Country	Number of Properties	Percent of Total	Number of Rooms	Percent of Total
New England	3,892	7.0%	111,774	6.0%
Middle Atlantic	6,741	12.1	360,895	19.5
East North Central	7,729	13.9	313,895	16.9
West North Central	6,053	10.9	172,515	9.3
South Atlantic	6,696	12.1	224,008	12.1
East South Central	1,934	3.5	59,449	3.2
West South Central	5,841	10.5	155,037	8.4
Mountain	6,111	11.0	137,193	7.4
Pacific	10,572	19.0	319,278	17.2
	55,569	100.0%	1,854,044	100.0%

Source: Laventhol & Horwath.

FACTORS AFFECTING GROWTH AND CHANGE SINCE 1950

A number of trends in demographics, in styles of life, and in development during the period since 1950 have exerted a direct impact on the growth and diversification of the lodging industry. Eight key trends influenced both travel destinations and the magnitude of room demand: population growth and shifts, household formations, rising family incomes, increased leisure time, construction of the interstate highway system, business development in the suburbs, airport construction and growing air service, and convention center construction. These movements did not occur independently of each other or sequentially in any given order; in many instances, two or more phenomena correlated with each other or developed simultaneously.

Population grew rapidly from 1950 through 1980, at a rate of 1.35 percent compounded annually. The populations of the South Atlantic, West South Central, Mountain, and Pacific regions increased significantly faster than that of other regions. (See Figure 1–4.) Population shifted dramatically toward the Sunbelt and western states, such as Florida, Texas, Colorado, Arizona, and California.

Not only did the population expand, but also it grew older, with more widespread family formation causing a rise in the number of households. With these phenomena, and with the dispersion of families throughout the country, a need emerged for families to travel more frequently. In addition to this trend toward relocation travel, a movement toward expanded pleasure travel occurred, thanks to increased leisure time and to improved family incomes.

If the above key trends acted as catalysts, the construction of the interstate highway system functioned as the primary medium by which the population would travel, creating a demand for lodgings in new locations. Congress authorized a 42,500-mile interstate system in 1944, but not until 1956 did the Federal Aid Highway Act authorize the funding for the system's construction and completion. (Figure 1–5 shows the number of miles completed for selected years.) The interstate system would eventually connect, in both rural and urban areas, most of the nation's cities having populations of 50,000 or more, and it would offer an unprecedented opportunity for the American public to explore the country.

The interstate system not only changed long-distance travel, but also eased travel within metropolitan areas. In many cities, the interstate system aided the development of new residential neighborhoods in the suburbs. These new residential projects, in turn, brought retail shopping centers, office buildings, recreational and entertainment facilities, as well as development opportunities for hotels, to these emerging suburban locations.

The number of vehicles registered in the United States rose rapidly as population grew, as disposable income increased, and as the interstate system expanded. (Figure 1–6 shows the rapid growth in vehicle registrations during the decades of the 1950s, 1960s, and 1970s.) The public's preference for travel by automobile, coupled with the availability of inexpensive fuel during most of this period, aided the rapid nationwide development of motor hotels along interstate highways.

Although many persons traveled by automobile, a growing number traveled by air after 1945. (See Figure 1–7.) Paradoxically, air travel both inhibited and encouraged growth in the lodging industry. On the one hand, the introduction of jets reduced travel time and therefore decreased the need for extended stays. Business negotiations could be concluded within a shorter period, reducing the need for lodging. On the other hand, jet travel enabled business concerns to bring people together for meetings and training sessions more frequently. Meanwhile, it opened up many new destinations for pleasure travel.

As air travel became more popular, new airports appeared and existing airports expanded, creating new business centers outside the downtowns. By the early 1980s, over 700 airports existed that had been certified by the FAA's Office of Safety and Compliance for scheduled passenger service. This number included 23 large hub airports, 35 medium hubs, and 62 small hubs. These 120 airports accommodated the vast majority of all U.S. air traffic and passenger movement.

The construction of convention centers resulted from the rapid growth of the U.S. economy, a growth that also served to increase the memberships of professional and fraternal associations. While this expansion was occurring in the number and size of associations, improvements in ground and air transportation brought more regions of the country into consideration for conventions and meetings. Some larger cities already had massive civic centers and auditoriums built to hold events for local residents. To market these buildings as facilities for conventions and trade shows

McCamly Square, the centerpiece for downtown revitalization in Battle Creek, Michigan, consists of a Stouffer hotel, a commercial center, the Kellogg Arena and convention facility, and a public commons with parking facilities. The city broke ground for the project in August 1979, and Stouffer, which had contributed $500,000 to the deal, opened the hotel in November 1981. The Kellogg Arena opened one month later.

FIGURE 1-4

POPULATION GROWTH AND SHIFTS

(000's)

Region	1950	1960	1970	1980	Annual Percent Change
New England	9,314	10,509	11,847	12,349	.94%
Middle Atlantic	30,164	34,168	37,213	36,788	.66
East North Central	30,399	36,225	40,263	41,670	1.06
West North Central	14,061	15,394	16,328	17,185	.67
South Atlantic	21,182	25,972	30,679	36,944	1.87
East South Central	11,477	12,050	12,808	14,663	.82
West South Central	14,538	16,951	19,326	23,743	1.65
Mountain	5,075	6,855	8,290	11,369	2.73
Pacific	15,115	21,198	26,548	31,797	2.51
	151,325	179,322	203,302	226,508	1.35%

Source: U.S. Department of Commerce, Bureau of the Census.

FIGURE 1-5

FIGURE 1-6

INTERSTATE HIGHWAY MILES COMPLETED

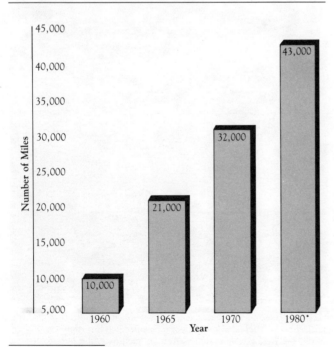

* As of 1980, the system was 95 percent completed. The only segments remaining to be built were beltways around cities.
Source: U.S. Department of Transportation.

VEHICLES REGISTERED IN THE UNITED STATES

Year	Number	Annual Compound Percent Change
1950	49,200,000	—
1960	73,900,000	4.15%
1970	108,400,000	3.91
1980	159,000,000	3.91

Source: U.S. Department of Transportation.

FIGURE 1-7

AIR PASSENGER GROWTH

Year	Passenger Movements	Annual Compound Percent Change
1945	6,687,968	—
1950	17,424,414	21.1%
1960	52,391,708	11.6
1970	155,097,644	11.5
1980	292,537,000	6.6
1945–1980		11.4

Source: Air Transport Association of America.

seemed a logical extension of their traditional uses. Although the convention facilities themselves often operated at a loss, the cities hosting the conventions received important economic benefits. Later, many medium-sized and small cities saw a chance to take part in this type of venture and constructed convention centers to accommodate state and regional groups.

The opening of convention centers strongly impelled the growth in demand for hotel rooms from the group/convention segment during the 1960s and 1970s. Facilities such as McCormick Place in Chicago, the Georgia World Congress Center in Atlanta, The Coliseum in New York, and the Gateway Convention Center in St. Louis generated a need for larger hotels to house convention delegates. This in turn encouraged the inclusion of large new hotels in urban mixed-use developments that also housed office, retail, recreational, and other types of space.

DIVERSIFICATION AND EVOLUTION OF THE INDUSTRY

Lodging chains such as Holiday Inns, Ramada Inns, Howard Johnson's, and TraveLodge emerged in the 1950s as their founders identified opportunities for new development at some of these new locations. Later, in order to grow faster, many chains became franchisors as well as developers and operators of company-owned facilities.

Hotel chains instituted for themselves standard designs, specific development parameters, management structures

Of all lodgings, resorts and budget hotels suffer the most during recessions. Facilities in strategic urban locations, however, typically are not hurt as badly during these periods. This 804-room, luxury Westin hotel represents the first phase of the 9½-acre Copley Place project in Boston. The 36-story hotel is of reinforced concrete with a precast concrete panel facade.

and systems, operating efficiencies, market-identified images, and referral networks. They also stressed uniformity of design for easy recognition by the traveling public. Hotel chains had their own signs, emblems, and slogans, giving themselves a necessary distinctiveness to aid in their advertising programs, sales promotions, referrals, and advance reservation services.

Holiday Inns, Inc., became one of the first chains to build standard, inexpensive lodging accommodations throughout the United States. Founded in 1952, Holiday Inns first concentrated on building along highways and interstates to serve the needs of vacationing families and of commercial travelers. Kemmons Wilson, the chain's founder, attracted attention and numberless guests with his offer of free accommodation for children under the age of 12 traveling with their parents. (The name "Holiday Inn" was inspired by a movie starring Bing Crosby as a hotel owner. Wilson's architect wrote the name of Crosby's hotel, Holiday Inn, across the blueprint, and it "stuck.") Holiday Inns have multiplied until today they compose the largest hotel chain in the world, with properties serving many types of travelers at their worldwide locations.

The Marriott Corporation entered the hotel business relatively recently, in 1957. In that year, Marriott decided that a site they had chosen for their corporate headquarters and for a commissary for food operations in Washington, D.C., would better serve as a site for hotel development. Marriott succeeded with this first property, and the corporation continued to expand, especially near major airports and in resort areas.

As the competition from chains grew in the 1950s and 1960s, and as the independents found it increasingly necessary to reserve their marketing efforts for staying competitive, referral organizations evolved. The most widely known of these organizations include Best Western International, Friendship Inns, and Superior Motels, Inc.

Referral organizations, in comparison to hotel chains, structure themselves on a nonprofit basis. Their members own and control them, voting on policies and electing directors. Through affiliation with a recognized referral organization, an independent owner/operator unites efforts and resources with other independents. With this type of affiliation, independent operators can benefit from reservation referrals, sales promotion benefits, and other advantages of chain operations without sacrificing individual control of their properties.

During the 1950s and 1960s, when most hotel development concentrated along the interstates and in outlying suburban areas, mature chains such as Sheraton and Hilton also began to franchise. Sheraton and Hilton needed to develop smaller roadside and suburban hotels in order to compete with the newer chains without diverting significant capital from larger projects in downtown and resort areas.

As a result of all this competition, the range of amenities and services offered kept enlarging. Indoor and outdoor swimming pools, restaurants, lounges, meeting and banquet rooms, valet service, complimentary limousine service, live entertainment, saunas, whirlpools, and free in-room movies appeared as facilities and services offered. Hotels that had proposed mainly to provide overnight sleeping accommodations evolved into entertainment, dining, and meeting complexes.

High inflation during the 1970s, however, exerted a reversing influence on this trend. As the purchasing power of the dollar shrank, room rates at most full-service hotels climbed to record highs. Travelers, more aware of their needs, realized they did not always use the facilities provided by full-service hotels, such as meeting rooms, recreational amenities, restaurants, and lounges. In addition, during recessionary years, businesses began to evaluate more closely their travel expenditures.

Although the "budget" or "economy" hotel appeared in the 1960s, this segment of the industry only began to grow quickly in the 1970s. Budget operators recognized the chance to "get back to basics," to charge a lower room rate, and to eliminate ancillary facilities. They found a niche in the market and responded with an appropriate product. Thus, hotels became more specialized as travelers grew more sophisticated and competition more intense.

The hotel products that arose to meet the emerging needs of varied travelers differed according to five salient traits: pricing structure, amenities and facilities provided, location, specific market(s) served, and distinctiveness of style or offerings. (Figure 1–8 clarifies the different categories.) A hotel in one category, clearly, may also fit into two or three additional categories. For instance, a hotel classified as "middle-market" may also occupy a suburban location and serve primarily commercial travelers. Marketing strategies gained in importance; they were now needed to communicate to the traveler the availability of the different types of hotels and the position of a particular property in the marketplace.

THE 1980s SETTING

Between 1948 and 1981, the national inventory of hotel rooms showed an increase of over 640,000 rooms. During the same period, however, the actual number of properties decreased by 1,434, as smaller hotels disappeared from the inventory and gave place to larger facilities. Figure 1–9 gives the distribution of rooms by property size and by number of rooms available in 1981. A comparison of Figure 1–9 with Figure 1–1 clearly indicates that properties with at least 100 rooms accounted for most of the guest rooms added in the 33-year period.

Although the number of rooms available in the United States rose by 35 percent between 1948 and 1981, the number of rooms demanded failed to keep pace, and occupancy decreased. (See Figure 1–10.) As of the mid-1980s, the occupancy level of 1948 has never been repeated. Overall annual occupancies in the 1960s have set the norm for the industry, year after year, with fluctuations depending upon the relationship between supply of and demand for rooms.

A comparison of the regional breakdown of properties and rooms in 1948 and in 1981 illustrates the fact that hotel development has followed population shifts. (See Figures

FIGURE 1-8

TYPES OF HOTELS, BY SELECTED DEVELOPMENT CRITERIA
(Generically Described)

Price

Budget/Economy Hotels
Rooms-only operations with little or no public space, no on-premise food and beverage facilities, and room rates 20 to 50 percent below the average for the market area.

Middle-Market Hotels
Operations offering a wide range of facilities and amenities, with room rates equal to or slightly above market-area averages.

Luxury Hotels
Hotels providing upscale decor and furnishings, concierge service, a limited amount of high-quality public space, a high ratio of employees to rooms available, and room rates substantially above market-area averages.

Amenities

Convention Hotels
Large hotels with 500 or more guest rooms, extensive meeting space, several restaurants and lounges; sometimes adjacent to convention centers.

Commercial Hotels
Operations emphasizing comfortable, functional guest rooms with ample work area, smaller meeting and conference rooms, and limited recreational amenities.

Location

Downtown Hotels
High-rise buildings with attached or covered parking; varying numbers of guest rooms and varying ranges of facilities and amenities, according to pricing and to market orientation of the property.

Suburban Hotels
Low- to mid-rise buildings with surface parking, interior corridors, recreational amenities, and meeting and banquet facilities.

Highway/Interstate Hotels
Low-rise structures having surface parking, exterior corridors, some food and beverage space, minimal banquet space, and an outdoor swimming pool.

Resort Hotels
Hotels that emphasize recreational amenities, food and beverage outlets, and meeting and banquet space; typically located in a picturesque setting.

Specific Markets Served

Executive Conference Centers
Facilities sited in secluded, countrylike settings with fewer than 300 rooms, a variety of well-planned small meeting rooms and classrooms, and modern audiovisual equipment. Meals and the use of athletic facilities are included in the quoted daily room rate.

Health Spas
Specialized hotels catering to specific needs such as to spend a concentrated, secluded period of time losing weight, reducing stress, or breaking a habit. These facilities usually have professional staffs including dietitians, therapists, physicians, and/or counselors.

Resort Hotels
Hotels that emphasize recreational amenities, food and beverage outlets, and meeting and banquet space; typically located in a picturesque setting.

Distinctiveness of Style or Offerings

All-Suite Hotels
Facilities characterized by larger-than-normal room size, a living/parlor area separated from the sleeping area, cooking and refrigeration equipment, residential-looking public space, and the aim of catering to long-term guests.

Renovated/Converted Hotels
Old, historic structures that were once grand hotels or other older facilities, refurbished to the original era's splendor and elegance. Most of these are considered classic hotels. An example of an unusual conversion is the Quaker Hilton Inn in Akron, Ohio, which was converted from an old Quaker Oats grain elevator.

Mixed-Use/Focal-Point Hotels
Components of large multi-use developments, serving to focus the other uses or to complement them. Architecturally significant and designed to be inward-facing.

FIGURE 1-9

LODGING PROPERTIES BY SIZE CATEGORY IN 1981

Size Category	Number of Properties	Percent of Total	Number of Rooms	Percent of Total
Fewer than 50 rooms	39,590	73.1%	690,000	27.6%
50–99 rooms	7,985	14.7	517,700	20.7
100–299 rooms	5,660	10.5	849,000	34.0
300 rooms and over	900	1.7	441,000	17.7
	54,135	100.0%	2,497,700	100.0%

Source: Laventhol & Horwath.

FIGURE 1-10

OCCUPANCY TRENDS IN THE U.S. LODGING INDUSTRY

	1948	1958	1963	1967	1972	1977	1981
Number of Establishments	55,569	70,535	64,276	65,579	58,688	51,861	54,135
Number of Rooms Available per Day	1,854,044	2,118,777	2,385,930	2,101,500	2,223,600	2,198,700	2,497,700
Average Number of Rooms Occupied per Day	1,575,669	1,437,553	1,448,630	1,297,800	1,317,500	1,451,200	1,570,700
Percentage of Occupancy	85%	68%	62%	62%	59%	66%	63%

Source: Laventhol & Horwath.

FIGURE 1-11

LODGING PROPERTIES AND ROOMS BY REGION OF THE COUNTRY IN 1981

Region of Country	Number of Properties	Percent of Total	Number of Rooms	Percent of Total
New England	3,455	6.4%	122,800	4.9%
Middle Atlantic	6,360	11.8	306,700	12.3
East North Central	7,345	13.6	311,400	12.5
West North Central	4,945	9.1	180,900	7.2
South Atlantic	11,185	20.7	560,700	22.4
East South Central	2,470	4.6	127,750	5.1
West South Central	4,590	8.5	238,500	9.6
Mountain	5,550	10.1	258,250	10.3
Pacific	8,235	15.2	390,700	15.7
	54,135	100.0%	2,497,700	100.0%

Source: Laventhol & Horwath.

1–3 and 1–11.) The South Atlantic region has replaced the Middle Atlantic as the region with the largest number of guest rooms. Major expansion of the guest-room inventory also occurred in the East South Central, West South Central, and Mountain regions. The number of rooms in the New England and West North Central regions grew minimally, while the number of rooms available in the Middle Atlantic and East North Central regions declined.

Regardless of regional location, though, a general trend existed toward chain affiliation between the late 1940s and the early 1980s. By the latter time, about 54 percent of all hotel rooms and 22 percent of all properties in the United States had affiliated themselves with some chain, franchise, or referral organization.

The ownership of hotels has also changed notably since 1948. Then, ownership primarily rested with the owner/operator. Although many operators still hold ownership positions, hotel corporations as well as institutions such as insurance companies and pension funds have established important new ownership positions in the industry. Also, individual investors who are not operators have entered into direct ownership through the use of limited-partnership interests.

The U.S. hotel industry has altered greatly over the last several decades, becoming more diverse and chain-dominated. Anyone considering the development of a hotel should possess a general understanding of hotel supply and demand trends, as well as knowledge of the development process and of alternative approaches to financing and structuring a project. The next four chapters deal with these issues, while the last chapter takes a look ahead to consider what might be expected in the future for the industry.

TRAVEL AND MARKETS

CHAPTER TWO

In the United States, where society has become exceptionally mobile in the last several decades, travel represents a major business, and hotels are the type of lodging establishment most frequently selected by commercial and pleasure travelers. A few statistics from the U.S. Travel Data Center's 1982 National Travel Survey indicate the vast size and some basic characteristics of the travel market:

◆ Americans took nearly 537 million trips, or 1.07 billion person-trips, during 1982. (A "trip" is defined as travel 100 miles or more away from home and then back, whether or not an overnight stay is involved, but excluding 1) travel as part of an operating crew on a train, airplane, bus, truck, or ship; 2) commuting to a place of work; and 3) student trips to or from school. A "person-trip" is counted every time one person takes a trip. If two people travel together, two person-trips and one trip are counted.)

◆ Trips (of 100 or more miles one way) averaged 790 miles round trip, with an average of 4.5 nights spent away from home.

◆ By the end of 1982, 64 percent of all U.S. adults had, at some time during their lifetimes, taken one or more trips 100 miles or more away from home.

◆ Travelers selected hotels, motels, and motor hotels (all generically referred to as "hotels" in this chapter) on 36 percent of the trips; they only used homes of friends or relatives more frequently (on 45 percent of all person-trips).

◆ Those on business/convention trips were likelier to choose hotels (68 percent in 1982) than those traveling for pleasure (32 percent).

Because of the size and diversity of the travel market, hotel developers and operators should know as much as possible about the major market segments that account for hotel room demand. Then they can design and operate properties well suited to meet the particular needs of different types of travelers. A number of questions deserve consideration before a developer can understand and respond to market demand:

◆ *Why are people traveling?* The purpose of a given trip often virtually determines hotel selection. The same person will select different kinds of hotels for different kinds of trips. A luxury downtown hotel, for example, might be the traveler's choice while on a business trip requiring that he or she project a certain image. The same traveler might choose a budget hotel on an interstate route during a pleasure trip with the family.

◆ *Who is traveling?* The age and income level of each traveler, and the number of persons in each party, all influence the type and variety of facilities, amenities, and services sought. Senior citizens, young families, 40- to 50-year-old businesspersons, younger business travelers, or women traveling alone have particular needs and preferences.

◆ *What are the origins and destinations of those traveling?* Understanding travelers' points of origin will provide

Americans took nearly 1.07 billion person-trips during 1982.

developers with useful direction for marketing efforts and may also help them plan appropriate amenities and services. A hotel serving many international guests, for example, may need interpreters and a currency exchange. Knowing where travelers are destined also represents a major element in facility planning, raising as it does the distinction between transient (in-transit) and destination guests.

◆ *What is the price sensitivity, or lack of it, of those traveling?* This will vary widely, depending on whether a traveler is on an expense account, the purpose of the trip, and the expected length of stay.

These critical questions exemplify the issues typically analyzed by hotel developers today. Overall, hotel developers and major chains orient themselves toward a degree of market segmentation and of product diversification that was unimagined 20 or 30 years ago. At that time, most commercial hotel rooms were small and basic—efficient, but not designed with the guest in mind.

Most recently, product differentiation has evolved as developers have attempted to reach a greater number of more specific markets. Thus, while product diversification resulted in categories such as budget hotels, conference centers, and all-suite hotels, it further segmented each category. All-suite hotels, for instance, have taken the form of urban, suburban, or residential properties, and each type has targeted a different market segment.

Since the concept of market segmentation is so basic to understanding the hotel industry in the United States, the first section of this chapter provides a basis for defining major

market segments and characterizes three primary segments. One of the characteristics discussed, seasonal demand, becomes the topic for the latter part of this chapter because it may determine the success or failure of so many hotels.

The concluding discussion in this chapter introduces the concept of a supply-induced market for a given type of hotel. Not all hotels are built to serve an already existing local demand for rooms. A resort hotel may bring travelers to a location they would never have visited otherwise; a convention hotel may attract an entirely new clientele to an area that could never have accommodated them before.

The need or desire to travel, and the resulting hotel markets, cannot be easily analyzed. By focusing on three important aspects—market segmentation, seasonality, and supply-induced demand—this chapter aims to give a perspective on "Product Response to Markets," the topic of Chapter Three.

MARKET SEGMENTATION

Most trips fall under one of two categories, business trips or pleasure/personal trips. Besides the purpose of the trip, however, two other questions influence a traveler's selection of a hotel:

◆ Will I be traveling independently, or as part of a larger group?

◆ Will I be in transit when I reach this particular market area, or will I have arrived at my final destination?

Responses to these questions also deserve consideration by those who wish to define the distinct demand segments available to a hotel in a certain market area.

Figure 2–1 summarizes the basic segmentation breakdown. The examples at the bottom of the chart indicate one type of guest who would be categorized in each subsegment. This segmentation could, of course, be taken further, to subdivide the travel market even more distinctly: a destination resort hotel might, for instance, target both independent and group travelers with special interests such as golf, tennis, or skiing. Or, a hotel with association meetings as one of its target markets would have to subdivide this market by size of group, according to its capacity to accommodate groups. The purpose of a trip, the independent- versus group-travel differentiation, and the in-transit versus destination distinction, then, are three key variables in understanding the general composition of hotel room demand.

Each subsegment of demand represented by the examples in Figure 2–1 possesses a distinct profile. A profile of a subsegment might include such demand traits as these:

◆ Fluctuations in demand, by day and by month;

◆ Single versus double occupancy (are there generally one, two, or more guests per room?);

FIGURE 2-1

MARKET SEGMENTATION

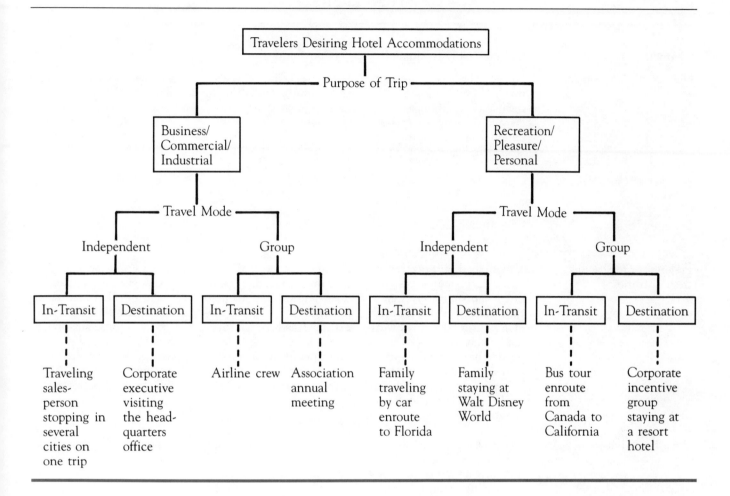

- ◆ Length of stay;

- ◆ Needs and preferences for meeting space, restaurants, recreational amenities, and other facilities and services;

- ◆ Price sensitivity;

- ◆ Extent of repeat patronage; and

- ◆ Specific sources of room demand, both from within the market area (which companies, attractions, schools, hospitals, and events generate local room demand?) and from outside the market area (what is the origin city or country for those now traveling to this area?).

Figure 2–2 summarizes a typical profile for three differing demand segments of destination travelers. As indicated, a wide range exists in some demand characteristics from one

segment to another, and, for some characteristics, variations even occur within the segment. The uninitiated developer might not recognize the need to understand market segmentation before moving ahead with a project, but, as can be seen, the demand for hotel rooms is not a generic one. Understanding this fact and analyzing the specific market potential for a proposed hotel through a detailed market study can prove to be crucial to the successful operation of that hotel. The market segments to be served should form the primary focus for the design, marketing, and operation of the new hotel.

FLUCTUATIONS IN DEMAND

Of all demand characteristics, fluctuation in demand is the one most frequently overlooked by developers inex-

FIGURE 2-2

TYPICAL PROFILES FOR SELECTED DEMAND SEGMENTS OF DESTINATION TRAVELERS

Characteristic	Commercial/Individual	Commercial/Group (Convention)	Pleasure/Individual (Tourist)
Fluctuations in Demand	Monday through Thursday nights. Limited monthly fluctuations, although demand decreases somewhat during summer months and around holidays.	Either weekdays or weekends. Spring and fall months most popular for large associations.	Summer months most popular overall. Seasonality varies widely, based on geographic destination and on activities to be pursued.
Number of Guests per Room	One.	Two.	Two or more.
Length of Stay	One to four nights.	Two to four nights.	Two to six nights or longer.
Preferences for Facilities/Amenities	Varies based on price sensitivity: corporate executive often wants quality restaurants, bars, perhaps a health club, and is concerned with image; traveling salesperson may be more price sensitive, wants convenience, reasonably priced restaurants, and lively bars. Highly location sensitive.	Specific need for varied amounts of meeting, banquet, and exhibition space; for flexibility in space; for excellent audiovisual support; for knowledgeable and proven convention coordinators; and sometimes for recreational amenities.	Often wants swimming pool, tennis, golf, game room, or other recreational amenities. Desire for a variety of restaurants and bars varies, based on extent of development and on alternative facilities in the surrounding area.
Price Sensitivity	Varies based on position and income level of the guest, and on whether or not guest is traveling on an expense account.	Little, because of discounts on room rates due to the volume of rooms booked, and due to the amount of food and beverage business generated.	Full spectrum—from high price sensitivity to none.
Extent of Repeat Patronage	Considerable amount of repeat business, because many commercial travelers must be in an area on a recurring basis. Also depends on incentives available for increasing frequency.	Frequently, rotation of one group through several geographic areas occurs, with large groups going from one property to another within a chain.	Repeat visits occur, but for each trip the tourist selects this destination, does not need to go there. Many competitive influences vie for this market: travel agents, advertising, recommendations of friends or relatives, and past experience.
Source of Room Demand	Influenced primarily by the specific demand generators located within the market area.	Varies from small meetings for local companies' salespeople, to large state or regional events, to national groups.	Fluctuates widely, based on the size of the resort, the facilities and attractions available, marketing efforts, and reputation.

perienced with hotel projects. They fail to recognize that the guest rooms and space a hotel offers are perishable; if these are not sold each day, sales cannot be made up at a later date. For a specific project, a careful analysis of demand trends for each segment of the market permits a realistic projection of annual occupancy.

Although commercial travel remains relatively consistent throughout the year, the volume of noncommercial or pleasure travel changes with the seasons. Pleasure travel peaks in the summer quarter, as many families vacation while children are out of school.[1] (See Figure 2–3.)

For the United States overall, August represents the month of peak demand, while June comes second, closely followed by October. (See Figure 2–4.) Room demand remains relatively strong in October because of the popularity of this month for meetings and conventions. The demand for rooms reaches its lowest point in December, as some business travel falls off due to the Christmas holidays.

The full range of U.S. geographic areas shows differing seasonal profiles, primarily because of weather conditions. In addition, one type of hotel will show a different demand profile from another. Hotels catering to commercial travelers, for instance, typically experience peak occupancy on Tuesday and Wednesday nights throughout the year, with Monday and Thursday nights only slightly less busy. Occupancy in such hotels, however, often falls to a very low point on Friday through Sunday nights. This cycle limits the annual occupancy potential at commercial hotels to the mid-60 to low-70 percent range, unless the hotel or the market area can be made attractive to noncommercial travelers, with their weekend travel patterns.[2]

The fluctuations in demand that occur in some resort destinations are extreme enough so that some hotels only stay open for part of the year. For 1983, these seasonal operations were estimated to represent about 11 percent of the total number of available guest rooms in the United States, a percentage that has not changed materially in the past 35 years.[3] Seasonal resorts exist in each part of the country: Florida's beach resorts, and Rocky Mountain ski lodges, only remain open during the winter, while New England's shore resorts open only during the summer.

Seasonal resorts suffer from some problematical operating situations:

✦ Seasonal operations make it difficult to keep good employees; most service personnel need and want to work all year.

✦ Physical maintenance of interiors can pose a problem if hotel operators turn off the air conditioning or heating for an extended period. The need for maintenance continues even when revenues cease for a season.

FIGURE 2-3

QUARTERLY DISTRIBUTION OF PERSON–TRIPS, 1981*

Quarter	Pleasure Trips	Business/Convention Trips
First	12.7%	23.5%
Second	28.7	25.7
Third	31.7	25.0
Fourth	26.9	25.8
	100.0%	100.0%

*Three persons traveling together count as three person-trips.

Source: U.S. Travel Data Center quarterly reports, from the *1981 National Travel Survey*.

FIGURE 2-4

U.S. NATIONWIDE SEASONAL ADJUSTMENT FACTORS

Month	Factor*
January	.820
February	.992
March	1.069
April	1.059
May	1.018
June	1.082
July	1.056
August	1.103
September	1.019
October	1.080
November	.943
December	.698

*Factors were based on monthly occupancies from 1973 through 1982. The closer a factor comes to 1.000, the more "average" the month.

Source: Laventhol & Horwath.

[1] These general patterns are reflected in the seasonal adjustment factors compiled by Laventhol & Horwath for their *National Trend of Business in the Lodging Industry*, a monthly publication that tracks trends in occupancy and sales. The seasonal adjustment factors were based on monthly occupancies over a 10-year period at the hotels included in the firm's data base.

[2] Laventhol & Horwath has compiled seasonal adjustment factors for these classifications: 1) *affiliation*—chain or independent; 2) *area*—Northeast, Southeast, North Central, South Central, or West; 3) *location*—center city, suburban, highway, airport, or resort; 4) *size*—fewer than 150 rooms, 150 to 299 rooms, 300 to 600 rooms, or over 600 rooms; and 5) *type*—hotel, motor hotel, or budget/ economy property.

[3] Source: Laventhol & Horwath.

- Seasonal resort operators must exercise careful budget and cash flow control, especially during periods when little revenue is coming in but many costs remain fixed (i.e., debt service).

For reasons such as these, seasonal operations are not growing in number. Some resorts have, however, made an effective transition from seasonal to year-round operations. Managements of such resorts have identified market segments that could be attracted to their properties in their off seasons. For example, a winter resort in the mountains has added meeting space and recreational amenities in order to compete for group meeting business outside the ski season. Similarly, a tourist-centered beach hotel in Florida has begun to market its facilities to local residents at reduced rates in the summer season.

Recognizing that seasonality does exist and knowing the seasonal patterns for the market segments currently demanding rooms in a given area will help a developer to evaluate the potential for a new hotel. A forward-looking analysis, however, cannot stop with current statistics for transient visitors. A new group must be identified—that comprising the potential visitors who may come because of population growth, new commercial or industrial development, new tourist attractions or recreational development, changes in transportation networks, or even new lodging facilities.

Developers may relatively easily observe and understand the direct link between new commercial, industrial, recreation, or transportation development in an area and an increasing demand for hotel rooms. But they may find it more difficult to grasp the idea of supply-induced or latent demand, namely, that new room demand can emerge simply because a new lodging facility becomes available.

SUPPLY-INDUCED DEMAND

Not all hotels are developed to respond to an existing demand for rooms. Some are planned, constructed, and marketed to attract people who otherwise would not have come or at least would not have stayed overnight.

Supply-induced demand most frequently involves pleasure travelers and business/convention group travelers. Throughout the United States, numerous examples exist of hotels whose development has relied primarily, if not exclusively, on their ability to bring people to the area simply because they, the hotels, are there. The following hotels, for instance, have induced their own demand:

- Marriott's Marco Beach Resort. With no base of commercial business, this hotel had to build its own occupancy by marketing to tourists—both individuals and groups—and to conventions.

- Opryland Hotel. Although the theme park, Opryland, and the Grand Ole Opry itself had attracted many pleasure travelers, the opening of the Opryland Hotel with its extensive meeting and exhibition space brought an entirely new segment of business to the area—large conventions that never could have met in Nashville before because of its limited facilities.

- Hilton Head Inn. One of the earlier developments on Hilton Head Island, this hotel was built, among other reasons, to accommodate prospective buyers of houses and condominiums on the island. It occupied an isolated site, and management needed to generate business

Walt Disney World's resort hotels and recreation areas each use individual themes. The Contemporary Resort Hotel combines over 1,000 guest rooms with convention facilities, restaurants, shops, tennis courts, and a marina. Monorail trains pass through the hotel at the fourth floor.

The Henley Park Hotel, a transformed 1918-vintage apartment building, aims to capitalize on the success of the nearby Washington, D.C., Convention Center. With 82 rooms and 16 suites, the hotel is trying hard to be British, with afternoon tea and rooms with four-poster beds. Single rooms command $95 to $135 per night; doubles, $110 to $155.

The Hyatt Regency at Reunion in Dallas, Texas.

through direct marketing efforts to tourists and convention/ meeting groups.

Supply-induced demand that involves commercial travelers may, for instance, target the businessperson who must go to a location for business but who plans the trip to avoid staying there overnight. If a first-class hotel opens in the subject location, this businessperson may now alter a previous travel decision and stay in the area.

Although potentially an essential source of business for many hotels, supply-induced demand is very difficult to quantify. The experience of an existing hotel that found itself in a similar position when it opened may act as a case in point for a developer or investor attempting to project the future of a new property. But these comparisons can be invalid. Such elements as timing and location differ. The developer proposing a "pioneer" project, one that will rely to a large extent on supply-induced demand, takes a risk. Frequently, such a developer must rely on profits from other activities, such as those from land development, if the hotel is to be successful. A chance of failure exists, but so does a chance for phenomenal success.

A CAUTION

In short, developers must decide on the markets to be targeted for any property under consideration. Market segments with specialized needs and preferences vary widely; some are compatible with others, some are not. Indeed, a great deal of overlap does exist between different segments. Yet, if developers and analysts become too theoretical and develop hotels that are too specific in their targets, an overbuilt hotel market may result. Travelers, who are after all people, are not that segmentable. The same person will choose different types of hotels on different trips. Further to complicate the issue, that same person will sometimes not even choose a place to stay but will be booked into a hotel by a business contact, a travel agent, or a meeting planner.

In addition, although the physical plant of a hotel may appeal to several compatible segments, management can rely too heavily on one segment. Or, it can derive a high percentage of its business from one source. Severe operating problems can ensue. For example, a highway location may allow a hotel to fill frequently with primarily transient traffic. But when a new interstate highway reroutes traffic, business may virtually dry up. Or, a first-class hotel in a major tourist destination may target its marketing heavily at tour groups from one foreign country. If new laws in that country limit the amount of currency that can be taken abroad, however, the hotel may suddenly have its "firmly" booked business for the next six months canceled, and its marketing department scrambling to replace it.

Successful hotels today typically target their marketing efforts at two or three specific segments, but retain enough flexibility to fill in periods of low demand with compatible business. Site selection and product development primarily grow out of the needs of these two or three targeted seg-

The Hyatt Regency at Waikiki Beach. Resort hotels usually provide a variety of experiences. Their surroundings, generally scenic or wilderness environments, are made pleasantly accessible because of the hotels' locations. As a rule, recreational activities play an important role. Resort hotel rooms afford picturesque views, and the designs of the buildings themselves induce relaxation and extended stays.

ments. Chapter Three outlines the various products that have resulted from this awareness of segmentation. In order to provide perspective on the new products now emerging, however, consideration should be given to general trends in future room demand.

THE MAGNITUDE OF FUTURE TRAVEL

A good illustration of some of the issues that influence the volume of future travel might involve commercial or business-related room demand:

✦ Employment shifts. Shifts occur, not only geographically, but between industries. New plants opened by large northern companies in lower-priced labor markets in the South can cause more demand for rooms in the South during personal visits by management. Growth in high-technology industries can mean more training sessions for staff and for users.

✦ Decentralization. Both the length and the frequency of state legislative sessions increase in a political environment that emphasizes decentralization over federal control. This results in a bigger hotel demand in state cap-

itals. Similarly, decentralized companies with local and regional branch offices generate a need for regional and national meetings—a need that does not exist in centralized operations.

✦ Education needs. Dynamic, quickly changing products and services require continuing education meetings and seminars, and create greater room demand.

✦ Technological advances. Teleconferencing now offers an alternative to face-to-face meetings and may deter travel.

✦ Industry expansion. The growth of new city franchises for sports teams, for instance, and the creation of new leagues, translate into increased room demand.

✦ The state of the economy. In recessionary periods, businesses may dramatically curtail travel by canceling travel plans, by reducing the length of each stay, or by trading down to lower-priced accommodations.

Although the state of the economy also influences personal travel, other factors affect the magnitude of travel in the pleasure category:

✦ Family income. Families with a larger amount of disposable income travel more. Thus, as the number of two-

24

wage families increases, the pleasure-travel volume should rise.

✦ Available leisure time. Growing amounts of leisure time, along with increased disposable income and the comparative ease of travel, should attract former nontravelers into the market.

✦ Age of population. With the aging of the U.S. population, more travel should take place, as retirees are exceptionally mobile pleasure travelers.

✦ Transportation factors. Bargain fares and seasonal promotions by U.S. air carriers can wield an impact on destinations selected and on durations of stay. New or extended interstate highways also dramatically increase pleasure travel.

✦ Currency exchange rates. As exchange rates fluctuate, some foreign destinations will gain popularity with U.S. travelers and will divert some domestic travel. Likewise, exchange rates will influence the incidence of travel to the United States by residents of foreign countries.

Although it is impossible to predict categorically that the demand for hotel rooms in the United States will continue its upward trend, many of the issues that affect the volume of both commercial and pleasure travel do mean an escalation in room demand. An important question is, will a saturation point be reached? Saturation of the market would not likely last long, but a developer must realize that economic cycles and a number of evolving issues can cause fluctuating occupancies for some projects. Thus, staying power, in addition to possible supplementary investments during lower cycles, may be required.

PRODUCT RESPONSE TO MARKETS

CHAPTER THREE

As a general rule, hotel development follows other types of real estate activity. Most hotels that opened in the United States during the first half of the twentieth century opened in downtown areas where office buildings, retail space, residential development, and many of the area's employers were already concentrated. With the coming of the interstate highway system and of beltways around major cities, and with the rapid expansion of air travel, development of commercial, retail, and residential projects moved out from the central core, and suburbia began to evolve. As the demand for hotel rooms grew, developers responded with new types of hotels in newly created suburban, highway, and airport locations.

The hotels built in such locations differed dramatically from the hotel products found in downtown business districts; conditions for and demands on development had changed. Land costs were lower in the suburbs. On the other hand, local zoning was often stricter, with limits, for instance, as to the building heights allowed. The costs of low-rise construction, of course, were substantially less than those of downtown high-rise construction; moreover, features such as elevators were often unnecessary. Parking grew in importance: frequently, guests did not arrive at suburban hotels via public transportation but in private automobiles.

In the 1960s and 1970s, in response to this changed demand, many new hotels went up outside the downtowns. As competition intensified, developers and chains began to pay attention to the needs of smaller and more specific subsegments of demand, and responded with different product offerings. Some concepts that emerged during these two decades include:

◆ *Budget or economy hotels,* intended to cater to the more price-sensitive travelers, those looking for an excellent price/value relationship.

◆ *All-suite hotels,* developed to provide a larger and more diverse guest unit by eliminating some public space (such as restaurants and meeting rooms) typically found in first-class hotels.

◆ *Executive conference centers,* targeted at those holding relatively small meetings and requiring a well-controlled environment with excellent audiovisual equipment, specialized meeting service, and related facilities.

By the 1980s, a number of major national hotel chains had begun to diversify their products to appeal to a wider range of travelers. Differing concepts arose within a chain to embrace the lower-, middle-, and upper-priced categories of products.

DOWNTOWN FACILITIES

GENERAL CHARACTERISTICS

The number of quest rooms in downtown hotels varies widely, but typically, downtown properties are larger than hotels in other locations. The larger size supports the rela-

SOME FACILITIES, AMENITIES, AND SERVICES AVAILABLE AT MAJOR DOWNTOWN HOTELS

+ Several restaurants and lounges ranging from coffee shop to gourmet restaurant, intimate lounge to show bar;
+ Extensive meeting and banquet space;
+ Full range of convention equipment, such as sound system, projectors, screens, lecterns, chalkboards, and a portable stage;
+ An exhibition hall with loading dock;
+ A gym or health club;
+ A swimming pool;
+ Retail shops, car rental desks, airline ticket offices;
+ A game room;
+ Translation and secretarial services; and
+ A concierge, able to arrange for theater tickets, babysitting services, city tours, or other guest needs.

tively high development costs inherent in constructing a building in a densely developed area, and accommodates a group meeting orientation. Downtown hotels are generally high-rise structures because of both high land costs and limited availability of land. Within a metropolitan area, downtown hotels often comprise the oldest and newest properties in the area. The grand old hotels, such as the Brown Palace in Denver or the William Penn in Pittsburgh, represent one-of-a-kind buildings with ornate detailing impossible to reproduce today. The new downtown hotels are usually parts of mixed-use projects that have helped to stimulate revitalization programs in major cities. The 1,100-room Westin Peachtree Plaza in Atlanta, for example—at 73 stories the world's tallest hotel—was developed along with office and retail space at the Peachtree Plaza. And the 2,019-room Hyatt Regency/ Chicago in Illinois Center forms part of an office/retail/residential complex.

Many downtown hotels offer guests an extensive array of facilities, amenities, and services. (See Figure 3–1.) Even with this variety, however, hotels in many downtown areas still often find it difficult to attract business on Friday, Saturday, and Sunday nights. As a result, average annual occupancy levels at downtown properties range from 65 to 72 percent. Annual occupancy in center city hotels was 67 percent in 1980 and in 1981, and slipped to approximately 64 percent in 1982. For a variety of reasons, however, average room rates at center city hotels generally exceed those in airport, suburban, or highway locations. The average annual room rate at some representative center city hotels in 1983 exceeded by 25 to 47 percent those at these other types of locations. Only hotels in resort settings reported a higher average room rate.[1] (Selected operating statistics for center city hotels appear in Figure 3–2.)

[1] Statistics from Laventhol & Horwath's annual study, U.S. Lodging Industry, for the years 1980 through 1983.

Income from the rental of guest rooms constitutes the major source of revenue at center city hotels, as it does for most hotels of any type. (See Figure 3–3.) Overall, the mix of guests at downtown hotels is fairly evenly distributed among businesspersons, tourists, and conference participants. (See Figure 3–4, which also includes other market data for center city properties.)

Although downtown hotels share a common type of location and some general traits, several styles of downtown hotels have evolved, as developers and chains have specialized in order to appeal to particular segments of a growing and diversifying market. An individual business traveler can feel literally lost in a 1,500-room hotel and totally frustrated by long waits and poor service when a group of 1,300 persons needs to be accommodated. To respond to the needs of varying types of guests, then, three distinct types of downtown hotels offer their services in most large U.S. cities: convention hotels, commercial hotels, and luxury hotels.

CONVENTION HOTELS

Downtown convention hotels generally contain 500 or more guest rooms and a large amount of meeting, banquet, and exhibition space. In addition, they often physically connect with or provide convenient access to large convention centers. Convention hotels frequently emphasize food and beverage facilities, with restaurants of differing styles and price rates from lower-priced coffee shops to mid-priced operations and gourmet rooms, and usually with an entertainment lounge and other bars. Many such hotels also include substantial retail space.

Convention hotels need large lobbies to handle the volume of check-ins and check-outs occurring in concentrated time periods and the amount of luggage carried by large groups. A number of guest rooms have two beds to allow for the high percentage of double occupancy typical of convention groups. From five to 10 percent of the guest rooms are suites in many convention hotels, as the sitting/living rooms permit use as hospitality rooms or as meeting spaces for small groups.

In an effort to accommodate individual guests better, and to cater to the upscale traveling executive, some large convention hotels have designated certain floors as special service floors, with personalized attention given to guests staying there. Examples include Hyatt's Regency Clubs, Marriott's and Radisson's Concierge Levels, and Hilton's and Sheraton's Executive Towers sections. The hotels control access to these floors and provide on them several, and sometimes all, of these features: a concierge; separate check-in/check-out desk(s); 24-hour room service; an honor bar; a lobby/lounge area; special in-room amenities such as extra-thick towels, bathroom scales, shower massages, complimentary toiletries, or terrycloth robes; turn-down service; complimentary daily newspapers; and continental breakfast/evening hors d'oeuvres.

Brief profiles of several convention hotels exemplify the scope of available facilities:

FIGURE 3-2

OPERATING STATISTICS FOR CENTER CITY PROPERTIES

	1981	1982
Occupancy	67.0%	64.2%
Double Occupancy	38.3%	36.0%
Average Room Rate	$48.48	$56.12
Ratio of Net Income before Income Taxes to Total Sales	10.4%	0.8%
Return on Total Assets	9.6%	0.6%

Source: Laventhol & Horwath's annual *U.S. Lodging Industry,* 1982 and 1983 editions.

FIGURE 3-3

COMPOSITION OF SALES FOR CENTER CITY PROPERTIES

	1981	1982
Revenue Sources		
Rooms	65.4%	61.6%
Food	20.6	23.8
Beverage	8.1	8.8
Telephone	2.9	2.9
Minor Operating Departments	1.4	1.3
Rentals and Other Income	1.6	1.6
	100.0%	100.0%

Source: Laventhol & Horwath's annual *U.S. Lodging Industry,* 1982 and 1983 editions.

FIGURE 3-4

MARKET DATA FOR CENTER CITY PROPERTIES

	1981	1982
	Percentage of Repeat Business	
	46.4%	41.7%
	Composition of Market	
Government Officials	5.8%	4.3%
Business Travelers	37.9	32.4
Tourists	18.0	28.7
Conference Participants	24.6	27.7
Others	13.7	6.9
	100.0%	100.0%
	Advance Reservations	
Percentage of Advance Reservations	83.9%	83.6%
Composition of Advance Reservations		
Direct	38.0	42.2
Reservations System	26.5	29.5
Travel Agents and Tour Operators	22.2	17.4
Other	13.3	10.9
	100.0%	100.0%
	Method of Payment	
Cash	25.6%	26.3%
Credit Card	50.6	52.6
Travel Agent or Tour Operator	7.8	4.8
All Other Credit	16.0	16.3
	100.0%	100.0%

Source: Laventhol & Horwath's annual *U.S. Lodging Industry,* 1982 and 1983 editions.

The Westin Bonaventure in Los Angeles contains 1,500 guest rooms; 10 restaurants and lounges; a ballroom for groups of up to 3,000 seated theater style, or 2,800 seated for a banquet; an exhibition hall of 25,116 square feet; and 19 smaller meeting rooms. Nonconvention amenities include a five-level shopping gallery, an outdoor pool, and eight nearby tennis courts.

The New York Hilton at Rockefeller Center comprises a grand total of 2,124 guest rooms; five restaurants and lounges; and 150,000 square feet of convention, exhibition, and meeting space. Its staff speaks 35 languages, and its lobby offers the convenience of several airline offices, a ticket agency, and an American Express office.

The Franklin Plaza in Philadelphia houses 800 guest rooms, eight restaurants and lounges, 16,500 square feet of exhibition space, and function rooms with a banquet capacity of 2,000 persons. Amenities consist of an indoor pool, racquetball and squash courts, a running track, and a health club.

The Memphis Hyatt provides 300 guest rooms, three restaurants and lounges, 21 meeting rooms, and 12,000 square feet of exhibition space.

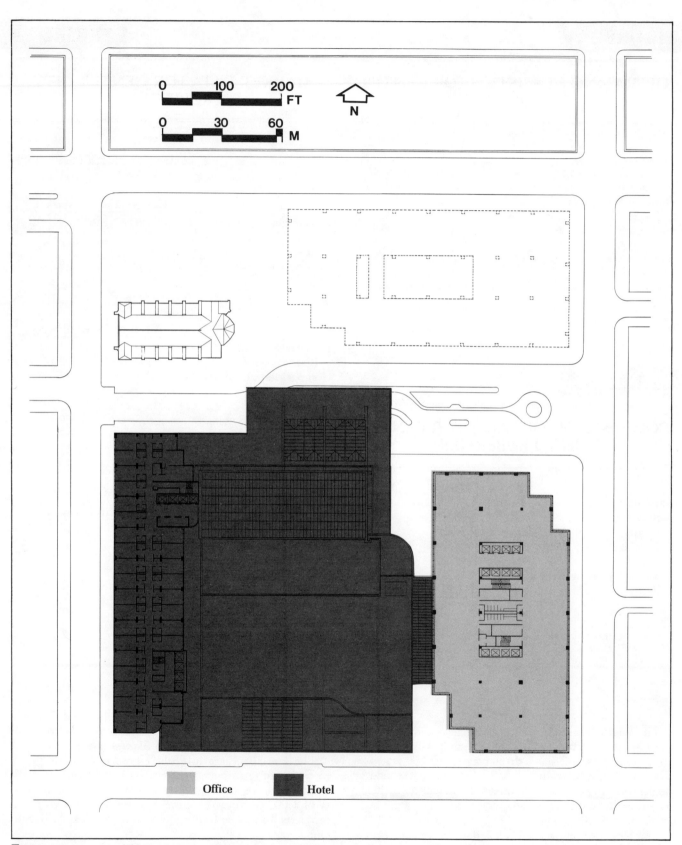

Franklin Plaza—a $97 million complex incorporating offices, a convention center, and an 800-room hotel—occupies one city block in downtown Philadelphia. The large lobby and pre-function area help in handling the large volume of check-ins and check-outs that occur in concentrated time periods, and aid in accommodating large meeting functions.

COMMERCIAL HOTELS

Downtown commercial hotels, somewhat smaller than convention hotels, generally offer 300 to 500 rooms. Conventions and meetings may constitute an important segment served by commercial hotels, but the groups are smaller. Not unusually, these hotels afford specialized meeting space, such as well-appointed boardrooms. Most such hotels make available a scaled-down amount of public space, with no more than two restaurants—a coffee shop and a higher-priced outlet—and limited retail space. The following are typical properties of this kind:

The Sheraton Plaza in Chicago, with its 336 guest rooms, also has one 120-seat restaurant and a 90-seat lounge; 21 meeting rooms, with the largest able to seat 275 persons theater style, or 240 for banquets; and an outdoor pool.

The Meridien Houston Hotel has 363 guest rooms; two restaurants of 125 seats each—one a gourmet room and the other a less expensive cafe; two lounges with a total of 140 seats; and 10,000 square feet of meeting/banquet space, including a ballroom of 5,600 square feet with a banquet capacity of 440. Guests can use one of three private health clubs in downtown Houston. They also benefit from the services of a concierge desk and enjoy the pleasant overall French flavor of the establishment.

The Holiday Inn in the Financial District/China Town area of San Francisco affords 562 guest rooms; two food outlets, one a 150-seat restaurant and the other a 75-seat

Toronto-based Four Seasons Hotels, Ltd., aims for the least price-sensitive trade, the top 10 percent of the hotel market. Its foray into the Washington, D.C., market is this hotel in Georgetown, which has 188 rooms and 20 suites. Four Seasons' equity partners include major insurance companies such as Equitable and AEtna, and prominent developers such as Urban Investment and Cadillac Fairview. Typically, Four Seasons' equity stake does not exceed 25 percent.

coffee shop; a 70-seat lobby bar and a 100-seat entertainment lounge; and 5,000 square feet of meeting space, the largest room of which measures 2,000 square feet and divides into three sections. A rooftop swimming pool provides an additional attraction.

Finally, the Best Western Motor Inn in Albuquerque contains 375 guest rooms, two restaurants and lounges, two pools, and banquet and convention facilities.

LUXURY HOTELS

Downtown luxury hotels are found primarily in the largest metropolitan areas of the United States, where sufficient numbers of discriminating potential guests pass through, who are willing and able to pay the high room rates charged. Typically, luxury hotels consist of 250 rooms or fewer, although some have as many as 400 or 500 rooms. These larger luxury hotels cater to top-echelon corporate travelers and to such tourists as are recognized and called by name by the hotel staff. All luxury hotels provide high-quality furnishings, a superior restaurant, and an extensive array of guest amenities and services. The emphasis on service results in a higher ratio of employees to guest rooms than is found in a lower-priced hotel with facilities of the same size. Luxury hotels may accommodate some meeting and banquet business, but, if so, they emphasize small groups.

The Whitehall in Chicago, for instance, offers 226 guest rooms and suites with furnishings in the style of the 18th century; the Whitehall Club, a private dining room open only to hotel guests and members; full concierge service, evening maid service, and more than one staff member per guest; and meeting and reception rooms to accommodate small groups (10 to 250).

The Four Seasons Hotel in Washington, D.C., provides 208 guest rooms and suites; the 125-seat Aux Beaux Champs restaurant, a 40-seat cafe, and the Garden Lounge, with 125

The 774-room J.W. Marriott Hotel on Washington, D.C.'s Pennsylvania Avenue should become a major presence as a commercial hotel, with its attached shopping mall and office building.

The Stanford Court Hotel in San Francisco exemplifies a return to the elegance of an earlier era. Built on the site of the Leland Stanford mansion on Nob Hill and originally operated as the Stanford Court Apartments, the hotel has 402 guest rooms, including 34 suites. The property aims to provide a first-class luxury hotel featuring understated elegance, residential decor, and outstanding service.

seats; and 8,200 square feet of meeting space, with a banquet capacity of 400. It maintains a guest history file and a 24-hour concierge service, and it employs a multilingual staff.

The Sheraton Grande Hotel in Los Angeles, with its 487 guest rooms, also houses Ravel, a 103-seat French gourmet restaurant; the Back Porch, a casual, indoor/outdoor 175-seat cafe on multilevel terraces overlooking the pool; a contemporary lobby bar; and an entertainment lounge. It makes available 24-hour room service, 24-hour valet service, concierge service, and a butler on every guest room floor. The bathrooms display marble floors, walls, and vanities; and limousine service and a helicopter pad give the hotel convenient transportation facilities.

The Carlyle Hotel in New York, similarly luxurious but in more of an old world style, makes available 250 rooms for both residential and transient occupancy; an English Regency–style dining room, a cafe, and cocktail lounges; two small conference rooms; and two meeting rooms. Banquet capacity is 175 persons. Every guest room provides either a kitchen or a pantry serving area, in this exclusive, European-style hotel with its emphasis on fine service.

DOWNTOWN FACILITIES IN SMALLER CITIES

Demand for hotel rooms in some smaller cities of the United States may be insufficient in size or in depth to support the variety of hotel products available in major cities. Consequently, properties must be designed and operated to serve a wide spectrum of guests. Hotels that fall into this category include:

Hotel	Location	Number of Guest Rooms
Amway Grand Plaza Hotel	Grand Rapids, Michigan	700
Stouffer's Five Seasons Hotel	Cedar Rapids, Iowa	282
Sheraton at St. Johns Place	Jacksonville, Florida	350
The Portland Hilton	Portland, Oregon	500
Hyatt Birmingham at Civic Center	Birmingham, Alabama	405

This brief listing shows that hotels located in smaller cities serving a variety of markets differ considerably in number of guest rooms. However, each emphasizes flexible meeting/banquet space and offers some recreational amenities. Such hotels often do a considerable amount of local food and beverage business, both in the hotel's restaurant(s) and lounge(s), and through banquets and other catering services. The managements of many of these properties need to be active in community affairs, since hotels in smaller cities often act as local social centers.

RESORT HOTELS

GENERAL TRAITS

Originally, resort hotels in the United States were sited near water (at either an ocean beach or a lakeside), in scenic mountain settings, or near natural wonders such as hot springs. They were operated as independent hotels and frequently on a seasonal basis only. They relied largely on the natural attractions of the area instead of on building an extensive selection of amenities or facilities. Guests attracted to these resorts were individual, "social" guests: those with money, power, and influence. Surviving examples of older resort hotels include the Boca Raton Hotel & Club, Boca Raton, Florida; The Broadmoor, Colorado Springs, Colorado; The Breakers, Palm Beach, Florida; the Grand Hotel, Mackinac Island, Michigan; The Greenbrier, White Sulphur Springs, West Virginia; the Grove Park Inn, Asheville, North Carolina; and the Hotel del Coronado, San Diego, California. Although these hotels originally served only the wealthy elite, they now cater to a wider spectrum of guests while still providing the ambiance on which they were originally marketed.

New resort hotels began to be developed in alliance with manmade attractions in the mid-20th century. The growth of interstate highways, the introduction of jet travel, the increase in leisure time, and the growing affluence of the American population, each helped to make vacation travel feasible for more Americans. Thus, a new and larger demand arose for hotel accommodations at resort locations.

Some resort hotels were constructed around golf and tennis, as were the Doral Hotel & Country Club in Miami, Florida, and The Lodge at Pebble Beach in California. Other resort hotels aimed to generate gaming business at Nevada casinos. During the 1930s, when licensed casino gaming first became legal in Nevada, only a few small casinos existed in Las Vegas, and these catered almost exclusively to local residents. By the late 1940s, Las Vegas began to promote tourism and to create business; hotels such as the Las Vegas Hilton, The Dunes, The Sahara, and The Stardust were built solely to attract and accommodate visitors who would then use the casino. Similarly, in the late 1970s, the legalization of casinos in Atlantic City, New Jersey, resulted in several major new hotels dependent on this manmade attraction. New resort hotels also grew up in natural destinations such as Hawaii (Hyatt Regency/Maui), the Rocky Mountains (Keystone Ranch), and the Caribbean (Rockresort's Little Dix Bay, Virgin Gorda, British Virgin Islands).

Resort hotels have also been developed in conjunction with theme parks. Events in central Florida after the opening of Walt Disney World in late 1971 provide the most dramatic evidence of this type of development. Two major hotels—the 1,047-room Contemporary Hotel and the 636-room Polynesian Hotel—were developed within Walt Disney World, while numerous hotels sprang up in the surrounding area to accommodate the millions of visitors attracted to this tourist destination yearly. The 870-room Buena Vista Palace, standing within the hotel plaza at Walt Disney World Village and open since early 1983, exemplifies this trend. By 1983, over 34,000 hotel rooms had become available in the greater Orlando area, with thousands more either under construction or proposed. The expansion of facilities within Walt Disney World (primarily the creation of EPCOT), the opening of the Orange County Convention Center, and the evolution of other attractions such as Sea World and Circus World all combined to generate the tremendous room demand that supports this hotel concentration.

Resort hotels vary widely in number of guest rooms and in facilities available, depending on their locations and on the types of markets served. In recent years, however, a trend has

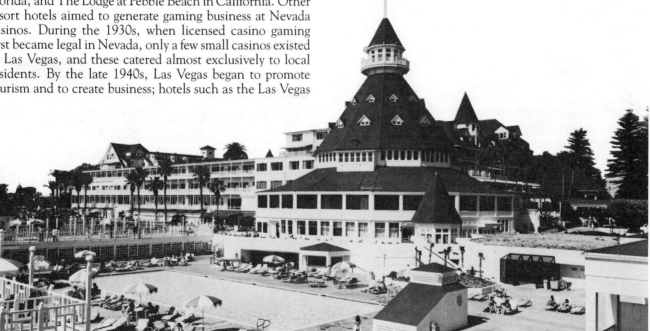

*P*oolside at the Hotel del Coronado in San Diego, California.

occurred toward active outdoor activities, reflecting the health and fitness boom within the American population since the 1970s. To support the variety of amenities and facilities provided, resort hotels today are typically open throughout the year. In addition, even old-line resorts such as The Greenbrier and The Broadmoor now cater to group convention business, as well as to their traditional market, the individual social guest.

Although tourists are the primary source of room demand for resort properties, conference participants embody an important secondary business source. (See Figure 3–5.) Another trait of resort hotels is that double occupancy is highest there, because of the tourist concentration. (See Figure 3–6 for double-occupancy and selected operating statistics for resort properties, and Figure 3–7 for the composition of sales for resort properties in 1981 and 1982.)

CHAIN RESORT HOTELS

In the 1960s and 1970s, major U.S. hotel chains such as Hilton, Sheraton, Hyatt, and Marriott identified an opportunity in the resort segment of the lodging industry. Such chains recognized that they could effectively accommodate

---

FIGURE 3-5

MARKET DATA FOR RESORT PROPERTIES

	1981	1982
	Percentage of Repeat Business	
	46.1%	36.2%
	Composition of Market	
Government Officials	2.1%	1.0%
Business Travelers	16.3	11.6
Tourists	53.3	56.9
Conference Participants	24.0	27.3
Others	4.3	3.2
	100.0%	100.0%
	Advance Reservations	
Percentage of Advance Reservations	88.4%	87.2%
Composition of Advance Reservations		
Direct	47.8%	43.8%
Reservations System	14.3	19.9
Travel Agents and Tour Operators	31.1	28.7
Other	6.8	7.6
	100.0%	100.0%
	Method of Payment	
Cash	39.4%	30.3%
Credit Card	32.2	40.3
Travel Agent or Tour Operator	17.1	18.2
All Other Credit	11.3	11.2
	100.0%	100.0%

Source: Laventhol & Horwath's annual U.S. Lodging Industry, 1982 and 1983 editions.

FIGURE 3-6

OPERATING STATISTICS FOR RESORT PROPERTIES

	1981	1982
Occupancy	64.2%	69.0%
Double Occupancy	75.0%	71.6%
Average Room Rate	$51.37	$55.62
Ratio of Net Income before Income Taxes to Total Sales	11.4%	5.0%
Return on Total Assets	10.4%	3.6%

Source: Laventhol & Horwath's annual U.S. Lodging Industry, 1982 and 1983 editions.

FIGURE 3-7

COMPOSITION OF SALES FOR RESORT PROPERTIES

	1981	1982
Revenue Sources		
Rooms	69.8%	61.9%
Food	17.0	22.6
Beverage	7.9	9.8
Telephone	2.6	3.0
Minor Operated Departments	1.1	0.8
Rentals and Other Income	1.6	1.9
	100.0%	100.0%

Source: Laventhol & Horwath's annual U.S. Lodging Industry, 1982 and 1983 editions.

both the individual-tourist and group segments of the market with proper facility planning. This would reduce severe seasonal fluctuations in demand and thus improve overall annual occupancy.

To the resort field, these major chains brought their traditional strategic advantages, including their extensive referral networks, their marketing expertise and seasoned experience in handling groups, and their chain images and mass appeal. Chains now own 41.9 percent of resort properties (a total of 757) and 53.1 percent of the available resort rooms (a total of 152,928).[2]

Marriott, for example, now has a number of resort hotels, such as Marco Beach Hotel Villas, Marco Island, Florida; The Camelback Inn, Scottsdale, Arizona; Rancho Las Palmas Resort, Rancho Mirage, California; and Marriott at Shipyard Plantation, Hilton Head, South Carolina. Similarly, Holiday Inns has the Acapulco Holiday Inn and the Holiday Inn Aruba, while Sheraton has the Sheraton Santa Barbara Hotel and Spa, and the PGA National Sheraton Resort.

CONDOMINIUM RESORT OPERATIONS

In the 1970s, the full-service resort hotel saw competition emerge from a new source. Condominiums in resort areas began to be sold as secondary or vacation residences whose owners then had the option of placing their units in a rental management system. A management company, selected by unit owners, would then manage the day-to-day operation of the resort that resulted. Unit owners could only use their resort residences for a limited period of time. They received the revenue from the rental of their units and paid the related expenses. Some of the condominiums at Sea Pines Plantation and Palmetto Dunes Plantation on Hilton Head Island, South Carolina, and at Keystone in Colorado typify this kind of operation.

Sometimes, the sale of the condominium units was registered with the Securities and Exchange Commission, and unit buyers were required to place their units in a mandatory rental pool. In this situation, revenue was pooled, and revenue and expenses were both distributed according to a predetermined formula. Innisbrook at Tarpon Springs, Florida, and Tamarron in Colorado both operate in this manner.

By the mid-1970s, some condominium developers had begun to offer some units on a timeshare basis. Typically, 50 one-week shares would be sold, with two off-season weeks reserved for annual repairs and maintenance. Buyers could purchase one or more shares, each of which entitled them to use a given unit during the same week each year, either for a specified number of years or forever. Buyers also could opt to join a trading system whereby they could exchange their week in their own unit for a week at an affiliated resort in another destination. The price of a share varied from the peak season to the low season, but fell within the financial capabilities of many Americans. Although some abuse of the

---

[2] Source: Laventhol & Horwath. These data are based on a total of 1,806 properties and of 287,754 rooms.

The Sheraton Maui on Kaanapali Beach in Hawaii.

PGA National is a 2,340-acre planned recreational and resort community in Palm Beach Gardens, Florida, that offers various facilities including the PGA National Golf Club and the Sheraton Resort. Opened in 1982, the Sheraton Resort comprises a 336-room hotel and conference center, with restaurants, lounges, a solar-heated swimming pool, and a sand beach on a 26-acre lake.

Mariners Inn is a 324-unit luxury condominium resort hotel located on a 13-acre waterfront site in Hilton Head, South Carolina. Each of the rooms provides features of a condominium, and each is sold to an individual buyer. Although the arrangement allows the investor to use the purchased unit for a total of 30 days a year, the purchaser cannot stay longer than 14 days at a time and still qualify for all the tax advantages offered by this type of investment.

concept has occurred, many excellent timeshare condominium complexes exist, and these have attracted some buyers who otherwise might have stayed at regular full-service hotels.

HIGHWAY/INTERSTATE FACILITIES

Highway or interstate hotels came into prominence in the 1960s. As the interstate highway system neared completion, Americans were becoming more mobile, and new chains were being born. Lodging chains such as Holiday Inns, Ramada Inns, Howard Johnson's, Quality Inns, TraveLodge, and Rodeway Inns expanded rapidly, primarily along interstates. Each developed an identifiable image and built a referral network as it grew.

Typically, highway facilities are two-story, exterior-corridor structures with 200 rooms or fewer, and with adjacent surface parking. Restaurants and lounges occupy separate commercial buildings that also contain the registration area, administration offices, and lobby. Banquet and meeting rooms are small, able to seat only 200 people or fewer, and situated next to the restaurant. Recreational amenities originally consisted simply of an outdoor pool.

As the highway concept evolved, recreational amenities became more varied. Enclosed courtyards that included a swimming pool, sauna, whirlpool, miniature putting green, and other games, as well as a patio food and beverage area, became prominent by the mid-1970s. Holiday Inns, Inc., went so far as to trademark this enclosed courtyard concept, calling it a "Holidome." Other chains and independents followed, in order to penetrate the weekend vacation market and to attract vacationing families who could supplement weekday commercial demand.

Highway properties are reasonably priced, although rates usually run higher than in economy establishments; highway hotels are also characterized by short lengths of stay, with one night being the average. (For occupancy, double-occu-

pancy, and other operating statistics for highway properties, see Figure 3–8. The market composition of guests at highway properties, the percentage of repeat business, reservation characteristics, and methods of payment appear in Figure 3–9.) As do other types of hotels, highway hotels derive most of their revenue from guest room sales, but a significant secondary portion does come from food and beverage sales. (See Figure 3–10.)

Examples of this kind of property are profiled below:

The Holiday Inn in Effingham, Illinois, contains 107 guest rooms in a two-story, exterior-corridor structure standing at the junction of Interstates 70 and 57 with West Fayette

FIGURE 3-9

MARKET DATA FOR HIGHWAY PROPERTIES

	1981	1982
Percentage of Repeat Business		
	50.8%	46.9%
Composition of Market		
Government Officials	3.1%	4.9%
Business Travelers	52.0	49.4
Tourists	25.8	28.8
Conference Participants	15.7	10.6
Others	3.4	6.3
	100.0%	100.0%
Advance Reservations		
Percentage of Advance Reservations	71.3%	59.2%
Composition of Advance Reservations		
Direct	35.1%	44.5%
Reservations System	34.0	32.5
Travel Agents and Tour Operators	20.1	12.5
Other	10.8	10.5
	100.0%	100.0%
Method of Payment		
Cash	37.1%	32.1%
Credit Card	48.2	54.8
Travel Agent or Tour Operator	3.6	6.9
All Other Credit	11.1	6.2
	100.0%	100.0%

Source: Laventhol & Horwath's annual *U.S. Lodging Industry,* 1982 and 1983 editions.

FIGURE 3-8

OPERATING STATISTICS FOR HIGHWAY PROPERTIES

	1981	1982
Occupancy	71.6%	66.0%
Double Occupancy	41.0%	41.0%
Average Room Rate	$34.63	$38.09
Ratio of Net Income before Income Taxes to Total Sales	13.7%	8.7%
Return on Total Assets	13.0%	7.4%

Source: Laventhol & Horwath's annual *U.S. Lodging Industry,* 1982 and 1983 editions.

FIGURE 3-10

COMPOSITION OF SALES FOR HIGHWAY PROPERTIES

Revenue Sources	1981	1982
Rooms	59.2%	57.6%
Food	24.0	24.8
Beverage	8.5	9.0
Telephone	2.0	2.1
Minor Operating Departments	3.7	4.4
Rentals and Other Income	2.6	2.1
	100.0%	100.0%

Source: Laventhol & Horwath's annual *U.S. Lodging Industry*, 1982 and 1983 editions.

Road. The inn includes the Red Oak restaurant, a cocktail lounge, and meeting rooms to accommodate up to 450 people. An outdoor swimming pool attracts travelers passing by.

The Ramada Inn in Davenport, Iowa, provides 183 guest rooms in a two-story, interior-corridor building at the junction of Interstate 90 and U.S. Highway 61. Facilities consist of a restaurant, a cocktail lounge, and meeting rooms for up to 300 people; amenities center on the enclosed courtyard, which contains a pool, sauna, whirlpool, and game room.

The Quality Inn in Madison, Wisconsin, offers 156 rooms in a two-story structure with interior corridors, on combined U.S. Highways 18-12 and Interstate 90. A restaurant, a cocktail lounge, and meeting and banquet space for 300 persons round out the facilities, while an indoor swimming pool provides an amenity for guests.

The Howard Johnson's in Kenosha, Wisconsin, is a 96-room, two-story structure with exterior corridors, sited alongside Interstate 90 at Wisconsin Highway 50. It features a restaurant, a cocktail lounge, meeting and banquet rooms for up to 100 persons, and an outdoor pool.

Finally, the Days Inn in Jackson, Mississippi, off Interstate 40, contrasts with the above-listed properties in that it offers 122 guest rooms but no on-site food service or swimming pool.

SUBURBAN FACILITIES

Interstate beltways around core downtown areas catalyzed, and the availability of land formed the medium for the development shift from center city to suburban locations. Large portions of the population migrated to suburban residential neighborhoods, with retail and office/industrial centers following. This migration created pockets of lodging demand within the ever-widening metropolitan areas, with the downtowns acting as the hubs and the major suburbs functioning as the spokes. Lodging chains saw an opportunity to expand and moved to suburban areas in the early 1970s.

Suburban land costs slightly exceeded those at interstate locations, but remained less than on downtown sites. Construction, therefore, took the form of mid-rise buildings of four to 12 stories containing between 200 and 500 rooms, with a median size of 300 rooms. With this kind of building's smaller footprint, any extra land offered itself for extensive public space that could serve the anticipated commercial meeting demand and the local food and beverage demand. Recreational facilities also appeared, often consisting of an enclosed pool, a sauna, and a whirlpool; these increased weekend transient demand.

The typical guest's length of stay increased beyond one night to an average of two nights, as commercial travelers remained longer, and as penetration into the meetings market became more significant. Conference participants now account for approximately 15 to 20 percent of total demand in suburban hotels. (See Figure 3–11.) Room rates are typically higher than or equal to those at highway facilities, but lower than those at downtown hotels. (Figure 3–12 shows operating statistics for typical suburban properties.)

The following profiles of suburban hotels will present a more detailed picture:

The Holiday Inn in Westlake, Ohio, a suburb of Cleveland, has 267 guest rooms in a five-story structure north of Interstate 90 on Crocker Road. It contains a 250-seat formal restaurant, Cahoon's; a 75-seat coffee shop; a 175-seat cocktail lounge; 9,700 square feet of meeting and banquet space, including a ballroom of 6,000 square feet that divides into four sections; a Holidome with an indoor pool, whirlpool, and game room; plus a health club.

The Marriott Hotel in Perimeter Center, Atlanta, Georgia, stands in a suburban office park adjacent to Perimeter Mall and Park Place. It is a 15-story hotel with 404 guest rooms, a 205-seat restaurant, a 140-seat lounge, 14 meeting rooms with a 400-person capacity for banquets, and facilities for saunas, tennis, swimming, and games.

The Hilton Inn in Naperville, Illinois, also sited in an office park, offers 160 rooms in an eight-floor structure with smoked glass windows and earthtone brickwork. A 150-seat Allgauer's restaurant, a 40-seat Greenhouse casual restaurant/cocktail lounge, and 5,300 square feet of meeting and banquet space afford food and beverage, as well as group-meeting facilities.

In St. Louis Park, Minnesota, the Sheraton Hotel is a 15-story structure with 307 guest rooms, featuring an elegant restaurant, Seasons in the Park, and a casual restaurant/lounge with live entertainment called Kelly's. The hotel also has a 7,500-square-foot ballroom, six additional function rooms, and an indoor pool.

AIRPORT HOTELS

Before it became a fact, the development of hotels at airports had often been encouraged by local airport authorities who would thereby receive lease income. Such

FIGURE 3-11

MARKET DATA FOR SUBURBAN PROPERTIES

	1981	1982
	Percentage of Repeat Business	
	45.7%	55.1%
	Composition of Market	
Government Officials	2.8%	4.1%
Business Travelers	56.3	52.6
Tourists	16.4	21.9
Conference Participants	20.8	17.6
Others	3.7	3.8
	100.0%	100.0%
	Advance Reservations	
Percentage of Advance Reservations	79.5%	79.4%
Composition of Advance Reservations		
Direct	45.6	38.7
Reservations System	33.2	30.9
Travel Agents or Tour Operators	12.1	13.7
Other	9.1	16.7
	100.0%	100.0%
	Method of Payment	
Cash	32.2%	26.3%
Credit Card	48.9	51.8
Travel Agent or Tour Operator	4.9	3.4
All Other Credit	14.0	18.5
	100.0%	100.0%

Source: Laventhol & Horwath's annual *U.S. Lodging Industry,* 1982 and 1983 editions.

FIGURE 3-12

OPERATING STATISTICS FOR SUBURBAN PROPERTIES

	1981	1982
Occupancy	70.7%	68.8%
Double Occupancy	35.7%	41.4%
Average Room Rate	$38.38	$38.09
Ratio of Net Income before Income Taxes to Total Sales	11.3%	12.4%
Return on Total Assets	13.9%	9.1%

Source: Laventhol & Horwath's annual *U.S. Lodging Industry,* 1982 and 1983 editions.

Artist's rendering of the Dallas/Fort Worth Airport Hilton.

hotels were needed to serve passengers and airline crews alike (although many crews preferred to stay downtown, closer to restaurants, retail shops, and other attractions). One of the first on-premise airport hotels was built within the Miami International Airport in 1959. These hotels most frequently appeared at larger airports, which handled a sufficient volume of traffic to support such operations.

Gradually, developers and operators foresaw the chance to serve the meetings market as well as passengers and crews. Because airports lie at a distance from central business districts, businesspersons could save time and the cost of ground transportation by meeting at airport facilities. Additional savings accrued because room rates were lower than those charged by hotels of comparable quality downtown. As busi-

ness, office, and industrial parks and, later, free trade zones and distribution centers were located near airports, these also stimulated airport hotel development.

The facilities provided at off-premise airport hotels closely resemble those at other suburban hotels. Hotels sited near airports, however, differ importantly in that they cater to a more diverse market. Their market includes guests associated with airport activity; passengers whose connections force them to stay overnight; passengers who are stranded due to weather conditions or to mechanical difficulties; and airline crews.

The number of guest rooms in hotels either on airport property or near to it varies considerably. Airport hotels, however, are generally somewhat larger than other suburban

FIGURE 3-13   FIGURE 3-14

OPERATING STATISTICS FOR AIRPORT PROPERTIES

	1981	1982
Occupancy	72.1%	66.0%
Double Occupancy	31.0%	29.0%
Average Room Rate	$38.58	$44.98
Ratio of Net Income before		
Income Taxes to Total Sales	20.4%	4.2%
Return on Total Assets	16.5%	3.0%

Source: Laventhol & Horwath's annual *U.S. Lodging Industry*, 1982 and 1983 editions.

hotels, averaging between 250 and 800 rooms. They also command somewhat higher room rates than do other suburban properties. As a result of air traffic patterns, many airport hotels are only low- to mid-rise structures. (For operating statistics and market data on airport properties, see Figures 3–13 and 3–14.)

The Marriott Corporation took an early lead in developing airport hotels because of the corporation's background in on-board airline feeding. The Hilton Corporation has also emphasized airport locations, both in major markets and near lower-volume airports.

The following profiles of airport hotels show an available range of facilities:

The Marriott Hotel, Kansas City International Airport, Kansas City, Missouri, with its 265 guest rooms, also offers the 150-seat King's Wharf restaurant and 145-seat Windjammer Lounge, 30 meeting rooms seating between 10 and 500 persons for banquets, and an indoor pool. Only one-quarter mile from the airport, the hotel drives its guests to and from their flights in a courtesy car.

The O'Hare Hilton, O'Hare International Airport, Chicago, Illinois, consists of 886 guest rooms, seven restaurants and lounges, and 60 conference and meeting rooms seating up to 400 persons. The hotel's enclosed moving sidewalk brings passengers to and from the airport terminal.

The Registry Hotel, Bloomington, Minnesota, houses 330 guest rooms in a 10-story structure two miles from the airport. Two restaurants and two lounges make available food and beverage service, while 15 meeting rooms—seating 30 to 700 persons with a banquet capacity of 600 persons—accommodate groups. Amenities include an indoor pool, sauna, and Jacuzzi, and the hotel runs a courtesy airport limousine as well.

ECONOMY FACILITIES

In the 1960s and 1970s, management and owners of many hotels upgraded their services and expanded their amenities in an attempt to attract business. Generally, they could raise

MARKET DATA FOR AIRPORT PROPERTIES

	1981	1982
Percentage of Repeat Business		
	43.8%	57.3%
Composition of Market		
Government Officials	4.6%	2.2%
Business Travelers	53.1	44.8
Tourists	21.6	33.1
Conference Participants	13.0	17.0
Others	7.7	2.9
	100.0%	100.0%
Advance Reservations		
Percentage of Advance Reservations	82.1%	76.7%
Composition of Advance Reservations		
Direct	34.8	37.4
Reservations System	39.1	33.9
Travel Agents and Tour Operators	18.8	15.4
Other	7.3	13.3
	100.0%	100.0%
Method of Payment		
Cash	40.1%	30.4%
Credit Card	42.6	50.8
Travel Agent or Tour Operator	6.0	3.9
All Other Credit	11.3	14.9
	100.0%	100.0%

Source: Laventhol & Horwath's annual *U.S. Lodging Industry*, 1982 and 1983 editions.

room rates without significant resistance or complaints from their guests, since business travelers on expense accounts constituted the largest segment of lodging demand. Hotelkeepers, of course, needed the rate increases to pay for new facilities and services, and to cover the inflationary increases that occurred in the 1970s, especially in such key areas as labor, energy, and construction. Meanwhile, however, many businesses became concerned with inflation and controlled travel expenditures more carefully. True, pleasure travel was expanding rapidly, but much of this expanded demand came from a price-sensitive portion of the market.

Economy properties emerged, then, as an alternative for value-conscious travelers who required only the lodging basics—clean, comfortable rooms at 20 to 50 percent below

The North Hills Comfort Inn in Raleigh, North Carolina, has 84 guest rooms, an apartment for the manager, a lobby and office, and laundry and storage space. Acquisition of the 1.1-acre site cost $250,000.

market-area average room rates. Instead of offering restaurants, extensive meeting and banquet space, recreational facilities and other ancillary amenities that many travelers did not use or wish to pay for, economy hotels concentrated on guest rooms, offering them at widely affordable prices.

Economy properties were originally built along interstate highways and on the outskirts of major metropolitan areas because land was inexpensive and readily available there. As economy properties evolved, they moved to suburban areas, resorts, airport vicinities, and, finally, downtown settings. Economy hotels usually followed full-service lodging properties into these locations. Originally, economy properties took the form of two-story, exterior-corridor structures with 50 to 150 rooms. Motel 6 was the first economy or budget hotel chain, starting in 1963. As the name implies, Motel 6 offered no-frills, rooms-only accommodation at a rate of $6.00 per night. Rooms had shower stalls but no bathtubs, and guests paid extra for the use of the television set. Telephones were not available in guest rooms.

The economy segment expanded rapidly—from 1970, when only six chains existed, with about 225 properties and 16,000 rooms, to 1983, when over 60 chains operated, with more than 2,400 properties and 250,000 rooms. This segment has grown not only in size but also in property differentiation. Economy products now differ according to the quality level of the facilities and to the price/value relationship to the guest. By the early 1980s, the economy industry had generated three distinct tiers.

The upper tier includes properties offering relatively upscale furnishings and decor. Such properties charge room rates that are closer to market-area average rates (20 to 25 percent below), and contain more rooms (100 to 150) than do other economy hotels. They also provide a 24-hour front desk, a small multipurpose room, interior corridors, and a toll-free ("800") reservation number. Examples of upper-tier facilities are LaQuinta Motor Inns, Drury Inns, Comfort Inns, Days Inns, Dillon Inns, Signature Inns, Skylight Inns, and Hampton Inns. (Hampton Inns is Holiday Inns' entry in the economy segment.) Specific descriptions of several properties representing upper-tier economy hotels follow:

The Signature Inn in Castleton, Indiana, has 126 guest rooms, each containing 312 square feet. All of its guest rooms have a large desk, and each single room contains a queen-size bed and a reclining chair. An adjacent Perkins Cake 'n' Steak restaurant and additional outlets nearby provide food and beverage service. A 918-square-foot professional conference room, free HBO movies, complimentary coffee, an "800" toll-free reservation number, and an outdoor pool complete the list of the hotel's offerings.

A Dillon Inn in Grand Rapids, Michigan, comprises 112 guest rooms, each between 321 and 364 square feet in size. All rooms are furnished with comfortable chairs and decorated in neutral and earth-toned colors; all singles have king-size beds. In a small conversation lounge, the hotel serves a complimentary continental breakfast and puts out the daily newspapers for guests to read. Guests may watch free movies, benefit from an "800" toll-free reservation number and a 24-hour desk, and dine at adjacent restaurants.

In Woodbridge, Virginia, the Comfort Inn offers a somewhat smaller number of rooms, each of which is in turn smaller in size than those listed above. On the other hand, there is a conference room, and some extra amenities are provided. The 95 guest rooms each contain between 240 and 320 square feet, and the conference room is 828 square feet in size. Two outdoor hot tubs and a game room offer relaxation, and a guest laundry provides a desirable convenience. Guests are entitled to complimentary coffee and can obtain food and beverages nearby.

Middle-tier economy facilities have 60 to 125 fully furnished guest rooms, room rates usually 25 to 40 percent below the market average, either exterior or interior corridors, and an "800" reservation number. Lodging chains belonging in this category include Red Roof Inns, Exel Inns, Thrifty Scot, Super 8 Motels, Budgetel Inns, Econo Inns, Knights Inns, and Regal 8 Inns. Descriptions of properties considered to be middle-tier economy hotels follow:

An Exel Inn, in Milwaukee, Wisconsin, contains 111 guest rooms, each 245 or 308 square feet in size. The rooms offer free HBO movies, ESPN and Cable News Network channels, complimentary coffee, and free local phone calls. The two-story brick structures have interior corridors.

The Red Roof Inn in Cedar Rapids, Iowa, is a two-story frame building with an exterior corridor. Its 109 rooms each comprise 251 square feet.

Lastly, the Thrifty Scot in Lincoln, Nebraska, with its 84 guest rooms ranging in size from 219 to 298 square feet, makes available to its guests a complimentary continental breakfast and a small meeting room off the lobby. A neighboring Perkins Cake 'n' Steak restaurant serves the guests' food and beverage needs.

The lower tier of economy properties is occupied by hotels offering the bare essentials in their guest rooms, with room rates about 50 percent below the market average. Lower-tier budget hotels range in size between 60 and 125 rooms, have exterior corridors, and limit their front desk hours. They do not accept credit cards, nor do they provide an "800" reservation number. Motel 6 is the dominant brand in the lower tier, with nationwide, year-round rates at all locations. (In 1983, these were $15.95 for a single and $19.95 for a double.) The rooms have no telephones, and guests must pay extra for television viewing. All locations do, however, feature swimming pools.

Overall, economy properties operate at higher occupancy levels than do full-service, middle-market hotels because of their smaller size and lower break-even level (the latter the result of lower fixed costs). Most economy properties employ only 15 full-time staff members per 100 available rooms. This compares to 56 equivalent employees per 100 available rooms in a full-service hotel.[3] By concentrating on room revenues and by keeping the average number of rooms per hotel between 100 and 125 units for optimal efficiency, economy hotels enjoy a significantly better profit margin and rate of return on total assets than do full-service hotels. (See Figure 3–15.)

[3] Source: Laventhol & Horwath's annual *U.S. Lodging Industry*, 1983 edition.

FIGURE 3-15

RETURN ON TOTAL ASSETS COMPARISON

	Full-Service Properties	Economy Properties
Net Income before Income Tax (Ratio to Total Sales, 1982)	7.0%	24.1%
Ratio of Return on Total Assets (Median, All Establishments, 1982)	7.2%	13.5%

Source: Laventhol & Horwath's annual *U.S. Lodging Industry*, 1983 edition.

Business travelers and tourists represent the two major user types for economy hotels. Proceeds from guest room rentals account for over 96 percent of total revenues. (Figure 3–16 shows the market mix of guests and other market data for several categories of economy properties, while Figure 3–17 summarizes the sources and uses of revenue for 1982.)

Economy properties were originally built along interstate highways and on the outskirts of major cities. The site for the 95-room Comfort Inn in Woodbridge, Virginia, lies approximately one-half mile east of the Woodbridge/Occoquan interchange of Interstate 95, some 20 miles southwest of Washington, D.C. The property, however, is not visible from the highway.

FIGURE 3-16

MARKET DATA FOR ECONOMY PROPERTIES

	Mean, All Establishments	Average Rate Tiers		
		Under $22.00	$22.00–$24.99	$25.00 and Over
		Percentage of Repeat Business		
	43.6%	47.8%	41.2%	48.3%
		Composition of Market		
Government Officials	3.5%	2.1%	3.2%	6.7%
Business Travelers	48.3	39.5	48.9	57.5
Tourists	34.9	41.8	33.9	30.0
Conference Participants	2.3	0.6	2.5	3.3
Others	11.0	16.0	11.5	2.5
	100.0%	100.0%	100.0%	100.0%
		Advance Reservations		
Percentage of Advance Reservations	21.7%	12.4%	21.0%	37.0%
Composition of Advance Reservations				
Direct Inquiry or Own Reservations System	97.6%	99.3%	97.5%	95.8%
Travel Agents and Tour Operators	0.8	0.1	0.9	1.7
Transportation Company	0.7	0.3	0.7	1.2
Other	0.9	0.3	0.9	1.3
	100.0%	100.0%	100.0%	100.0%

Method of Payment (Mean, All Establishments)

Cash	61.2%
Credit Cards	35.4
All Other Credit	3.4
	100.0%

Source: Laventhol & Horwath's annual *U.S. Economy Lodging Industry*, 1983 edition.

ALL-SUITE FACILITIES

All-suite hotels have as their predominant trait a larger-than-normal guest space (500 to 800 square feet, compared with a conventional hotel room of 300 to 400 square feet), accommodating a combination living room/parlor as well as a sleeping area. Cooking and refrigeration equipment are often provided in the guest space.

The all-suite concept resulted from efforts to meet the needs of specific demand subsegments. Businesspersons who travel frequently find these rooms spacious, homelike, and functional for use as work and display areas, as lounges for entertainment and relaxation, and as interview centers. Many businesswomen prefer all-suite hotels because they can conduct business there in a parlor rather than in a bedroom setting. Corporate personnel who are relocating, international travelers, conference participants, and others who need a long-stay facility appreciate the multiple usefulness of the suites. Many pleasure travelers also prefer suites, especially when traveling with children, because the guest spaces provide separate rooms for adults and children without the extra cost incurred in a conventional hotel.

Regardless of the specific source of market demand, however, all-suite hotels are generally well received in the marketplace. Indications of the strength of this market appeal are the relatively high incidence of repeat patronage, and the strong local reputations often achieved by all-suite properties.

Many all-suite hotels operate at higher annual occupancy levels than do conventional hotels because they have successfully penetrated the weekday transient commercial demand, the long-term demand, and the pleasure and mini-vacation demand segments. Room demand from the latter two segments frequently occurs over the weekend and may account for as much as 20 percent of the total demand in an all-suite hotel. Moreover, guests generally stay longer in an all-suite hotel, with length of stay ranging between three and five days. These properties usually command higher average room rates than do hotels offering only typical guest rooms in the same market area. While the concept varies widely from property to property, all-suite hotels take three basic forms: urban, suburban, and residential.

Urban all-suite hotels are mid- to high-rise structures containing 200 to 300 suites. This size is preferable because it retains the perceived residential atmosphere and because management can provide the desired level of personal service.

Washington, D.C., is a case in point, encompassing as it does a variety of all-suite hotels in an urban setting. Most of

these opened in the late 1970s and early 1980s. Some have small restaurants (50 to 80 seats) and lounges (20 to 50 seats), but others offer only room service, or no food and beverage service at all. (See Figure 3–18.)

Most suburban all-suite hotels stand between four and eight stories tall and are found among office building concentrations, near airports, or adjacent to retail centers. Granada Royale Hometels dominates the suburban locations and is the largest all-suite chain. With Holiday Inns' recent acquisition of Granada Royale, the latter will likely remain the market leader.

The first Granada Royale appeared in Phoenix in 1969. Since then, their concept has evolved so that Hometels now look less like apartments but still retain a residential atmosphere. Hometels characteristically use a Spanish architectural style, but some recently opened properties in the chain have departed from this precedent. The St. Paul and Minneapolis Hometels reflect an old world and a contemporary design, respectively. These hotels keep to the suburban all-suite average of four to eight floors and have 180 to 300 suites surrounding a landscaped atrium/courtyard. Granada Royale's trademark in the lodging industry has involved its morning tradition of a complimentary American-style breakfast cooked to order, and its evening provision of unlimited cocktails during a two-hour open bar for Hometel patrons and their guests. With these practices, the chain has hoped to strengthen its local market presence through word-of-mouth advertising.

The first Hometels offered no food and beverage service, other than the complimentary service in the courtyard and the very limited meeting catering. The designs of subsequent Hometels, however, incorporated full-service restaurants that were leased to experienced outside operators.

Each guest room comprises a two-room suite, with living area and separate bedroom. The living space offers a sitting area with a queen-size hide-a-bed; a wet bar; a galley kitchen with range, refrigerator, and utensils; and a dining area with

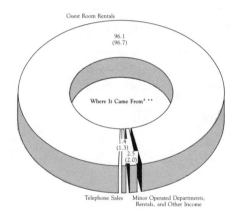

FIGURE 3-17

THE U.S. BUDGET LODGING INDUSTRY DOLLAR, 1981

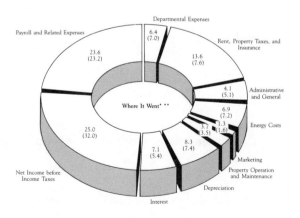

*Based on the arithmetic mean.
**1980 amounts (in parentheses).

The 125-suite Guest Quarters on Pennsylvania Avenue in Washington, D.C., has no meeting space and no lounge but does offer room service.

a large table that doubles as a conference table. Both the bedroom and the dining area have a telephone and a television set.

A recently built property is the Granada Royale Hometel in Bloomington, Minnesota. Its 219 suites surround a sky-lighted atrium/courtyard. The room mix consists of 85 "king suites" with 522 square feet, 120 "double/double" suites with 556 square feet, and 14 "executive" suites with 1,030 square feet. (The executive suites differ primarily in that they feature an attached boardroom for eight to 12 people.) Guests can dine at a 140-seat, upscale restaurant called Woolley's with its adjacent lounge that overflows into the courtyard; browse at a gift shop; enjoy an indoor pool, sauna, steam room, and whirlpool bath; and park for free in a 425-car facility.

Clearly, Granada Royale Hometels can compete directly with mid-market lodgings such as Holiday Inns, Marriott Hotels, Sheraton Inns, Hilton Inns, and Ramada Inns.

In contrast to these two earlier kinds of all-suite properties—urban and suburban—residential all-suite hotels usually sprawl in two-story complexes and offer a larger number of in-room amenities, though fewer in-hotel support services. In 1977, Brock Residence Inns pioneered this concept in Wichita, Kansas. Residence Inns typically are low-rise, garden-apartment or townhouse-style complexes, without restaurants or other major hotel amenities. The properties range in size from 64 to 290 suites. Because of their low-rise configurations, Brock Residence Inns require larger sites than do properties in other all-suite chains. Most of the suites are one-bedroom studio units of approximately 500 square feet. The bedrooms are not walled off from the kitchen and living areas as they are in other all-suite chains; furnishings, however, are more residential in nature. Kitchens are fully equipped with a full-size refrigerator/icemaker, dishwasher, garbage disposal unit, electric range/oven, blender, popcorn popper, coffeemaker, toaster, and table settings for four persons.

This chain prefers to locate its properties in suburban areas near standard full-service hotels. Thus, guests can use the amenities offered by the full-service hotels while staying

FIGURE 3-18

PROFILES OF SELECTED ALL-SUITE HOTELS IN WASHINGTON, D.C.

Property	Number of Suites	Restaurant	Lounge	Meeting Space (Sq. Ft.)	Swimming Pool
General Scott Inn Rhode Island Avenue, NW	65	No	No	No	No
The Canterbury N Street, NW	98	Yes	Yes	1,300	No
Guest Quarters New Hampshire Avenue	107	Room Service	No	No	Yes
Guest Quarters Pennsylvania Avenue	125	Room Service	No	No	No
River Inn 25th Street, NW	128	Yes	No	350	No
Quality Inn/Downtown 16th Street, NW	136	Yes	Yes	1,250	No
One Washington Circle Washington Circle, NW	152	Yes	Yes	800	Yes
Capitol Hill Hotel C Street, SE	153	No	No	900	No
Ramada Central Rhode Island Avenue, NW	186	Yes	Yes	1,600	Yes
Washington Circle Inn Pennsylvania Avenue, NW	201	No	No	1,750	No

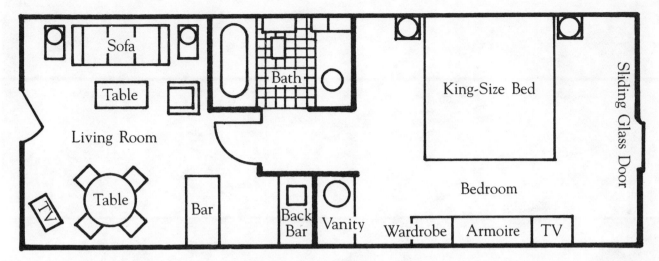

The site plan for the Park Suite Hotel in Denver typifies those of upscale hotels concentrating on room rentals and not on commercial and meeting space. The one-bedroom suite contains 500 square feet and the two-bedroom suite, 800 square feet. Public space is limited.

at the Residence Inn. Additionally, Brock Residence Inns make their appearance on sites where they can attract guests planning a long stay. Such sites may include those near corporate training centers, medical centers, and corporate parks, which have a high incidence of employee turnover and relocation.

Specifically, the Brock Residence Inn in Tulsa, Oklahoma, consists of 136 suites—104 studio suites of 504 square feet each, and 32 penthouse suites of 824 square feet each. The Inn provides a swimming pool, a Jacuzzi, and a sports court, and its gatehouse accommodates a commercial laundry, a guest laundry, a small conference room, and a sitting area. Free parking for 140 cars is available on the grounds.

A typical Brock Residence Inn. These properties have between 64 and 290 suites.

EXECUTIVE CONFERENCE CENTERS

Evolving as a distinct type of conference center during the 1970s and 1980s, executive conference centers have emerged primarily to fill the requirements of specialized meetings such as upper-management planning meetings and education/training seminars. Groups using executive conference centers include business concerns, professional organizations, and associations that look for quality rather than price in their accommodations and service. Room rates often cover overnight accommodations, three meals, conference set-up, and service charges.

Executive conference centers provide sophisticated audiovisual equipment and meeting aids, and are staffed by professional conference coordinators. These centers have between 100 and 300 lodging rooms, a number of specially designed meeting rooms, and a larger number of breakout rooms. The operations are characterized by personalized, friendly service and by high-quality food. The typical facility stands in a rural or suburban setting, about 30 miles or three-quarters of an hour's drive from an airport.

This kind of conference center generally offers conference planning assistance, videotape equipment, tape recorders, film and slide projectors, closed-circuit television, secretarial services, messenger services, and graphics services.

As might be expected, executive conference centers most depend upon conference participants for their business. (See Figure 3–19 for the customer market mix at these centers, and Figure 3–20 for a profile of a typical meeting.)

Executive conference centers normally make available to their guests tennis, swimming, and game room facilities. Sometimes, the centers also contain a gym and exercise room, a sauna, a steam bath, a racquetball area, or all of these. Golf sometimes constitutes one of the recreational amenities provided, although, in the 1982 study that generated Figures 3–19 and 3–20, only 42 percent of the respond-

The Scanticon-Princeton Executive Conference Center and Hotel constitutes a major part of the 1,604-acre Princeton Forrestal Center, a university-owned multi-use office and research park in Princeton, New Jersey.

ing centers reported golf as one of their amenities.

Three executive conference centers, briefly profiled, will exemplify this type of lodging. The Scanticon Executive Conference Center & Hotel in Princeton, New Jersey, consists of 300 sleeping rooms, at least one function room large enough to seat 458 persons theater style, and a total of 26 meeting rooms. The somewhat smaller Harrison Conference Center Inn in Southbury, Connecticut, offers 121 sleeping rooms, a function room that can seat 200 persons theater style, and 24 meeting rooms in all. Finally, Arrowwood of Westchester in Rye, New York, like Scanticon, houses 300 sleeping rooms, but accommodates 500 people theater style in its largest function room, and has 31 meeting rooms.

MULTITIERED MARKETING STRATEGIES

Throughout the 1960s and 1970s, most hotel chains were established within a well-defined market segment. An informed onlooker could clearly distinguish between those chains that appealed to the economy, middle, executive, or luxury markets. While an occasional property might position itself to cater to a nontraditional market segment, the focus of the parent company remained unchanged.

A recent phenomenon appears to be gathering momentum as a result of intense competition from "upstart" chains siphoning off specific lodging demand segments. This phenomenon is the diversification of major lodging chains into markets above or below their usual focus. Quality Inns first attempted a multitiered marketing strategy by introducing Comfort Inns and Quality Royale to complement its Quality Inns line. Others followed quickly, either by developing differing brand labels to target new segments, or by buying other existing chains (as Holiday Inns did with Granada Royale Hometels). (See Figure 3–21.)

Several causes have impelled this sudden interest in product diversification. These include:

◆ The need to recognize and to identify clearly the variations among existing properties within a chain;

◆ A belief held by some chains that, to achieve their aggressive growth plans, the chains must widen the markets to which they had appealed;

◆ High development costs in some markets, which precluded the implementation of all but upscale properties there;

◆ Until the last three to five years, the limited number of available franchisors serving the executive market (primarily, only Hilton, Sheraton, and Marriott); and

◆ Pressure from major franchisees, who were starting to secure franchises from either upscale or economy franchisors, or who were, in some cases, developing their own upscale or economy chains. (Servico with Royce Hotels, Brock with Park Suite and Residence Inns, and High Country Corporation franchising not only from Holiday Inns but also from Econo Travel, typified this trend.)

As a response to these pressures, the tiered approach not only increased a chain's potential market but also allowed it to position a property more precisely in a given market area. Some potential problems, however, exist with this continuing strategy. First, the traveling public may not be able to differentiate between the various product offerings, at least at first. Second, upscale and economy properties being built in markets where traditional properties in the same chain already operate may exert an adverse impact on the existing properties.

FOREIGN HOTEL AFFILIATIONS

Adding to the wide variety of domestic chains competing to satisfy the room demand from all segments of the lodging

---

FIGURE 3-19

EXECUTIVE CONFERENCE CENTERS: PERCENTAGE OF ROOMS OCCUPIED BY MARKET SEGMENT

Conference Participants	82.3%
Social (vacationers)	3.2
Transients	8.2
Others	6.3
	100.0%

Source: Laventhol & Horwath, *The Executive Conference Center: A Statistical and Financial Profile 1982.*

FIGURE 3-20

EXECUTIVE CONFERENCE CENTERS: PROFILE OF A TYPICAL MEETING

Size (number of persons)	140
Duration (days)	5
Meetings per Week	50
Size of Day Meetings (number of persons)	19
Maximum Number of Conferences Possible per Day (without detracting from the operation)	284
Percent of Conference Participants Staying in Single-Occupancy Rooms	74%

Source: Laventhol & Horwath, *The Executive Conference Center: A Statistical and Financial Profile 1982.*

FIGURE 3-21

CHAIN MULTITIERED BRAND MARKETING STRATEGIES

			Marketing Tiers		
Chain	Economy/ Limited-Service	Middle-Market	Executive	Luxury	All-Suite
Holiday Inns, Inc.	Hampton Inns	Holiday Inns	Crowne Plaza Hotels		Embassy Suites/ Granada Royale Hometels
Brock Hotel Corporation	—	Holiday Inns	—	—	Park Suite and Residence Inns
Hospitality International	Scottish Inns	Master Host Inns and Red Carpet Inns	—	—	—
Hyatt Corporation	—	Hyatt House	Hyatt Regency	Park Hyatt	—
Marriott Corporation	Courtyard	Marriott Inns	Marriott Hotels	Marquis Hotels	—
Ramada Hotel Group	—	Ramada Inns	Ramada Hotels	Ramada Renaissance	—
Quality Inns International	Comfort Inns	Quality Inns	Quality Royale	—	Quality Choice Suites

The 340-room Washington Plaza Hotel is one of six "mid-priced luxury hotels" that the Howard Johnson's hotel group plans to open by early 1985. Within five years, the company plans 60 hotels in the Plaza Hotel chain, which will compete directly with the Ramada Hotel chain in price and quality. Plaza Hotels will offer rooms in the $50- to $70-per-night category, which represents a tilt upscale from Howard Johnson motor lodges at $35 to $50 a night. The "new" hotel was the 343-room International Inn until the Inn was renovated at a cost of $5 million.

market, foreign companies have recently made efforts to be represented in major cities around the United States. Foreign affiliations offer a developer an international polish that may succeed in setting a hotel apart from those with domestic affiliations in its market area. Prominent entries in this field are Four Seasons from Canada, Meridien Hotels and Sofitel Hotels from France, Trusthouse Forte and Rank Hotels from England, Regent International Hotels from Asia, and Oberoi Hotels from India. These chains all represent upscale or luxury facilities. At another end of the spectrum, Sara Hotels of Sweden and Ibis Hotels of France are considering entering or have entered the U.S. lodging market in the economy sector of the industry.

Demonstrably, the lodging industry is a dynamic one—with its many markets, and its widely differing products designed and priced to meet the needs of these markets. A developer cannot simply decide to build "a hotel" without careful planning and an analysis of what type of hotel best suits a particular market area and site.

Questions such as these require answers:

◆ Which lodging market(s) will the hotel serve primarily?

◆ Do these lodging-market demand segments exist in the area where the hotel will be built?

◆ How large is the demand base? Is it growing? Against whom will the hotel compete?

◆ What services, amenities, and facilities will accommodate the market's needs?

◆ Would an independent or a chain operation be more appropriate? If a chain, which brand label would be best?

◆ How can the hotel be financed?

In the development process, such questions and many more must be dealt with and answered. A cadre of consultants, architects, and management companies can provide valuable insights into and assistance in making a developer's ideas into a business reality, and a successful one at that.

THE DEVELOPMENT PROCESS

CHAPTER FOUR

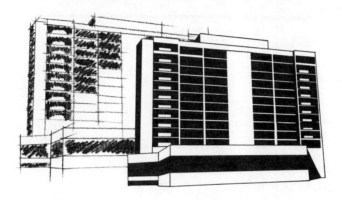

H otel development is essentially an integrated process that links the investor/owner, the developer, and the operator with the public they serve. The process founds itself on the principle that successful projects have typically met or exceeded the development objectives of their investors and owners; been compatible and complementary with the natural resources of their sites and with the surrounding land uses; secured financial gain for those associated with them; provided the type and quality of products and services desired by their guests; and enhanced the quality of life and the needs of the communities they serve. Hotel development requires a reciprocity between members of the development team, as well as between the public and private sectors in which they operate, and between the market segments that will ultimately decide the feasibility of the process.

The challenging development environment of the 1980s demands familiarity with the process by which hotel projects are analyzed, financed, developed, marketed, managed, and regulated. This chapter will discuss and assess the hotel development process—what it is, whom it involves, and how it is most effectively carried out.

The process of developing a lodging facility—regardless of type, size, location, or orientation—requires setting in motion and accomplishing five distinct phases of activity: (1) conceptualization, planning, and initiation; (2) feasibility analysis; (3) commitment; (4) design and construction; and (5) management/operation. (Figure 4–1 illustrates the sequential relationship of these phases.) In some cases, too little effort goes into the planning and feasibility phases.

Budgets are restricted, timing is short and often constraining, and the perceived need to get started overrides discerning in a careful, comprehensive manner what needs to be done. What results is a lodging product that fails to meet the expectations of its investors, performs poorly, is overbuilt or underbuilt for the market, and may threaten the financial credibility of its owners. In addition, examples exist throughout the United States of hotel projects that show insufficient attention to the construction and management/operation phases.

The developer, investor, and operator must therefore thoroughly understand the development process, know when to seek professional advice, and be able to integrate each member of the development team effectively to produce a successful project. (Figure 4–2 shows the interlocking functions of the process phases.)

AN OVERVIEW OF THE DEVELOPMENT PROCESS

CONCEPTUALIZATION, PLANNING, AND INITIATION

The conceptualization, planning, and initiation phase brings together the key members of the development team to:

FIGURE 4-1

THE HOTEL DEVELOPMENT PROCESS

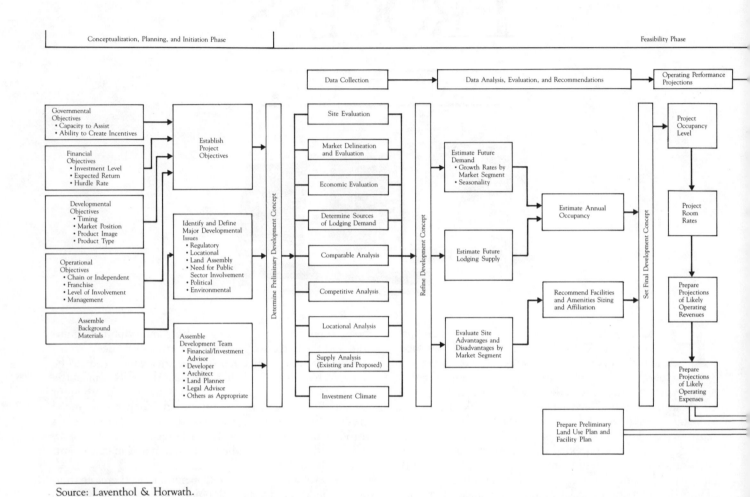

Source: Laventhol & Horwath.

- ◆ Establish objectives—financial, developmental, operational, and governmental.

- ◆ Identify and define developmental issues—regulatory, legal, locational, and managerial concerns; political and environmental issues; synergy of project components with one another; land assembly questions; development incentives; and other major issues.

- ◆ Formulate a preliminary development concept—one that responds to the constraints and opportunities of the site; that shows sensitivity to the needs of the community; that complements the surrounding land uses; and that minimizes market risk.

- ◆ Complete the assembly of the development team—a team sufficiently experienced both to initiate and to implement the overall project successfully.

Seasoned real estate professionals allocate a generous amount of time and resources to this phase, since the project's objectives and planning will serve as a framework within which to measure the progress and success of the development process.

FEASIBILITY ANALYSIS

Conducting a market and financial feasibility analysis for a proposed hotel is essential to determining the "go/no-go"

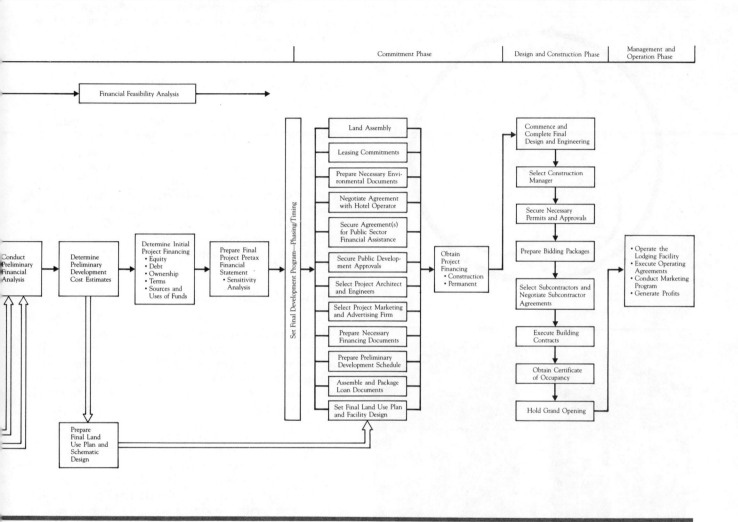

	Commitment Phase	Design and Construction Phase	Management and Operation Phase

Financial Feasibility Analysis

Conduct Preliminary Financial Analysis → Determine Preliminary Development Cost Estimates → Determine Initial Project Financing
• Equity
• Debt
• Ownership
• Terms
• Sources and Uses of Funds → Prepare Final Project Pretax Financial Statement
• Sensitivity Analysis → Set Final Development Program—Phasing/Timing

Prepare Final Land Use Plan and Schematic Design

Land Assembly
Leasing Commitments
Prepare Necessary Environmental Documents
Negotiate Agreement with Hotel Operator
Secure Agreement(s) for Public Sector Financial Assistance
Secure Public Development Approvals
Select Project Architect and Engineers
Select Project Marketing and Advertising Firm
Prepare Necessary Financing Documents
Prepare Preliminary Development Schedule
Assemble and Package Loan Documents
Set Final Land Use Plan and Facility Design

Obtain Project Financing
• Construction
• Permanent

Commence and Complete Final Design and Engineering
Select Construction Manager
Secure Necessary Permits and Approvals
Prepare Bidding Packages
Select Subcontractors and Negotiate Subcontractor Agreements
Execute Building Contracts
Obtain Certificate of Occupancy
Hold Grand Opening

• Operate the Lodging Facility
• Execute Operating Agreements
• Conduct Marketing Program
• Generate Profits

status of the project. The finished assessment of market potential for the project discloses the level of demand for its use by each market segment, the suitability of the site, the estimated growth of and changes in market demand, the special locational characteristics of the project, and some resultant facilities specifications, sufficiently detailed to begin a formal architectural program. With the changes occurring today in the hotel development climate, a timely and thorough examination of market potential must be made before the final decision to proceed is taken.

The final step in the feasibility phase involves determining the preliminary development costs, identifying and selecting the best financing structure, and preparing operating and consolidated financial statements that can respond to change. Ultimately, a feasibility analysis aims to recommend

a product that will meet or exceed the economic, financial, developmental, and operational expectations of the project's investors, developers, and operators.

COMMITMENT

At the conclusion of the feasibility phase, preliminary design and development schedules must be generated, enabling all parties concerned to negotiate and execute documents and to begin development proceedings. These proceedings might involve:

◆ Securing project funding, either a sufficient amount to cover front-end costs and land assembly, or a total commitment on a construction or a permanent loan;

FIGURE 4-2

THE FIVE PHASES OF THE HOTEL DEVELOPMENT PROCESS

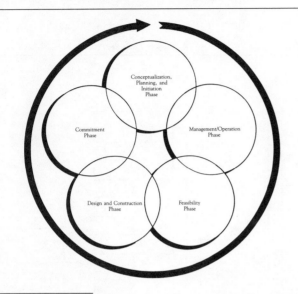

Conceptualization, Planning, and Initiation Phase

Commitment Phase

Management/Operation Phase

Design and Construction Phase

Feasibility Phase

Source: Laventhol & Horwath.

The Hyatt Regency Hotel at Illinois Center, a mixed-use complex on Chicago's lakefront.

◆ Concluding the commitment for land assembly and control;

◆ Determining the nature and extent of public and private sector funding and assistance;

◆ Completing any development agreements necessary to begin the project; and

◆ Executing, if necessary, either a preliminary management agreement with an experienced hotel operator, or a franchise agreement.

DESIGN AND CONSTRUCTION

The design and construction phase should create the public image or signature for the project. Necessarily, it also greatly influences the operating performance and marketability of the product. The final design, the phasing and timing of development, the preparation, negotiation, and execution of construction management documents, and the actual building of the hotel, together compose the construction phase. The goal of this phase is to complete the project according to the design, market, operational, and cost guidelines already established.

MANAGEMENT/OPERATION

The ability to manage and market the project effectively upon completion will determine its long-term success. Because currently a need exists for a new hotel to affiliate with a professional management firm, or to have access to a national or international reservations network, or both, this phase takes on added importance for the project's debt and equity investors.

Successful hotel developers acknowledge the desirability of starting to consider this phase early in the development process. Income-producing properties such as hotels must strike a balance between the external forces of fluctuating market demand, changing growth and development cycles, and sensitive capital markets; and the internal elements of marketing, staff resources, and operating performance. Monitoring the management/operational phase minimizes the development risk while maximizing the value and life of the facility. Without appropriate and skilled management involved in the early stages of the process, the chances for a profitable, efficient project decrease.

Hotel development—although constrained by uncertainty regarding future conditions, governed by ever-shifting market segments, and subject to the increasingly higher expectations of all those involved—nevertheless frequently offers a more challenging, exciting prospect than that of developing another kind of land use project. In developing a hotel, the developer, investor, and operator create both a business and a real estate venture. The development process links five distinct, though evolving, phases that sequentially provide a blueprint for action. Each of the five phases deserves close attention if the product is to meet the challenges satisfactorily.

Recognizing the vitality of the area around Union Station in Washington, D.C., the owner of the Hotel Commodore decided to upgrade the facility, which has now been renamed the Phoenix Park Hotel. In addition to refurbishing the rooms, the owner/developer has added another restaurant to complement The Dubliner, an Irish pub.

CONCEPTUALIZATION, PLANNING, AND INITIATION (PHASE I)

After initial conceptualization, an optimal development program begins by creating the framework within which the progress and final success of the project will be judged. Generally, one of the following nine parties initiates the program:

◆ An equity investor, an investment group, or an institutional investor acting on behalf of a trust, an investment fund, or a landowner.
◆ A property owner or owners recognizing a development opportunity.
◆ A developer seeking or seizing an opportunity, interested in expanding his or her real estate portfolio, or needing a cash-producing investment.
◆ A developer needing a hotel as an integral element of a multi-use development project.
◆ A hotel development or management company seeking to expand its product into new demand segments or geographic markets.
◆ A local nonprofit, tax-exempt development corporation.
◆ A public or quasi-public agency (redevelopment authori-

ty, planning department, development corporation), a citizen advisory committee, or a special community task force.
◆ A special interest group, an organization of local businesspersons, or a merchant association.
◆ A for-profit partnership or corporation that uses investor equity to develop projects.

One, two, or three of these parties conceive an idea that a hotel project is needed, sometimes specifying the site, type, size, preferred operator, and physical characteristics (number of stories, amenities, design guidelines, etc.) of the proposed hotel. But eventually, one individual or one group emerges as the motivator behind the initiative to develop the hotel. It is in this individual or group—typically the landowner, developer, or investor—that the hotel development process is vested.

The planning and initiation phase starts with the setting of overall objectives. According to leading professional hotel consulting firms, lending institutions, and attorneys, the major problem encountered at the outset of the hotel development process is a lack of attention to the expectations for a project. Some developers and investors attempt a project without considering their levels of commitment, their abilities to carry out and finance the project successfully, or their

Developers should consider whether surrounding land uses will be compatible with a hotel. Conventions at the Georgia World Congress Center (foreground) provide a stimulus for the existence of the Omni Hotel in Atlanta (right of center).

expectations of financial gain from and positions in the project. This is often the case, for instance, if a developer is building a hotel within a mixed-use project. Many times, a perceived community need will override good planning practices and consensus on expectations. Answering the following questions will aid the team at this point:

✦ *Financial.* What are the project's financial objectives? Do they involve long-term, residual, or value appreciation goals? Is the aim to realize capital gains? To create an operating entity? To create development profits? Or to achieve a combination of these? What are the priorities of the developer regarding these goals? How much equity can be invested? Can the developer finance a project of this magnitude? What return on investment will be acceptable? What will be the level of commitment in terms of time, money, and resources?

✦ *Developmental.* What are the existing constraints and opportunities of the site? Are the surrounding land uses, both existing and proposed, compatible with the development of a hotel? What is the existing condition and image of the site? Who will serve as the developer? Is this the first hotel project for this developer? If so, how familiar is he or she with the hotel development process, and what advice or guidance is needed? Does this project intend to make a special statement—to be one of a kind or to have a distinctive design, for example? Is the site large enough to carry the development? How accessible is the site?

✦ *Operational.* What type of hotel management structure will be best—franchise, affiliate, company-owned? Can the developer or owner manage the hotel, or will this function require the services of a professional hotel operator? What level of involvement in the hotel's operation is desirable or even possible?

✦ *Governmental.* What policies govern development on or near the site? Do those policies encourage development or discourage it? What public sector financing incentives exist? How will the public react to the development of the project? How long will all of the governmental processes take?

These questions and many more deserve consideration and response before primary development objectives can be established. By analyzing and discussing these questions fully, the development team will grow in its ability to make consistent qualitative decisions. This growth will allow the hotel development process to occur in a climate without disappointments and surprises.

The determination of overall project objectives, however, continues after these questions have been answered. Considerable public concern has arisen recently over the development process as it affects quality of life, historic preservation, the environment, and legal and regulatory constraints. The structure of the subsequent development phase often depends upon dealing with some of these major issues in the planning and initiation phase:

✦ Will the land assembly require condemnation or relocation? If so, how will this action affect the timing and public relations of the project?

✦ Will public hearings be necessary to discuss the project? Which active, influential, and vocal community groups exist that might constrain development? Can their concerns be remedied or mitigated?

✦ Can the development team exercise any control over the development or redevelopment of adjoining land parcels?

✦ Do political issues exist regarding the desirability of this development? If so, what contingency plans must be made in case the political climate changes?

✦ What other developments or activities, current or proposed, would have a positive or negative impact on the project?

✦ Is the host community committed to an aggressive marketing program that encourages economic development and travel to the area?

✦ What incentives or disincentives will encourage or deter the development process? Which funding sources might be approached? Which financing vehicles are available for use (revenue bonds, tax increments, tax abatement, etc.)?

✦ Is there room for future growth?

Florida's promotion of itself as the place to have fun in the sun ("When you need it bad, we've got it good") has doubtless helped hotels such as this Holiday Inn on Brickell Avenue in Miami.

◆ What kind of economic and investment climate does the host community offer? Is it an active one? Does it primarily influence or, on the other hand, respond to changing conditions? How has the community reacted during periods of economic downturn and stagnation?

The common thread throughout these questions is the need to identify and deal with the major influences on development by formulating objectives. These must respond to existing and likely future conditions. A lack of timely access to important data, public agencies, lending institutions, developers, syndicators, bankers, hotel operators, and architects may hinder or prevent an optimal development program.

The final step in the planning and initiation phase entails completing the assembly of a full development team. For most hotel projects, for instance, retaining the services of an overall financial and development advisor during this phase is important. Early selection of this individual or firm particularly matters on complex projects. Depending on the sophistication and experience of the project initiator, this advisor will:

◆ Identify other potential members of the development team for one or all of the project phases;

◆ Coordinate the preparation of the development objectives;

◆ Advise and guide the other involved parties as the project progresses;

◆ Undertake and complete a market and financial feasibility analysis;

◆ Research examples of hotel projects that have been successfully analyzed, financed, developed, and operated;

◆ Maintain regular contact with hotel operators, developers, architects, and others directly associated with the lodging industry;

◆ Augment the project's credibility with the financial community;

◆ Proceed as quickly or as slowly as the project requires; and

◆ Perform all of the above services without having a vested interest in obtaining future work from the project.

Other members of the development team during various project phases may include architects, engineers, attorneys, developers, government relations advisors, marketing advisors, management advisors, public finance advisors, appraisers, accountants, tax advisors, and land planners.

On completion of the conceptualization, planning, and initiation phase, the initiator should have established a set of development objectives; formulated an initial development concept; become aware of the major opportunities and constraints of the project; addressed each of the principal issues inherent in the hotel development process; retained the services of a professional financial and development advisor; assembled other members of the team necessary to begin the project; and established a timetable for the feasibility analysis.

Adding finishing touches to the Regent Hotel in Washington, D.C. The new copper-domed, $45 million project aims at the wealthy traveling executive with such extras as a health club, an executive business center, and butlers.

FEASIBILITY ANALYSIS (PHASE II)

All parties to the development process must accept some degree of risk, since the decision to proceed with a project rests on a set of assumptions, analyses, and expectations—that is, on beliefs regarding events that have not yet occurred. The level of risk varies according to the nature of the project, the reliability of the data base, the team's confidence in its ability to control future events and conditions, and the expected level of financial gain and commitment. The decision to build and operate a hotel requires an accurate assessment of current and future economic and market conditions, a structure that insulates the project from uncontrollable conditions, a management group committed to maintaining the quality of the investment, and a feasibility study that is pragmatic, timely, and responsive to all potential influences on the hotel's performance.

At this stage, the development team's ability to control the project's pace and financial commitment remains significant. To maintain this control, the team must now undertake a preliminary feasibility study to determine the "go/no-go" status of the proposed project. A preliminary feasibility study may be done by experienced project team members, by a hotel operating company, or by a real estate consulting firm that specializes in hotel development. Conducting a preliminary analysis internally makes for an initial cost savings. These analyses, however, usually lack the level of detail required by most lenders to be considered for funding, or by most hotel operators to be considered for potential management or affiliation relationships. Investing in an analysis by a hotel consulting firm may permit the project team access to a national resource base that can provide continuing financial development advice and thus save time and resources.

Determining a project's feasibility calls for a two-step process. The first step involves assessing the market feasibility of the project. The second step requires preparing a cash flow statement that responds to the market findings and that enables a potential lender to assess the amount of cash available before debt service and income taxes.

ASSESSING MARKET SUPPORT

For many years, developers, investors, and operators of hotels concluded that "if the location was good, the project would be successful." This traditional approach to hotel development worked in many instances because the hotel market was typically undersupplied, and because developable land was oversupplied. Today, however, many urban and suburban areas throughout the United States are experiencing a cyclical oversupply of hotel rooms, as well as of office, industrial, and retail space. The feasibility of a hotel in one of these markets requires analysis of several factors, only one of which is location. Accurately quantifying lodging demand calls for a close look at several interrelated circumstances:

+ Location of the subject site with regard to market demand generators;

+ The sources and strengths of transient visitation;
+ Location of competitive properties, and their physical and operational characteristics;
+ Current and future travel patterns;
+ Economic growth within the market area;
+ Regulatory and legal issues;
+ Site characteristics; and
+ Special local conditions and trends.

The project initiator or hotel consulting firm must collect the quantitative data that will form the basis for future development decisions. This party will need to:

Develop a Data Base

This data base will serve as a reference point for making project recommendations, and will guide comparisons of the subject property's projected performance with actual results obtained at similar existing properties. The development team should keep all information collected during the research process for future reference.

Delineate the Market Support Area

The market area for a lodging facility is the geographic region containing its major sources of demand. To determine the boundaries of this market area, a feasibility study should evaluate:

+ The location of competitive hotels, and the segmentation and origination of their major business sources.

+ The distance from the proposed site to the major sources of travel demand (office concentrations, convention centers, recreational activities, and others).

+ The travel patterns and trends of the commercial, convention, and vacation visitors to the area and to the proposed site.

+ The distance between the proposed site and major recreational centers (theme parks, public parks, ski slopes, oceans or lakes, golf courses, tennis facilities, and the like).

+ Expenditure patterns of area visitors.

+ The existing socioeconomic boundaries.

Determine the Sources of Lodging Demand

This step in the assessment of market support for a lodging facility usually begins while the delineation of the market support area is still underway. The sources of demand for a lodging facility may be segmented into three major categories: (1) commercial travelers; (2) convention travelers; and (3) vacation or pleasure travelers. To identify and assess the sources of lodging demand, this methodology might be followed:

✦ Interview representatives from the local tourist and conventions bureaus and chambers of commerce to identify the number, length of stay, expenditure patterns, typical group size, lodging demand, and seasonality of tourists and convention delegates. (Note that these agencies do sometimes overstate this information. Also, they frequently do not maintain a research program that adequately quantifies travel patterns.)

✦ Interview officials from major ground transportation firms (car rental agencies and bus companies, for example) to determine the source, seasonality, and profile of their principal users.

✦ Interview corporate travel officers, meeting planners, association executives, wholesale tour operators, travel agents, brokers specializing in group or corporate travel, incentive-travel organizers, and spokespersons for travel clubs in feeder cities. Determine their clients' lodging needs, perceptions of the area, frequency of visits to the area, primary reasons for visiting, typical group size, and seasonality of travel plans. Find out how these clients view the competitive strengths and weaknesses of existing properties in the area; what services and amenities they seek; how large their typical lodging budgets are; their

The Grand Ole Opry and Opryland nearby serve as demand generators for the Nashville Holiday Inn at Briley Parkway.

future travel plans; the strengths and weaknesses of other market areas in their opinion; and their perceptions of the need for additional local lodging facilities. (American Express's "Lodging Market Analysis" report, interviews with major air and ground carriers, and consultations with local operators will aid in the identification of feeder cities.)

✦ Identify and speak with officials of comparable hotels to determine their properties' number of guest rooms, average annual occupancy, average annual room rate, market mix of guests, and type and class of facilities. If no comparable properties exist in the market area, locate similar facilities in nearby market areas, and then adjust their data for the subject location.

✦ Talk with representatives from local redevelopment agencies, planning departments, real estate brokerage firms, office-space leasing firms, and major development concerns to discover the existing and future supply of office space and the profile of incoming office tenants. Will they require lodging facilities?

✦ Speak with representatives of government agencies and public institutions such as colleges and universities to assess their current and likely future needs for lodging facilities.

✦ Obtain the traffic count of travelers along the major thoroughfares from which the proposed hotel will be seen. Identify how many cars per day, per month, and per year go past the site, with any seasonal variations that imply increased pleasure travel.

✦ Assess the existing capacity and arrival/departure patterns at the major airport within the market area; then determine the mix, seasonality, and growth rate in the number of airport passengers.

✦ List the major tourist attractions, community special events, regional and state fairs or expositions, athletic contests, and the like, and determine their typical needs for lodging facilities. Interview attraction or event organizers, hotel operators, tourist bureaus, and others.

✦ Characterize the employment profile and trends in the market area, and evaluate the scope of a region's economic activity. Meet with economic development officials and review the current employment statistics.

(Figure 4–3 analyzes business sources by location for the U.S. industry.)

Evaluate Existing and Proposed Lodging Supply

An inventory of the existing and proposed competitive lodging supply in the market area will help to predict the likely impact of a new lodging facility on the operating performance of that supply. For each existing and proposed

FIGURE 4-3

SOURCES OF BUSINESS FOR THE U.S. LODGING INDUSTRY IN 1981

	Location				
	Center City	Airport	Suburban	Highway	Resort
Source of Business					
Domestic	82.2%	85.1%	95.3%	90.4%	84.3%
Foreign	17.8	14.9	4.7	9.6	15.7
	100.0%	100.0%	100.0%	100.0%	100.0%
Percentage of Repeat Business	46.4%	43.8%	45.7%	50.8%	46.1%
Composition of Market					
Government Officials	5.8%	4.6%	2.8%	3.1%	2.1%
Business Travelers	37.9	53.1	56.3	52.0	16.3
Tourists	18.0	21.6	16.4	25.8	53.3
Conference Participants	24.6	13.0	20.8	15.7	24.0
Others	13.7	7.7	3.7	3.4	4.3
	100.0%	100.0%	100.0%	100.0%	100.0%
Advance Reservations					
Percentage of Advance Reservations	83.9%	82.1%	79.5%	71.3%	88.4%
Composition of Advance Reservations					
Direct	38.0%	34.8%	45.6%	35.1%	47.8%
Reservations System	26.5	39.1	33.2	34.0	14.3
Travel Agents and Tour Operators	22.2	18.8	12.1	20.1	31.1
Other	13.3	7.3	9.1	10.8	6.8
	100.0%	100.0%	100.0%	100.0%	100.0%
Ratio of Travel Agent Commissions to Room Sales	0.6%	0.7%	0.4%	0.3%	1.1%

*Based on those supplying detail.
Source: Laventhol & Horwath.

---

lodging facility that, because of its location, size, and room rate, will compete with the subject hotel, the initiator should quantify the following findings:

◆ Size (number of rooms);
◆ Location;
◆ Affiliation (chain or independent);
◆ Orientation (convention delegates, business travelers, vacationers, etc.);
◆ Amenities;
◆ Room rate (average annual);
◆ Occupancy (average annual);
◆ Whether leased or owned; and
◆ Competitive strengths and weaknesses.

Interviews with hotel operators and meeting planners—as well as a review of the *Hotel and Travel Index* and of earlier studies conducted by public agencies—will all furnish this kind of information.

Evaluate the Suitability of the Site for Development

The competitive market strengths of the site must be examined to determine the probability that a hotel developed on that site will capture its "fair share" of the lodging demand. At this stage in the feasibility process, it is not necessary to conduct an engineering or environmental study; the site should simply be evaluated with regard to its competitive position. The following questions arise in studying site suitability:

◆ Is the site easily accessible from major highway arteries? Is it near public transportation (subway or bus lines)?

◆ What is the existing zoning on the site? Is the site in a redevelopment area or historic district? What is the allowable development potential of the site?

◆ Is the site near and accessible to market demand generators?

◆ What are the physical characteristics of the site? Does it need significant site preparation?

◆ Have the major infrastructure improvements been made to the site (water, sewer, electric, roadways, etc.)?

◆ Will the surrounding land uses be compatible with the proposed hotel? Complementary? Competitive? Is there room for future growth of the project?

◆ Are there existing plans or proposals to modify the site, the area surrounding the site, or the major roadways leading to the site? Will any of these plans help or hinder the project?

For purposes of analysis, the development team's ability to mitigate any negative site characteristics deserves consideration equal to that given the characteristics themselves.

Analyze Market Demand

The most important step in assessing support for a hotel from each market segment is to analyze all data collected, and then to translate the total demand into measurable units. Analysts should determine and quantify:

◆ The seasonality of lodging use. Do existing hotel occupancies rise at certain periods of the year? Can these higher occupancies be attributed to specific market segments? (For example, Florida's higher hotel occupancies in winter are attributable to tourists leaving the cooler states in the central and northeastern regions for warmer climes.)

◆ Daily variations to market-area hotel occupancies. Do weekend occupancies rise at certain times of the year? Do weekday occupancies fluctuate by season? Can these daily occupancy patterns be attributed to specific market segments?

◆ Likely market segmentation for the proposed hotel. What is the estimated percentage by season of commercial, convention/group, and vacation/tourist markets using existing hotels? (Most of these data may be derived from the comparable and competitive lodging-supply analyses conducted earlier.) What is the estimated demand base, or total number of occupied room/nights, in the com-

The Franklin Plaza office and hotel project in Philadelphia is part of the larger Franklin Town redevelopment area.

petitive hotel supply? What is the estimated percentage of guests from each major market segment? (Figure 4–4 shows a market segmentation analysis conducted for a proposed 275-room first-class hotel in Florida.)

✦ The demand growth by market segment. Has the lack of available rooms constrained growth? Has "excess" demand been referred to hotels in other market areas? (By using the research conducted earlier, analysts may develop a projection of annual growth rates for a 10-year period by market segment. They should, however, recognize the impact that all area factors have on growth and should reflect all of these factors in their determinations of annual growth rates for each market segment. Elements to be considered might include presence or absence of a convention center, stabilization or upturn in the local economy, opening or closing of a major tourist attraction, expansion or scaling-down of airport facilities, and building or closing of a major highway leading to the site).

✦ Probable future lodging supply. Will proposed lodging facilities actually be built?

Recommend Facility Sizing and Amenities

By using the market research and projected market segmentation analyses already conducted, the development team may determine the optimal size and the best choice of amenities for the hotel. To improve the hotel's ability to satisfy the present and future needs of the available market segments, to respond to the opportunities and constraints of the site, to compete with other facilities, and to grasp development opportunities, the hotel must be properly sized. (See Figure 4–5 for a typical range of hotel sizes by facility category.)

Prepare Projections of Occupancy Level

Although a number of methodologies exist for projecting the likely occupancy of a proposed hotel, the most successful method and the one most endorsed by lenders is the "fair share" penetration technique. By using a quantitative analysis, the analyst can project a hotel's ability to capture its fair share of future demand—that is, the share proportional to its percentage of the competitive room supply. The ability to capture a fair share percentage of the market depends on the lodging property's physical and operating characteristics, location, room rates, amenities, relation to competitive facilities, status or image in tourists' or commercial travelers' perceptions, affiliation, and nearness to market demand generators.

Fair share is the ratio of the proposed hotel's available guest rooms to the total market support. For example, if there were 1,400 available rooms in the competitive market, plus a new 200-room hotel under construction that should be considered competitive, and if the subject property was to

FIGURE 4-4

ESTIMATED LODGING DEMAND BASE AND MARKET SEGMENTATION FOR A PROPOSED 275-ROOM FIRST-CLASS HOTEL (FLORIDA)
(Rounded)

Segment	Season Occupied Room/ Nights	Percentage	Off-Season Occupied Room/ Nights	Percentage	Annual Occupied Room/ Nights	Percentage
Commercial	52,400	50%	111,000	66%	163,400	60%
Convention/ Group	6,200	6	11,300	7	17,500	6
Vacation/ Tourist	46,800	44	46,300	27	93,100	34
	105,400	100%	168,600	100%	274,000	100%
Occupancy Percentage		77%		61%		66%

Source: Laventhol & Horwath.

have 250 rooms, the fair share would be 14 percent (250 divided by 1,400 + 200 + 250). This fair share percentage remains constant throughout the projection period unless new additions to the competitive supply occur.

In order to define the analysis further and to provide a more sensitive approach to predicting occupancy, the development team should factor some additional elements into its projections. According to a proposed facility's competitive strengths and weaknesses, it may achieve more or less than 100 percent of its fair share. A sensitivity analysis can often predict this likelihood. Experienced hotel consultants and operators should assist in sensitivity analyses. And they should take into consideration that occupancy rates may take the first three to five years of a hotel's operation to stabilize. (See Figure 4–6 for a fair share sensitivity analysis conducted for a proposed 275-room hotel.)

Inexperienced analysts often overlook several important dynamics of the marketplace. For instance, the potential of a hotel that carries an image sufficient to generate its own (supply-induced) demand cannot be measured solely by this analysis technique.

Prepare Projections of Room Rates

These typically derive from published room rates achieved at competitive properties, published room rates at similar projects in similar markets, known discount rates necessary to attract price-sensitive guests, and any influences or events unique to the market area. Use of questionnaires aids in this investigation.

PROJECTING REVENUES

After assessing the potential market support, deciding on the size and type of hotel that would be appropriate for the market area, and projecting average annual occupancies and room rates, an analyst should quantitatively predict likely revenues for each department. (The sources and uses of funds for the lodging industry appear in Figure 4–7.)

Room Revenue

Assessments of potential room revenue result from three factors: (1) projected number of available guest rooms; (2) projected average annual occupancy; and (3) projected average annual room rates. Thus, for a 300-room hotel with a projected annual occupancy of 70 percent and a projected average annual room rate of $70, room revenue would be $5,365,000 (300 rooms × 365 days × 70 percent occupancy × $70 average room rate).

Projecting room revenue is the single most important step in compiling financial projections for a hotel. Room sales typically represent the largest source of income for a hotel. Thus, determining room revenues requires careful analysis and is critical to the success of a hotel.

FIGURE 4-5

TYPICAL NUMBER OF ROOMS IN SPECIFIC HOTEL CATEGORIES

Category	Average Range of Hotel Rooms per Facility
Location	
Center City	500–700
Suburban	200–350
Highway	100–250
Airport	250–550
Resort	200–400
Convention	700–1,000
Casino	600–800
Type	
Luxury	150–250
First-Class	100 or more
Economy (Large)	350–600
Economy (Small)	150–350
Budget	75–150
Motor Hotel	100–150
Inn	50 or fewer

Source: Laventhol & Horwath.

Food and Beverage Sales

The volume of food and beverage sales is a function of the daily occupancy of the hotel, the type and number of guests staying there, and the incidence and nature of banquets, special events, and walk-in trade. Thus, the type, size, and mix of restaurants, bars, coffee shops, and banquet facilities must closely fit the needs both of the market-segment mix and of the walk-in trade. Food and beverage sales range from 30 to 35 percent of total lodging sales. To project these, an analyst must consider:

✦ The type and size of the hotel;

✦ Its location (a resort hotel may be the only place for overnight guests to eat, while a downtown hotel may attract a high-volume banquet and walk-in trade);

✦ Its market mix of guests (a convention hotel will generally incur a high volume of banquets, while a commercial hotel may incur a high volume of breakfast meals as business travelers prepare for a day of meetings);

✦ The quantity and quality of competitive food and beverage outlets;

FIGURE 4-6

PERCENTAGE OF FAIR SHARE:
SUMMARY OF PENETRATION RATES FOR A PROPOSED 275-ROOM HOTEL
(1985–1989)

Year	Season Commercial	Vacation/ Tourist	Convention/ Group	Total	Off-Season Commercial	Vacation/ Tourist	Convention/ Group	Total	Commercial	Vacation/ Tourist	Convention/ Group	Total
1985	100%	120%	165%	113%	100%	110%	180%	109%	100%	115%	175%	110%
1986	98	122	168	113	98	118	183	110	98	120	178	111
1987	95	126	170	114	95	128	185	111	95	130	180	112
1988	93	124	173	112	96	127	188	111	95	130	183	112
1989	90	120	173	109	97	125	191	112	95	130	185	110

Base: 100 percent.
Source: Laventhol & Horwath.

◆ The level of support and resources dedicated to marketing;

◆ The average check expected for each meal period;

◆ The number of "turns" a restaurant seat can accommodate comfortably; and

◆ The size, quality, and versatility of the meeting and banquet rooms.

When preparing projections of likely food and beverage sales, a development team should use data from comparable hotels, from yearly publications and special studies by leading hotel firms, from national restaurant and volume-feeding publications, and from local restaurant owners and operators.

Telephone Revenue

Telephone revenues—generally representing between 2 and 3 percent of total sales—result from charges to guests for their local and long-distance calls. Telephone sales are calculated as an amount per occupied room and reflect the mix of hotel guests. (Commercial travelers, for example, use in-room telephones heavily to arrange meetings or confirm appointments, while tourists less often need this convenience.)

Income from Other Departments

Within most middle-market and luxury hotels, some income derives from the operation of a guest laundry, gift shop, a newsstand, valet service, in-room movies, and other such departments. This income should be projected as net income after cost of goods, payroll, and related expenses have been deducted. If the proposed hotel will have other operating departments that will generate significant revenues (tennis club, exercise club, parking garage, golf course, etc.), then sales and expenses for each of these departments should be projected separately.

Food and beverage sales in hotels represent between 30 and 35 percent of total lodging sales.

FIGURE 4-7

SOURCES AND USES OF FUNDS FOR THE U.S. LODGING INDUSTRY, 1982

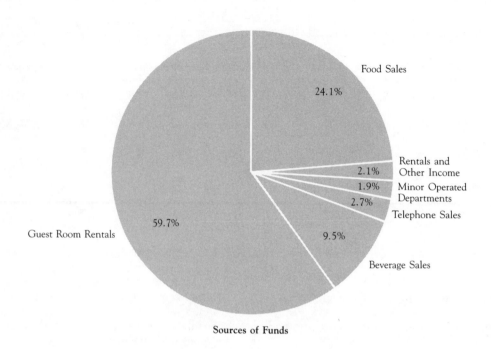

Sources of Funds

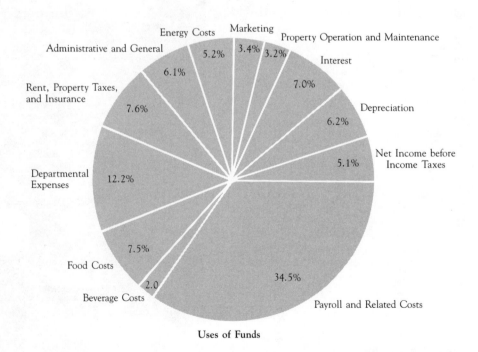

Uses of Funds

Source: Laventhol & Horwath.

Rental and Other Income

This income category, which provides between 1.5 and 2.5 percent of total sales, includes revenue from the rental of retail space in the hotel. Other income may involve commissions on sales, interest income, vending machine revenues, game room revenues, and other types of income from miscellaneous elements. Generally, a determination of expected income from leased retail space should consider the size, nature, and need for the shop, as well as the prevailing lease rates for such space at comparable facilities. (Some hotel operators have been able to obtain rents based on a percentage of sales above a minimum base rent.) In turn, a determination of specific space allocations for such retail outlets as clothing stores, souvenir shops, jewelry stores, travel agencies, airline reservation desks, and car rental outlets should consider the expected dominant market segment, and the type of area in which the proposed hotel will be located.

PROJECTING OPERATING COSTS AND EXPENSES

Projections of operating costs and expenses for all hotel departments result from assessing the relationships among the following: (1) the proposed facilities design; (2) prevailing local base rates for salaries and wages, utilities, and other related costs; (3) costs and expenses incurred by comparable facilities in comparable markets; (4) expected staffing needs; (5) requirements of the proposed hotel operator; and (6) predicted level of occupancy.

Operating expenses have both fixed and variable components. Fixed expenses are those that remain the same despite the rate of operations, while variable costs change in direct proportion to this rate. Rent, property taxes, insurance, and replacement costs for fixed assets, for instance, constitute the major fixed expenses. When preparing financial projections, expenses should be divided into their fixed and variable components, according to the *Uniform System of Accounts for Hotels*. (Figure 4–8 shows the range of fixed and variable expenses by category.)

Be aware that projecting costs and expenses requires an in-depth knowledge of how hotels operate. No standard industry rules of thumb apply to all hotels. As do other steps in the development process, predicting operating performance requires care and the involvement of experienced hotel consultants or operators.

The following are cost and expense categories that should appear in an operating statement:

◆ *Cost of food sales.* The cost of all food served to guests, less the cost of food served to employees. Ranges between 30 and 40 percent of sales, depending on the size and type of the hotel.

◆ *Cost of beverage sales.* The cost of all beverages served to guests, less the cost of beverages served to employees. Ranges between 17 and 25 percent of total beverage sales, depending on the size and type of the hotel.

Resort hotels can often supplement their room revenues with equipment rentals.

◆ *Cost of telephone calls.* The total amount billed by the telephone company for local and long-distance calls, and for equipment rental.

◆ *Payroll and related expenses.* Salaries, wages, payroll taxes, employee meals, and related expenses. Ranges from 29 to 39 percent of total sales.

A detailed payroll staffing schedule should be prepared for each department for the initial five years of operation. This will involve pinpointing the positions necessary in each department, the number of persons who will occupy each position, and the percentage of expenditures allied to cash payroll that will constitute "related expenses." Good sources for wage surveys include the U.S. Department of Labor/Bureau of Labor Statistics and various state departments of labor.

To validate the results of the payroll analysis, comparisons should be made, in percentages, to departmental sales and total sales, as well as to amounts per occupied room and to amounts per available room. These findings should then be cross-checked with data compiled on similar facilities.

Payroll categories include rooms, food and beverage, telephone, minor operating departments, administrative and general, marketing, and property maintenance. Payroll expenses should be determined as precisely as possible, while related expenses (uniforms, laundry, china, glassware, linen, travel agent commissions, etc.) should be projected as: (1) a percentage of department sales; (2) a percentage of total sales; (3) an amount per occupied room; and (4) an amount per available room.

FIGURE 4-8

GENERAL GUIDELINES ON RANGE OF FIXED AND VARIABLE EXPENSES BY CATEGORY

	Percent Fixed	Percent Variable
Rooms		
Payroll and Related	60–70%	30–40%
Other	25–35	65–70
Food and Beverage		
Payroll and Related	60–70	30–40
Other	60–70	30–40
Administrative and General		
Payroll and Related	90–100	0–10
Other	60–70	30–40
Marketing		
Payroll and Related	90–100	0–10
Other*	90–100	0–10
Energy	70–90	10–30
Property Operation and Maintenance		
Payroll and Related	90–100	0–10
Other	60–80	20–40

Source: Laventhol & Horwath.
*Franchise fees fall within this category and usually vary with sales.

♦ *Undistributed operating expenses.* General and administrative, marketing, energy costs, property operation costs, and maintenance expenses.

Note that many circumstances influence the identification of undistributed operating expenses, including the type, size, location, age, occupancy level, and orientation of the hotel.

PREPARING A CASH FLOW STATEMENT

After projecting all revenues and expenses, analysts will need to prepare a statement of projected cash flow from operations before debt service and income taxes. This should be presented in constant and current (inflated) dollars and should cover the initial five years of operation. The preparer of this statement will need to apply specific rates of inflation for each revenue or expense category. In the current business environment, rates of inflation vary significantly from year to year, as well as from one locale to another. In

the same way, their importance varies with the targeted guest mix, the price sensitivity in the marketplace, the quality of a hotel's management, and the operating category (e.g., energy costs, payroll costs, or food and beverage costs). Because of the complexity of this material, most experienced hotel analysts use microcomputers to formulate, test, and format these statements. (Figure 4–9 gives the ratios of sources and uses of funds to total sales, covering various types of lodging facilities. Figure 4–10 consists of a sample projected cash flow statement.)

DETERMINING PRELIMINARY DEVELOPMENT COSTS

In order to prepare the pre-tax cash flow statement needed for a feasibility analysis, preliminary development costs must first be determined. Of course, development costs for hotels vary according to type, size, location, amenities, and quality. But for purposes of analysis, an "order-of-magnitude" estimate of development costs may be prepared, based upon general industry standards; it can then be adapted to respond to local conditions. (See Figure 4–11 for the general range of hotel development costs on a per-room basis.)

A more refined development cost estimate may be obtained from the architect or developer on the project's team. Of a project's total cost, a developer should expect to spend 10 to 20 percent for land, 50 to 53 percent for construction, 13 to 14 percent for furnishings, and 13 to 18 percent for miscellaneous costs. In addition, some often-overlooked yet critical costs to include in the estimates are those associated with the provision of infrastructure to the site; the development of parking garages; site preparation; construction of roadways, retaining walls, sea walls, and the like; and the purchase, if desirable and justifiable, of higher-grade furnishings.

DETERMINING PRELIMINARY FINANCING STRUCTURE

Arriving at a preliminary financing structure aids both in the preparation of a pretax cash flow statement and in the execution of internal rate of return and cash-on-cash analyses. Because Chapter Five describes in detail the process of financing for hotel development, this section will only list the basic guidelines needed to evaluate feasibility.

Six major groups engage in hotel financing today: (1) lenders, including commercial banks, life insurance companies, pension funds, credit companies, and savings and loan associations; (2) developers; (3) hotel operating companies; (4) brokers and mortgage bankers; (5) government agencies; and (6) syndicators and passive investors. Most hotel financing deals involve more than one partner. This "layering" effect creates a variety of financing arrangements and a diversified array of financing terms.

Regardless of the lender category, the basic concern of any lender is the project feasibility. Unlike the performance of an office building that may be preleased, or of a residential project that may be presold, the performance of a hotel is dependent on day-to-day sales. Consequently, most lenders require a market study with financial projections. They also need a full statement of the assumptions used to establish the operating statement and the preliminary cost estimates. Most lenders use the first stabilized operating year to assess the cash flow available for debt service and for management incentive fees. Normally, debt service coverage primarily determines the principal amount of the loan, the combination of fixed and contingent interest components, and the terms. Debt coverage ratios of 1.20 to 1.35 have been accepted by most lenders. Debt coverage ratios for lodging facilities, however, often exceed those for other income-producing properties such as office, industrial, and retail facilities. This is because of hotels' dependency on the operation of a business rather than on the guaranteed cash flow typically found in office or industrial buildings, with their 10- to 15-year leases at rates cushioned against inflation.

Unless the ownership or financing structure has been finally negotiated and firm commitments obtained from all financing partners for their shares of the package, most analysts prepare a consolidated operating and development statement that includes:

✦ An operating cash flow statement;

✦ Estimates of total development costs;

✦ Financing assumptions (normally, a permanent loan at prevailing market rates, amortized over 28 to 32 years, payable monthly, and with a value of 80 percent of the development cost);

✦ Depreciation figures (generally obtained by the straight-line method);

✦ Management incentive fees (typically, 8 to 20 percent of income before fixed charges); and

✦ Loan origination fees (in most cases, 1 to 4 percent of the loan value).

Using the internal rate of return (IRR) as a measure constitutes one of the more common methods of analyzing project returns. The "hurdle IRR" is the minimum acceptable rate of return on investment that potential investors look for. Today, the hurdle IRR for freestanding hotels ranges from 15 to 22 percent, while that for hotels in mixed-use projects may be lower by one or two percentage points.

After evaluating the project's IRR, the project analyst must conduct a number of sensitivity tests to foretell how it would perform under different sets of assumptions (e.g., higher or lower inflation rates, differing interest rates, varied occupancy and room rates, etc.). Often, changes in the financing, development costs, or ownership structure will dramatically alter the overall financial performance of a project and thus affect the returns to the project's equity investors.

*T*he Vista International Hotel in the nation's capital is run by Hilton International.

COMMITMENT (PHASE III)

On completion of the phase just described, the overall feasibility of the project has been established, preliminary development costing and design have been prepared, a complete pro forma analysis has been undertaken, and a preliminary timetable has been set up for the project's construction. The commitment phase (sometimes called the packaging phase) involves final negotiation of the:

✦ Land assembly/site acquisition.

✦ Agreements from any public entities for development and funding assistance.

✦ Selection of and agreements with a hotel operator for franchise rights, affiliation, and/or management assistance.

✦ Development rights for, on, and, if necessary, over the site.

✦ Selection of a project architect and engineer.

✦ Selection of a project developer.

✦ Refined project development costs, both directs and indirects.

✦ Agreement among the funding, developing, and operating entities.

✦ Financing and ownership structure.

FIGURE 4-9

RATIOS TO TOTAL SALES FOR THE U.S. LODGING INDUSTRY, 1981*

Rooms	Age of Property				Size of Property				Occupancy				
	Built Before 1940	Built 1940–1959	Built 1960–1969	Built After 1970	Under 150 Rooms	150–299 Rooms	300–600 Rooms	Over 600 Rooms	Under 50%	50–59%	60–69%	70–79%	80% & Over
Sales	100.0%	100.0%	100.0%	100.0%	100.0%	100.0%	100.0%	100.0%	100.0%	100.0%	100.0%	100.0%	100.0%
Departmental Expenses													
Payroll & Related Expenses	19.2	18.5	17.3	16.4	19.1	17.3	16.5	16.6	23.6	19.4	17.9	16.4	17.6
Other	7.9	8.1	8.3	7.6	6.0	6.9	7.5	8.0	8.3	7.8	6.8	6.8	5.9
Total	27.5	27.0	26.3	24.2	25.3	24.2	24.1	25.5	33.8	27.9	24.9	23.1	23.9
Departmental Income	72.5	73.0	73.7	75.8	74.7	75.8	75.9	74.5	66.2	72.1	75.1	76.9	76.1
Ratio to Total Sales	39.5	52.0	47.0	44.0	56.4	50.4	44.1	42.5	42.3	44.2	46.9	50.5	58.7
Food & Beverage													
Sales													
Food	72.9	72.4	71.7	71.6	70.9	69.9	72.4	72.0	72.5	71.7	71.4	70.5	72.1
Beverage	27.8	32.2	28.4	28.5	30.9	30.5	27.6	28.0	27.5	28.4	29.8	29.8	28.1
Total	100.0	100.0	100.0	100.0	100.0	100.0	100.0	100.0	100.0	100.0	100.0	100.0	100.0
Cost of Sales													
Food	31.5	36.7	36.5	35.6	36.0	36.4	33.6	31.8	37.6	36.0	35.5	34.8	34.1
Beverage	20.9	23.3	23.3	23.2	23.2	23.0	21.1	19.1	26.6	22.9	23.0	21.4	20.6
Total	28.6	33.0	32.0	31.5	32.2	32.0	30.2	28.3	34.7	31.8	32.0	30.4	30.3
Gross Profit	71.4	67.0	68.0	68.5	67.8	68.0	69.8	71.7	65.3	68.2	68.0	69.6	69.7
Public Room Sales	2.7	2.4	2.3	2.2	2.4	2.8	2.7	1.4	2.2	2.8	2.3	2.8	2.7
Other Income	0.9	0.4	0.9	0.8	0.1	0.2	0.6	1.0	0.3	0.3	0.3	0.6	0.3
Gross Profit & Other Income	75.3	70.9	70.6	71.2	70.0	71.1	73.6	74.1	68.3	71.3	71.2	72.9	73.2
Departmental Expenses													
Payroll & Related Expenses	43.5	38.4	41.5	40.4	42.5	40.6	41.9	43.3	44.2	44.1	41.1	39.9	41.3
Other	10.7	13.0	13.0	12.4	10.8	13.0	11.3	11.0	16.7	12.9	11.4	11.8	10.1
Total	54.5	55.0	55.2	55.3	54.5	54.6	54.2	52.3	59.5	56.5	53.2	53.1	52.9
Departmental Income	14.8	14.5	15.0	17.1	16.3	17.2	19.8	22.1	9.0	15.1	18.4	20.4	20.1
Ratio to Total Sales	6.0	2.8	4.5	5.5	4.4	4.4	6.2	7.3	2.8	4.3	5.6	5.6	5.1
Telephone Departmental Income	(1.2)	(0.4)	(0.8)	(0.4)	(0.3)	(0.4)	(0.6)	(0.7)	(0.9)	(1.1)	(0.6)	(0.4)	(0.3)
Net Income from Minor													
Operated Departments	0.4	1.6	0.1	0.1	0.3	0.2	0.3	0.3	(0.4)	0.2	0.3	0.2	0.4
Rental & Other Income	2.1	1.7	1.0	0.9	1.4	0.8	1.3	1.8	1.2	1.3	1.1	0.8	1.6
Gross Income	49.5	53.5	52.8	52.6	61.2	55.7	53.0	53.4	47.8	51.5	54.3	56.7	64.0
Undistributed Operating Expenses													
Administrative & General													
Payroll & Related Expenses	4.7	4.2	4.5	4.5	3.8	3.7	4.0	4.0	5.4	4.5	4.0	3.7	3.2
Other	5.3	5.5	4.9	4.7	4.6	4.7	4.2	3.9	6.2	4.7	4.6	4.2	4.3
Total	10.1	10.8	8.5	9.3	6.8	8.4	8.2	8.3	10.7	9.1	8.2	7.7	6.2
Marketing	4.5	3.5	4.0	4.8	2.3	4.3	4.4	4.4	4.7	5.0	4.2	4.2	2.1
Energy Costs	4.9	5.5	5.5	5.1	5.5	5.5	4.7	4.9	7.7	6.2	5.7	4.9	4.3
Property Operation & Maintenance	8.2	5.8	5.8	4.7	5.4	5.7	5.3	5.7	8.1	7.0	5.7	5.1	4.8
Total Undistributed Expenses	28.0	27.4	24.8	24.3	21.6	24.0	22.9	24.2	32.1	27.8	24.1	22.4	18.5
Income Before Management Fees	21.9	29.5	27.9	28.4	40.8	30.9	31.0	29.3	14.7	22.4	30.4	34.6	45.3
Management Fees	1.9	2.7	3.2	3.3	4.6	3.9	3.0	3.0	4.0	3.9	4.3	3.7	4.5
Income Before Fixed Charges	21.7%	26.8%	25.0%	25.9%	37.0%	28.4%	27.9%	26.7%	10.4%	20.3%	25.4%	31.7%	42.1%

*All amounts are medians and do not necessarily add up to the totals shown. All ratios are based on total sales, except those of the rooms and of food and beverage departments. Cost of sales is shown as a percentage of the corresponding sales. Food and beverage departmental expense ratios are based on combined food and beverage sales.

Source: Laventhol & Horwath.

FIGURE 4-9 (CONT'D)

RATIOS TO TOTAL SALES FOR THE U.S. LODGING INDUSTRY, 1981*

Rooms	Northeast	Southeast	Area North Central	South Central	West
Sales	100.0%	100.0%	100.0%	100.0%	100.0%
Departmental Expenses					
Payroll & Related Expenses	17.8	16.8	18.8	18.1	16.6
Other	7.3	7.0	6.8	6.2	7.2
Total	24.2	24.3	25.6	24.4	24.7
Departmental Income	75.8	75.7	74.4	75.6	75.3
Ratio to Total Sales	48.3	49.8	45.6	55.9	46.9
Food & Beverage					
Sales					
Food	68.7	69.9	70.0	73.8	73.3
Beverage	31.4	30.1	30.8	27.2	26.7
Total	100.0	100.0	100.0	100.0	100.0
Cost of Sales					
Food	35.4	35.9	36.0	35.5	33.4
Beverage	20.9	23.3	22.8	22.7	20.6
Total	30.7	31.5	31.7	31.8	30.2
Gross Profit	69.3	68.5	68.3	68.2	69.8
Public Room Sales	2.9	1.4	2.8	2.0	3.2
Other Income	0.8	0.6	0.2	0.1	0.4
Gross Profit & Other Income	73.2	70.7	71.4	70.4	73.9
Departmental Expenses					
Payroll & Related Expenses	40.9	39.6	41.3	41.5	43.8
Other	12.6	13.0	12.4	11.4	9.9
Total	55.4	53.1	54.8	54.8	53.4
Departmental Income	17.8	18.1	17.1	17.0	20.7
Ratio to Total Sales	5.5	5.1	5.6	3.9	6.5
Telephone Departmental Income	(0.6)	(0.6)	(0.6)	(0.2)	(0.5)
Net Income from Minor					
Operated Departments	N	0.3	0.4	0.4	0.2
Rental & Other Income	1.1	1.2	0.9	1.0	1.4
Gross Income	55.0	55.0	53.1	61.3	55.9
Undistributed Operating Expenses					
Administrative & General					
Payroll & Related Expenses	3.8	3.9	4.0	3.6	3.8
Other	4.2	4.6	5.0	4.4	4.2
Total	7.9	8.1	8.8	6.6	7.9
Marketing	4.6	4.4	4.3	2.0	3.6
Energy Costs	6.1	5.8	5.5	5.2	3.9
Property Operation & Maintenance	5.7	5.2	5.8	5.6	5.0
Total Undistributed Expenses	25.1	23.0	24.7	20.6	21.6
Income Before Management Fees	29.9	32.8	28.2	41.5	32.3
Management Fees	3.9	3.9	3.9	4.6	4.0
Income Before Fixed Charges	27.7%	29.0%	24.5%	38.1%	30.1%

*All amounts are medians and do not necessarily add up to the totals shown. All ratios are based on total sales, except those of the rooms and of food and beverage departments. Cost of sales is shown as a percentage of the corresponding sales. Food and beverage department expense ratios are based on combined food and beverage sales.

Source: Laventhol & Horwath.

FIGURE 4-10

STATEMENT OF PROJECTED CASH FLOW FROM OPERATIONS, BEFORE DEBT SERVICE AND INCOME TAXES, FOR A PROPOSED 200-ROOM HOTEL
(In Thousands of 1983 Dollars)

	1986		1987		1988		1989		1990	
Revenues	Amount	Percent	Amount	Percent	Amount	Percent	Amount	Percent	Amount	Percent
Rooms	2628	54.20	2935	55.30	3110	55.85	3197	56.10	3373	56.57
Food and Beverage	2047	42.21	2179	41.07	2255	40.50	2293	40.23	2369	39.73
Telephone	131	2.71	147	2.76	155	2.79	160	2.80	169	2.83
Minor Operated Departments Net	4	0.08	4	0.08	5	0.08	5	0.08	5	0.08
Rentals and Other Income	38	0.79	42	0.79	44	0.78	44	0.78	46	0.78
	4849	100.00	5307	100.00	5569	100.00	5699	100.00	5961	100.00
Departmental Costs and Expenses										
Rooms	679	25.82	712	24.26	731	23.50	740	23.15	759	22.51
Food and Beverage Departments	1609	78.61	1668	76.53	1697	75.24	1719	74.96	1763	74.44
Telephone	139	105.50	149	101.79	155	100.00	159	99.18	165	97.66
	2426	50.04	2529	47.66	2583	46.39	2618	45.93	2687	45.08
Gross Operating Income	2422	49.96	2778	52.34	2986	53.61	3082	54.07	3274	54.92
Undistributed Operating Expenses										
Administrative and General	411	8.47	426	8.02	434	7.80	439	7.70	447	7.50
Marketing	255	5.26	263	4.95	267	4.80	270	4.73	274	4.60
Base Management Fee	145	3.00	159	3.00	167	3.00	171	3.00	179	3.00
Energy Costs	194	4.00	198	3.73	200	3.59	201	3.53	203	3.41
Property Operation and Maintenance	176	3.63	198	3.73	220	3.95	220	3.86	220	3.69
	1181	24.36	1244	23.43	1289	23.14	1300	22.81	1323	22.20
Cash Flow from Operations Before Fixed Charges, Replacement of Fixed Assets, Debt Service, and Income Taxes	1242	25.61	1534	28.91	1697	30.47	1781	31.26	1951	32.72
Property Taxes and Insurance										
Property Taxes	164	3.38	164	3.09	164	2.95	164	2.88	164	2.75
Insurance	20	0.42	20	0.38	20	0.36	20	0.36	20	0.34
	184	3.80	184	3.47	184	3.31	184	3.23	184	3.09
Cash Flow from Operations Before Replacement of Fixed Assets, Debt Service, and Income Taxes	1057	21.81	1350	25.44	1513	27.16	1597	28.02	1766	29.63
Replacement of Fixed Assets	48	1.00	106	2.00	167	3.00	171	3.00	179	3.00
Projected Cash Flow from Operations Before Debt Service and Income Taxes	1009	20.81	1244	23.44	1346	24.16	1426	25.02	1587	26.63
Statistics										
Occupancy Percentage	60%		67%		71%		73%		77%	
Rooms Occupied	43800		48910		51830		53290		56210	
Average Room Rate	60.00		60.00		60.00		60.00		60.00	

Notes: Percentages of departmental expenses are to departmental revenue; all other percentages are to total revenue.
Totals may not add, due to rounding.

Source: Laventhol & Horwath.

FIGURE 4-11

TYPICAL DEVELOPMENT COSTS PER HOTEL ROOM, 1983

Category	Improvements	Furniture, Fixtures, and Equipment	Preopening	Operating Capital	Total Expenditures Excluding Land
Luxury	$100,000–150,000	$25,000–35,000	$4,000–6,000	$4,000–5,500	$150,000–200,000
Deluxe	80,000–100,000	20,000–25,000	2,500–4,000	2,500–4,000	110,000–150,000
First-Class	30,000– 80,000	8,000–20,000	1,500–2,500	2,000–2,500	50,000–110,000
Economy	15,000– 30,000	5,000– 8,000	1,000–1,500	1,000–2,000	25,000– 50,000
Budget	10,000– 15,000	2,500– 5,000	500–1,000	500–1,000	16,000– 25,000

Source: Laventhol & Horwath.

♦ Necessary environmental documents.

♦ Preliminary development schedules.

♦ Design development drawings (preliminary design and design development can account for as much as 60 percent of the total design effort).

♦ Overall land use plan.

These commitments may be formal agreements, letters of intent or understanding, or other binding legal documents. All members of the project team normally take part in the closing of all agreements and in the decision to commit the project's investors to the documents that start the development process. Real estate attorneys should also take part at this point, because the agreements reached in the commitment phase are binding and firmly guide the project's development.

The most important step in the commitment phase is securing project financing, both construction and permanent financing. The funding sources and financing methods available for lodging properties, described in detail in Chapter Five, must undertake to cover both direct and indirect costs. Direct costs include those of land assembly and construction. Indirect costs, on the other hand, include legal and design fees; interest on loans during construction; the developer's profit; the developer's salaries and overhead; contingency and reserve funds; fees for permits, licenses, and inspections; consultant and tax advisory fees; and commissions. To meet these costs, the project team will need to obtain construction and permanent financing and some equity financing.

The methods used to obtain debt and equity financing will depend on the project team's demonstration of their property's viability. Often, lodging properties initially unable to generate much lender or investor confidence are developed in stages. Even if this is the case, as the commitment phase gears down and the construction phase approaches, the project team must still negotiate the final financing terms and relationships before beginning actual development.

DESIGN AND CONSTRUCTION (PHASE IV)

By the time final approval to begin construction has come down, the final site, architectural, and engineering plans will have been completed. These plans, of course, assign amounts of square footage to each use within the hotel complex. Space allocations vary considerably with the type of hotel being built—whether, for example, an economy motel on an interstate highway or an urban convention hotel—and with the specific market area. Even within one chain, hotels will not necessarily be carbon copies of one another, but will each be designed to complement the market for which it was built. (Figure 4–12 provides rough guidelines on space allocations for five basic uses within a middle-market hotel complex: site area, guest rooms, public facilities, support services, and administration.)

Parking is another element that should be decided upon in the preconstruction phase. Zoning requirements frequently dictate the minimum number of spaces that must be provided unless a variance has been obtained. In addition, or when parking is not set by local zoning, several other factors deserve consideration; the number of parking spaces required at a hotel varies with the mode of transportation of arriving guests, with the volume of walk-in patrons served in the food and beverage outlets, and with the amount of function space in the hotel. An airport hotel, for instance, might need very little parking if the majority of its business derives from air passengers either passing through or meeting others. In contrast, a suburban motor hotel that largely attracts local business through its meeting and convention services and its restaurant and "hangout" trade, might find that parking will be inadequate when the house is full and when a large local event is proceeding at the same time.

FIGURE 4-12

SPACE ALLOCATION GUIDELINES FOR HOTEL FACILITIES

I. **Site Area.** The site area depends on parking requirements and height restrictions.

	Acres
✦ Urban hotels	1.0–2.0
✦ Suburban or highway hotels with on-site parking	1.0 per 50 to 75 guest rooms

II. **Guest Rooms.** The total square footage of the guest room block usually equals 65 to 75 percent of the total floor area of the hotel.

✦ The net guest room area (including living space, bathroom, and closet) for a typical room is:

	Square feet
Budget hotels	200–275
Standard hotels	275–325
First-class hotels	325–375
Luxury hotels	375–450

✦ To determine the total square footage of the guest room block (including corridors, elevators, stairways, linen closets, vending areas, and storage), generally add 50 percent to the net guest room area. (This assumes a double-loaded corridor.)

1) For atrium hotels, add 60 percent to the net guest room area. (This assumes a single-loaded corridor.)

2) For some unusually efficient hotels, add as little as 35 percent to the net guest room area. (This assumes a double-loaded corridor.)

3) Very inexpensive hotels differ from each other too dramatically for a general rule; consider them on a case-by-case basis.

The minimum finished width of a room is about 12 feet.

✦ The minimum finished width of corridors on guest room floors is about 6 feet. If the guest room doors are recessed, this figure may go down to 5 feet.

III. **Public Facilities.** The amount of space assigned to the various public facilities shown below will fluctuate greatly. Except in budget hotels, however, and except in those hotels with no restaurant or meeting facilities, this space normally approximates 10 to 20 percent of the total floor area of the hotel.

A. **Lobby.** The lobby typically accounts for 2 to 6 percent of the hotel's total floor area.

	Square feet per guest room
Main lobby (general circulation)	7.0–10.0
Seating area	0.7– 1.0
Front desk and related	3.0– 4.0
Baggage storage	0.5– 1.0
Public washroom (lobby)	0.5– 1.0

B. **Retail Shops.** A gift or sundry shop usually contains 1.0 to 1.5 square feet per guest room. The size of other retail outlets may range from 100 to 1,200 square feet or more, depending on whether these outlets are simply desk operations for car rentals or airline tickets, or full-fledged shops. Recommended space allocations for shops depend on market requirements.

C. **Dining rooms and lounges.** Most dining and lounge facilities account for 4 to 6 percent of the total floor area of the hotel. Their size will depend on the market and on expected use.

	Square feet required per seat
Coffee shop	15–18
Specialty restaurant	18–20
Formal dining room	20–22
Cocktail lounge	15–18

D. **Function space.** This kind of space can range from little or none to extensive, depending on market requirements. Most meeting space provides between 1.0 and 2.0 meeting seats per guest room.

	Square feet required
Ballroom	10–12 per person (seat)
Meeting room	10–12 per person (seat)
Boardroom/hospitality suite	12–16 per person (seat)
Prefunction area	25–40 percent of ballroom area
Public washroom	
Men	0.4 per meeting seat
Women	0.6 per meeting seat
Coatroom	0.4–0.5 per meeting seat

FIGURE 4-12 (CONT'D)

SPACE ALLOCATION GUIDELINES FOR HOTEL FACILITIES

E. <u>Recreational facilities.</u> These, too, range from little or none to extensive, depending on market needs.

	Square feet required
Swimming pool and deck	10–20 per guest room
Lockers/shower/toilet area	2.0 per guest room
Health club	2.0 per guest room
Putting green	1,500

F. <u>Circulation.</u> An amount equal to 15 to 20 percent of the above total public area, excluding the ballroom, should be added to allow for circulation. (Circulation related to the ballroom was included above, under "prefunction area.")

IV. <u>Support Facilities and Services.</u> The amount of space allocated to support facilities and services will vary considerably according to the nature of those facilities included, the hotel's concept of operation (e.g., full-service or no-frills), and the number and types of facilities provided for employees. The usual range is between 10 and 15 percent of the total floor area of the hotel.

A. <u>Food preparation.</u>

	Square feet required
Coffee shop kitchen	10–25 percent of coffee shop
Main dining room kitchen	30–45 percent of dining room area
Banquet kitchen	20–30 percent of ballroom/meeting room space
Room service	1.0 per guest room
Food and beverage storage area	35–45 percent of total kitchen space

B. <u>Receiving.</u>

	Square feet required
Office	0.3–0.5 per guest room
Platform	100–250 per bay

C. <u>Hotel employee facilities.</u>

	Square feet required
Lockers/restrooms	6–10 per guest room
Cafeteria	4.0 per employee
Lounge (if any)	1.0 per guest room

D. <u>Housekeeping.</u>

	Square feet per guest room
Laundry	7.0
Linen storage (not on guest floor)	3.0
Guest laundry	0.8–1.5
Uniform issuing	1.0

E. <u>Other storage, maintenance, and miscellaneous.</u>

	Square feet required
Hotel general storage	3.0–7.0 per guest room
Ballroom/meeting room storage	1.0–1.5 per seat or 10–20 percent of ballroom area
Miscellaneous storage (garbage, empty bottles)	1.0–1.8 per guest room
Telephone switchboard/equipment	1.3–2.0 per guest room
Computer room	1.0–1.5 per guest room
Mechanical, electrical, and air handling rooms and systems	13–18 per guest room
Maintenance shop	5.0 per guest room
Security	0.3–0.6 per guest room
Circulation	10 percent of total area for support facilities and services

V. <u>Hotel Administration.</u> The amount of space reserved for administrative offices ordinarily varies between 1 and 2 percent of the hotel's total floor area. It includes the executive offices as well as the sales, accounting, personnel, and other administrative support offices. As a rule, a total of 10 square feet per guest room is allotted to this category.

Source: Laventhol & Horwath.

Parking—its amount and type—is a function of a hotel's location. At suburban hotels, surface parking may be sufficient, while in downtown locations, a parking garage may be required. This garage also serves an adjacent office building.

Parking is more a function of a hotel's location than of its price category. The availability of off-site facilities can have a significant impact. Sharing of parking with other uses in a mixed-use development also eases a hotel's burden of parking requirements.

Providing parking can be very costly. While too little allowance for it may severely impair the success of a project, too much space allocated to it may constitute an economic burden, both at the feasibility stage and in operation. A good general rule allows for one space per room, one space for every three or four restaurant seats, plus one space for every three employees.

After the design decisions have been made, the construction manager comes to the forefront of the development team. The services of an experienced construction manager are critical during this phase of a project. During construction, this person must:

✦ Initiate and administer contracts,
✦ Develop working drawings and specifications,
✦ Secure necessary permits and approvals,
✦ Direct the bidding selection process and conduct the negotiations with each subcontractor,
✦ Advise the project team of construction progress,
✦ Monitor change orders,
✦ Handle contract claims and disputes,
✦ Coordinate on-site facilities,
✦ Schedule construction activity,

✦ Monitor the construction activity and process,
✦ Obtain a certificate of occupancy on completion, and
✦ Assist in bringing the project in on time and on budget.

MANAGEMENT/OPERATION (PHASE V)

This phase usually begins 12 to 18 months before the hotel opens, continues when the hotel becomes operational, and involves the following functions:

✦ Preparation and implementation of an aggressive sales and marketing campaign;

✦ Recruitment, training, and retention of staff;

✦ Provision of services according to agreements negotiated during the commitment phase;

✦ Management of each operating department;

✦ Continuing control and reduction of operating costs and expenses; and

✦ Generation of operating profits, maintenance of facilities, and enhancement of the hotel's image in the marketplace.

Achieving the primary objective of the management/operation phase, which is to ensure the long-term success of the project, requires an experienced management team. Because lodging properties are viewed and financed as a combined business and real estate venture, the success of a project rests squarely on the strength and expertise of the operating entity. As a result, the number of investor/owners who operate their own lodging properties has decreased. Chain and independent operating companies will likely control the hotel management process for some time to come. In a highly competitive lodging environment, a paramount need exists for experienced hotel operators, as well as for good marketing and sales representatives.

Until very recently, the hotel development process appealed to many developers, investors, and operators. The constantly changing business and investment climate has forced many to rethink their decisions to develop lodging properties. Those who understand the hotel development process, however, will still likely recognize and grasp the numerous opportunities awaiting the right team.

FINANCING IN THE LODGING INDUSTRY

CHAPTER FIVE

Obtaining financing for a lodging property calls for creativity, tenacity, and flexibility. Today, hotel developers and operators find themselves aggressively competing for a constantly changing pool of funds (both equity and debt), and then having to deal with the increasingly complex terms and conditions for the use of those funds. In addition, recent federal tax legislation has provided new incentives for real estate investment; these have, in turn, resulted in a diversified array of financing methods and structures. Formerly passive lenders, for example, have, because of uncertainty over long-term inflation rates, become active partners in many development projects, while high interest rates and a soft market have reduced the number of financed hotel projects. Joint ventures of various types are increasingly accepted as a structure for developmental real estate transactions. The constantly changing and often unpredictable economic and investment climate in the United States has catalysed the formulation of new risk-sharing financing terms. Financing for lodging properties is now in a period of transition and will continue to be in flux.

Today's dynamic hotel financing environment contrasts sharply with the relatively stable conditions of the 1960s or 1970s. Less than 10 years ago, real estate financing remained an orderly, standardized process that matched developers with investors and lenders. Inflation and interest rates fluctuated only slightly, and project teams simply wanted to speed up the process. Today, however, the financing process involves incentive fees, national and international investors and lenders, project layering with multitiered financing vehicles initiating projects, and often volumes of computer-based analyses. At stake is the ability to structure a deal that satisfies the needs of all equity and debt partners. Major lenders are demanding higher real yields or various hedges against uncertain interest and inflation rates. Real estate financing for income-producing properties frequently calls into play variable interest rate loans, shorter terms, sale leaseback, convertible mortgages, and call provisions. Many lenders are now taking participating positions in properties to guard against inflation. These participating positions may include: (1) income participation, which includes sharing the effective gross revenue, net operating income, cash flow after debt service, or a percentage of increases over a base income; and (2) equity participation, which includes sharing in the proceeds of sale or of refinancing, or sharing in the tax benefits, depending on the institution or investor concerned. Following on the increased participation requirement in hotel financings, lower levels of equity returns, brought about by increased equity ownership, will likely result; thus, the real appreciation of a hotel property will probably not increase as rapidly as it did in years past. Estimates predict that 50 percent of all U.S. commercial real estate will be owned by institutions of various types by the year 2000. Lenders concern themselves less with default risk than with protecting the value of the invested principal, and consequently, they are taking partial or full ownership positions.

The financing of lodging properties does not resemble that of office, industrial, or residential projects. Lodging properties, which rely on the success of a business, are often viewed as high-risk investments with tremendous upside potentials. Opinions on the degree of this risk vary. For example, in the opinion of

Gary Wilson, executive vice president and chief financial officer of The Marriott Corporation:

> It seems clear to our company that investors are viewing hotels on a much more comparable basis with other forms of real estate. I think there are two reasons for this. First, during a period of very high inflation, hotels have a history of increasing room rates directly with inflation, thereby maintaining profit margins. Office buildings and retail establishments frequently do not have that benefit, considering the fixed nature of their leases. This is the reason institutions have actually been more interested in hotels than in other forms of real estate over the past five years. Second, investors are beginning to realize that a well-conceived hotel managed by a major chain takes some of the locational risk out of the real estate product. In the typical office or retail project, location is everything—and if a project happens to be poorly located, it is automatically a loser. However, with a major hotel chain, the marketing effort of that chain brings group business to the hotel—even if it is in a secondary or tertiary location. This does not mean that you can fill a poorly located hotel, but it does mean that location is not the primary issue that it is in other forms of real estate.

> Insurance companies are making 10-year bullet loans on many real estate projects, and the rate differential between an office building and a chain-managed hotel is slight. The difference today might be 25 basis points, whereas 10 years ago, it might have been 150 basis points.

Lodging properties characteristically involve lender participation because of the upside potentials. Lenders, however, regard lodging properties as risky ventures and typically finance only those projects that are well-conceived and well-located, and that involve experienced developers and operating companies. The cash flow available for debt service from a lodging property depends on economic downturns, quality of management, and unpredictable travel patterns.

Currently, the financing characteristics of lodging properties are constantly changing. Traditional lenders to the lodging industry, such as life insurance companies, are reducing future participation, as their portfolios in real estate are already heavily weighted with hotels. Depository thrifts have withdrawn almost totally because their charters ban equity investment. The major hotel chains and independent operating companies have discovered that, in order to achieve continued growth, they must find new financing methods. The Marriott Corporation, for instance, has raised approximately $1 billion since 1975 by selling equity interests in hotel properties to institutions such as Equitable Life Assurance Society, Massachusetts Mutual, and Prudential Life Insurance Company. Roy D. Burry, an analyst at Kidder Peabody & Company in New York, revealed that "Marriott makes almost as much money in managing as in owning hotels."

International investors have aggressively entered the financing marketplace, although only limited amounts have at this writing been put into direct hotel financing. (It should be noted that mixed-use developments that include hotels have been more attractive to foreign funds to date.) In 1982, foreign pension funds held over $5 billion in U.S. equity real estate.

Large and small syndicators are offering private real estate limited partnerships in order to take advantage of the tax laws to raise equity capital. Because some developers and syndicators find that they must put from 25 to 50 percent equity into a hotel project, a significant number of recent hotel financings have met their equity requirements through the sale of limited partnerships.

Financing has always been and still is forthcoming for well-conceived and well-located lodging properties. No standard industry rules of thumb exist, however, for financing hotel projects. Owners, developers, and investors now require an understanding of the financial vehicles available to a development project, plus creativity, willingness to negotiate and to share the equity benefits, and a project plan that will generate sufficient cash flow to permit flexible financing terms and conditions.

MAJOR SOURCES OF FINANCING

Seven primary sources of financing exist for lodging properties: (1) institutional lenders; (2) institutions acting as intermediaries; (3) syndications; (4) developers; (5) hotel operating companies; (6) brokers and mortgage bankers acting as intermediaries; and (7) government.

The Willard Hotel, a landmark structure on Washington's Pennsylvania Avenue, suffered through several development proposals that were stymied by a lack of financing. The new Willard is scheduled to reopen in 1986.

INSTITUTIONAL LENDERS

Institutional lenders principally comprise life insurance companies, pension funds, commercial banks, credit companies, and, to some extent, savings and loan associations. These lenders increasingly seek equity kickers in addition to interest income on loans to quality projects, in order to provide themselves a hedge against inflation. They attempt to avoid development risk by purchasing existing hotel projects of proven quality. In new projects, these lenders prefer properties that are well-located, that possess proven chain affiliation, and that have professional management. For lodging properties with these traits, lenders are devising new financial structures, such as equity takeouts and participations.

Recently, as the supply of proven hotel properties has declined, these lenders have been assuming more development risk and a share of the upside potentials. Accordingly, they have been pricing and assembling their financing packages with conditions that provide a buffer against inflation and development risk.

Life Insurance Companies

Insurance companies, which have provided a significant portion of the debt financing for hotel development, have recently reduced their involvement because of:

♦ The perceived overbuilt status of several hotel markets and products throughout the United States.

♦ A decline in monies available for lending, principally caused by policyholders' borrowing against the cash value of their accounts, and by the lack of the whole life policies that have provided good cash flow in the past.

♦ A desire to become equity partners in new hotel financings, and to receive the benefits of an equity owner as a nonnegotiable condition of financing.

♦ A lack of quality, seasoned hotel properties for funding.

♦ The availability of other, more secure investments (stock market, quality office buildings, retail or industrial facilities).

♦ A preference for financing hotel projects that have at least 300 rooms or that are parts of overall mixed-use projects in active commercial centers.

♦ A preference for making a minimum investment in the range of $20 to $30 million—which excludes smaller properties.

Over the past few years, life insurance companies have markedly reduced their issuance of long-term, fixed-rate mortgages. Today, most insurance companies require some form of participating mortgage, involving either a joint venture or their own assumption of a developer/owner posi-

tion in the project. In the current marketplace, lenders expect between 25 and 75 percent of the economic benefits from a property. True, life insurance companies have continued to provide debt financing on those projects that possess existing permanent loans. The primary objective of these companies, however, is to retain their dominant positions in the financing community; thus, they are willing to evaluate each hotel project on its own merits. To achieve their objective, they choose with care the properties they finance, and they seek an active part in the projects' overall development and management.

Pension Funds

According to several industry sources, pension funds will likely represent a major funding source for hotel development during the next two decades. Although pension funds have not yet committed themselves to financing many lodging projects, several analysts believe that these funds will move toward greater participation in this field. In 1983, pension funds worldwide had an asset value of approximately $700 billion, and, with an average annual growth rate of 12 percent, this figure should rise to a value of $1 trillion by 1985 and $2.7 trillion by 1992. Currently, only about 1 to 1½ percent of U.S. pension funds' assets are invested in real estate, while in Europe, this amount approaches 25 percent. If U.S. pension funds increased their involvement in real estate financing to 5 percent of their assets, the total Ameri-

The J.W. Marriott Hotel is a joint venture among The Marriott Corporation, Quadrangle Development Corporation, and AEtna Life & Casualty Company.

can involvement of this kind would amount to about $50 billion by 1985 or $135 billion by 1992.

Major pension fund managers have, however, been reluctant to increase their investment in real estate and, in some cases, have actually reduced their involvement level. This decline likely derives from the preferred liquidity of money market instruments, from the higher anticipated returns available in the stock and bond markets, from the generally perceived overbuilding of the hotel market, and from those state laws that prevent real estate equity investment.

In December 1980, an amendment to the federal tax law enabled pension funds to invest tax-free in leveraged real estate. This amendment specified that the income and capital gains of qualified trusts from debt-financed real estate projects may be tax-exempt, however, only if these trusts adhere to certain provisions and avoid such conditions as sale and leasebacks; equity participation loans; low-interest seller financing; and open-price sales.

During the past few years, pension fund managers have tended to transfer their investment responsibilities to major life insurance companies, brokers, and mortgage bankers. Public pension funds (state employee or teacher pension funds) need not adhere to ERISA regulations for investment, that is, to the "prudent man" concept; these public funds, however, are often subject to unusually restrictive controls for investment and, as a result, view each potential real estate venture with some concern and skepticism.

Most pension fund managers desire a balance of types of real estate investments and historically have preferred office buildings to hotels because of the fixed lease commitment. When pension fund managers evaluate a hotel project for financing, they:

◆ Prefer medium-sized to large-scale hotel projects—generally, properties with 250 rooms or more.

◆ Favor retention of an operating company and strongly desire chain affiliation.

◆ Prefer hotel projects within mixed-use developments to "stand-alones."

◆ Will finance on a debt or an equity basis.

◆ Require some form of participation in revenues, cash flow, and/or capital appreciation.

◆ Look for seasoned, well-located properties with proven operating performance.

◆ Will compare the return on investment to that offered by non–real estate investment opportunities.

Recent surveys of pension fund managers reveal that most pension funds involved in hotel investment are providing participating mortgages (either debt or equity); convertible mortgages (generally, with an interest rate two to three points below the market rate, and with the right to convert the mortgage to ownership of 50 percent or more of the property); or bullet loans (typically, with interest rates one to two points below market, depending on the term, which may run from three to 10 years).

Commercial Banks

The trends shared by life insurance companies and pension funds toward equity positions, revenue-sharing opportunities, and reduced mortgage terms have forced commercial banks to increase the length of their debt instruments. Thus, banks now capture a larger share of the real estate financing market. Commercial banks offer hotel developers construction loans, interim loans, open-ended construction loans, bullet loans, and gap loans without an equity participation requirement, when the developers can show that their projects are well sponsored and do not benefit from permanent takeouts. Commercial banks are willing to fix interest rates to one of several floating indices (the London Interbank Offered Rate—LIBOR, the prime rate, the T-Bill rate, those offered by certificates of deposit, etc.) and to negotiate interest rate caps, accrual provisions, and other interest-rate fixing options. Currently, the Federal Reserve prevents commercial banks from taking an equity position with their borrowers.

The commercial banking industry has, in recent years, been the major source of debt financing for projects in the $5 to $25 million loan package range. Often, the larger amounts of debt are raised by a consortium of banks. Most commercial banks have by now reexamined, or are in the process of reexamining their existing loan packages to determine the extent or mix of hotel projects they want in their portfolios.

Credit Companies

Credit companies, which historically have provided construction and standby loans for hotel properties, now represent important sources for bullet loans, wraparound mortgages, interim or minipermanent loans, and land development loans. These loans, except for the wraps, carry interest rates that are one to three points above the prime rate. They often function as financing vehicles for projects that carry high development risks.

Savings and Loan Associations (S&Ls)

S&Ls, once significant financing sources for smaller lodging properties, now play the same role for larger hotels. A September 1983 survey of 42 of the largest S&Ls in the United States revealed that 86 percent of the respondents act as joint venture partners in real estate, 69 percent as mortgage bankers, 52 percent as developers, and 26 percent as syndicators. More of these associations, the study predicts, will likely get involved in mortgage banking, real estate development, and syndication. The desire to balance investment portfolios with income-producing properties has motivated S&Ls to diversify their investments. The following recent events exemplify this trend:

♦ Gibraltar Savings & Loan Association formed a new subsidiary, Gibraltar Community Builders, to acquire, develop, and sell residential, industrial, and commercial properties.

♦ Great Western Financial Corporation, the parent of Great Western Savings & Loan Association, acquired Walker & Lee, a full-service real estate brokerage firm.

♦ American Diversified Savings & Loan Association (ADS&L) acquired American Development Company. ADS&L intends to provide project financing through its ability to raise debt instruments from private and institutional investors.

♦ A consortium of S&Ls committed $350 million to finance Marriott's New York Marquis Hotel.

INSTITUTIONS ACTING AS INTERMEDIARIES

A large influx of institutional capital has somewhat offset the decline of insurance company funds available for financing real estate ventures. This institutional capital comes from: (1) pension funds that are diversifying under ERISA guidelines; (2) foreign investors and foreign pension funds that seek a more stable investment climate; and (3) foundations and endowments.

Prudential Insurance Company of America's PRISAs (Property Investment Separate Accounts), the largest commingled funds in the United States, and others, have begun to purchase properties and to manage portfolios for other institutions, primarily pension funds. Set up in 1970 to provide pension funds with a real estate investment vehicle, PRISA I owned over $4 billion in income-producing properties by 1982. In 1980, Prudential established a second fund, PRISA II, that differed from the original separate account in that it had no geographic preference and was designed to purchase only the higher-value properties. PRISA I and II do

The Hilton Hawaiian Village in Honolulu, with the Rainbow Tower to the left and the convention center and parking garage to its right. The Ocean Tower is in the foreground, and the Diamond Head Tower stands to its right. The Tapa Tower, recently completed, is not shown.

*T*hree-quarters of the rooms at the Vista International Hotel overlook the atrium.

not get involved in the development process, but do provide their "pooled" clients with a share of the entire national portfolio of investments, prefer finished products, and permit trading of shares to increase liquidity of ownership. Similar separate accounts are offered by other insurance companies and banks, including Equitable Life Assurance Society of the United States, AEtna Life & Casualty Company, and Citibank. Most funds look for overall return rates that are at least 3 to 5 percent above the inflation rate; they are attracted to quality commercial properties that generate high income and that possess cushions against inflation and economic uncertainty. Although lodging properties have not traditionally been preferred investments for most separate accounts, in a recent study lodging outperformed all other forms of real estate in separate accounts over the past decade.

Insurance companies are also placing Guaranteed Investment Contracts (GICs) on certain hotel properties. GICs—fixed-rate monies normally placed on behalf of a pension fund by a life insurance company—carry guarantees that for a given term between five and 10 years, the fund will receive a fixed return. Reciprocally, the insurance company takes a mortgage on the property and makes a profit on the loan. GICs normally apply to existing hotel properties and not to forward commitments on construction projects.

Foreign investors and foreign pension funds compete directly with commingled funds for the acquisition of quality commercial properties. Both usually pay all cash rather than leverage their investments through borrowing. Foreign pension funds in the United States, principally those headquartered in Great Britain and Holland, have formed Delaware-based or Netherlands Antilles–based investment structures, or have created a commingled fund sponsored by several pension funds. In 1982, over $5.4 billion in foreign pension fund monies, managed by U.S. institutions, went into real estate equity.

In 1983, estimates placed the assets of foundations and endowments in the $85 to $100 billion range. Although foundations and endowment funds do not traditionally invest in real estate, several institutions (Interfirst Bank of Dallas, Prudential Life Insurance Company, and JMB Institutional Realty Corporation) offer real estate investment funds exclusively for foundations and for endowment money.

SYNDICATIONS

The decline of traditional debt financing and the high cost of capital have forced developers to raise equity. In addition, the recent change in tax legislation that increases depreciation write-offs has both encouraged and helped developers to raise equity. One of the most popular methods has been syndication. Real estate syndication is growing at an accelerated rate to provide the needed equity that enables developers to obtain construction and permanent financing. The 1981 Economic Recovery Tax Act (ERTA) and the 1982 Tax Equity and Fiscal Responsibility Act (TEFRA) provided the syndication industry with a variety of incentives, including shortened depreciation schedules and generous rehabilitation tax credits. According to D. Michael Kelly of the syndication firm Consolidated Capital, "Syndicators are now providing 30 to 50 percent of the equity for both new and existing projects." Total investment volume for public and private offerings has grown to nearly $21 billion annually. The Real Estate Securities & Syndication Institute (RESSI) estimates that by 1985, the annual volume for public and private syndications should reach $50 billion. By 1993, public and private syndications will likely raise nearly $100 billion annually.

Within the lodging industry, syndications represent an appealing option for smaller properties in emerging markets and locations—properties that do not often attract the interest of the major institutional lenders. The continued higher equity demands for property development; the decline in traditional debt financing; the inherent tax shelter, cash flow, and appreciation potential of hotels; the expected growth of the market with funds (albeit limited) for investment; and the availability of Individual Retirement Accounts (IRAs) and Keogh plans, will probably result in increased syndication activity. Lodging properties, traditionally not the products sought by large syndicators, are now viewed as opportunities for investment because of the good tax shelter potential that they represent.

The general partner in a typical syndication receives 10 to 30 percent of all cash raised as an acquisition fee; a property management fee equal to 4 to 6 percent of gross annual income; a 10 percent general administration fee; a 5 percent commission on the sale of the property; plus other percentage returns (up to 50 percent) after the original investors have received their initial investments back. Investors can expect yields of between 10 and 12 percent. Competition in the syndication market is high, with an estimated 50,000 active syndicators and 50 large national and regional firms sponsoring new offerings.

Recently, Balcor/American Express, one of the nation's largest real estate syndication firms, announced the formation of a subsidiary that will make short-term loans to real estate developers and investors. The new company, known as Balcor/American Express Real Estate Finance, Inc., makes Balcor the first major syndicator to enter the short-term real estate lending business. The formation of this subsidiary also marks the first time that investments by Balcor are being funded from sources other than limited partnerships and group trusts. The new company will also serve the market for partnership note financing.

Similar to syndication, the condotel concept is a funding mechanism that has been in use since the late 1960s. The creation of a condotel involves the sale of hotel units, each with an undivided fee interest in the common elements of the building, and the structuring of a voluntary or mandatory rental agreement (rental pool, leaseback, or individual unit rentals). The degree of ownership of public facilities and recreational amenities differs for each property, depending on the desired level of sponsorship involvement. Although the condotel financing mechanism has existed for nearly two decades, it remains an uncommon method, and nearly one-third of all condotel projects once filed with the SEC have been withdrawn from registration. An attraction to the developer, however, is that the condominium owners individually finance their own units. Among the better known condotel projects are The Camelback at Scottsdale in Arizona, and Innisbrook at Tarpon Springs in Florida.

DEVELOPERS

Although generally not a substantial funding source for hotel projects other than their own, developers have provided a relatively common financing solution for lodging

Interior of a unit at Mariners Inn, a condotel at Hilton Head, South Carolina.

projects with a total development value, excluding land, of less than $10 million. Generally, "developers' equity" has taken the form of the value of the land that they control and that they propose for use. Most developers have resisted the demand for equity positions on the part of institutional lenders; as a result, these developers have raised their needed equity through syndications. The combination of this equity with the value of the land proposed for development constitutes the principal financing package, which is then leveraged to raise the additional funds.

HOTEL OPERATING COMPANIES

A major hotel operating company will generally provide equity for a new hotel development in which it will retain the management contract, some form of ownership, and a share in the cash flow and/or appreciation of the property that bears its name. Hilton Hotels Corporation, for example, recently raised $150 million with two debenture offerings to provide partial funds for their $270 million Atlantic City casino hotel. Hilton, which expects to add 15,000 new hotel rooms in the non–equity-managed or franchise category by mid-1985, has funded new hotel projects through the sale of existing properties, through company profits, and through debentures. Hilton has one of the most conservative capital structures in the lodging industry (31 percent debt, 69 percent equity, as of an adjusted March 31, 1983, balance sheet). By 1986, Hilton will likely have approximately $400 million in cash for reinvestment.

The Marriott Corporation, on the other hand, has embarked on an expansion program to increase its hotel rooms to 92,000 by 1985. (In 1983, Marriott had 46,000 rooms.) Marriott has funded this aggressive growth by raising over $1 billion since 1975 through sales of equity interests in hotel properties to institutions while retaining management contracts; by selling limited partnerships; by selling company profits; and through other sources. In 1981, for instance, Marriott raised $18 million by selling interests to over 1,000 limited partners; then, on behalf of the partnership (Potomac Hotels, Ltd.), it secured a $456 million loan from a consortium of banks to finance 11 new hotel properties. Investors in this partnership will be able to shelter $9.00 for each $1.00 invested. After selling off equity interest in several hotel properties, Marriott owned 25 percent of its inventory in 1983, compared with 80 percent in 1968.

Other hotel operating companies have involved themselves in financing structures similar to those of Hilton and Marriott Corporations. The only way in which chain and independent operating companies can continue and can achieve their projected growth rates has been to act as funding catalysts. In this capacity, these operating companies: (1) provide assistance to franchisees by "opening doors" to lenders and brokers; (2) offer limited partnerships to raise equity; (3) seek joint venture agreements with developers or investors to acquire existing properties; and (4) obtain long-term Industrial Revenue Bond mortgages. The competition for debt and equity financing among the leading hotel operating companies will probably reduce the number of funding opportunities for independent lodging properties.

BROKERS AND MORTGAGE BANKERS ACTING AS INTERMEDIARIES

Both during periods of economic uncertainty and in times of economic growth, brokers and mortgage bankers have played active roles in the financing of commercial projects. These individuals and firms "find" debt financing, ordinarily from pension funds, for their clients. For the most part, brokers and mortgage bankers provide longer-term debt instruments for small to medium-sized development firms. The ability of a broker or a mortgage banker—to gain access to many funding sources, to locate and match a developer with a money source and vice versa, and to attract monies for real estate ventures—represents the principal measure of success for one of these intermediaries. Their role is growing in importance in today's highly volatile financing market.

GOVERNMENT

To stimulate private sector investment in either the deteriorating or the designated growth areas of communities, federal, state, and local governments have enacted various programs for financing. These government agencies use the following criteria to evaluate a project's eligibility for public financing assistance: (1) the project must have a public purpose; (2) the project must stimulate economic growth through job creation, increase property values, and attract new monies into the economy; and (3) it must conform to the community's planning and development guidelines. The principal sources and vehicles for public assistance in hotel funding include:

✦ Issuing *tax-exempt revenue bonds* (usually Industrial Revenue Bonds). Industrial Revenue Bonds are being used by developers and by hotel chains with strong credit ratings. They have a $10 million loan limitation. IRBs are normally amortized over 25 to 30 years, and the loan principal ranges from 40 to 100 percent of project cost. The issuance of an IRB may require a variety of guarantees, depending on the parties and the project involved.

✦ Financing infrastructure improvements through *special assessment districts*.

✦ Funding land assembly, relocation, land cost writedowns, infrastructure improvements, and debt service by *tax increment financing*.

✦ Obtaining a federal grant from the *Urban Development Action Grant (UDAG)* program. UDAGs provide the final financing necessary to implement a project. Over 1,000 projects have been awarded UDAG funds since the program's inception in 1977. A $6.5 million UDAG, for example, was used to finance Riverfront Center in Flint,

Michigan, a $61 million mixed-use project that included a 400-room Hyatt Regency hotel. UDAGs are available to over 3,400 qualifying large and small cities in the United States, and lodging properties have always been primary recipients of these grants because of the large number of jobs they create.

✦ Acquiring a grant from the *Community Development Block Grant (CDBG)* program. These grants are typically not used in downtown hotel financings. To receive a CDBG, a municipality must demonstrate private funding commitments of at least $2.50 for every $1.00 from the desired grant.

✦ Obtaining some form of *tax abatement*. The 1,407-room, 30-story Grand Hyatt Hotel in New York City, adjacent to the Grand Central Terminal, exemplifies the use of tax abatement to finance the acquisition and revitalization of an existing hotel. The developer, Donald Trump, determined that bringing the old 1,900-room Commodore Hotel up to the quality of a Hyatt would cost more than $60 million. As a result of the rehabilitation, the real estate taxes on the property would increase from $2 million to $7 million annually. Fortunately, the New York City Board of Estimate passed a financial assistance plan that permitted Penn Central to sell the Commodore to the Trump/Hyatt joint venture for $10 million. In turn, Trump/ Hyatt sold the property to the New York State Development Corporation for $1.00 and then leased it back for 100 years with an option to repurchase after 40 years. Rather than pay higher property taxes to the city, the owners were required to pay rent on a sliding scale until the 41st year, when the hotel would pay full taxes. As a result of this tax abatement, a financing package was successfully assembled.

Most hotel financing that entails issuing revenue bonds or obtaining federal grants involves a redevelopment agency. An excellent source of information on the mechanisms currently available within the public sector for financing assistance, the redevelopment agency has led all public entities in forming public/private partnerships.

Finally, recent tax legislation has provided financial incentives for the rehabilitation of historic structures by allowing developers and investors to depreciate property over a shorter period and to receive the benefits of a generous investment tax credit (ITC). The Barbizon Hotel in New York illustrates the work of the 1981 ERTA and 1982 TEFRA tax laws in awarding the new tax benefits. Placed on the National Register of Historic Places, the Barbizon Hotel, owned by Teitelbaum Holdings, Ltd., raised 30 percent of its equity through a partnership syndicated by Bache Halsey Stuart Shields; the balance came from debt financing through Manufacturers Hanover Trust Company. Under the new tax laws, the Barbizon syndication retained an 85 percent share of the profits and losses, tax credits, and cash flow, and should realize an internal rate of return of about 80 percent for its investors.

Front view of the Hotel Vintage Court in San Francisco. The hotel, which provides stylish rooms at moderate rates, cost about $60,000 per room to rehabilitate—substantially less than the current average for new first-class hotel rooms.

SELECTING THE PROPER FINANCING METHOD

No standard methods of financing lodging properties exist; nor do standard financing packages. Developers, investors, and operators of lodging facilities revealed in a recent nationwide survey of major hotel financings[1] that no two project funding arrangements are alike, and that nearly every project involves separate debt and equity partners. All survey participants, however, did use some combination of short- to intermediate-term debt instruments, long-term debt instruments, and one of three equity structures.

According to the survey, the most common short- to intermediate-term debt instruments are:

+ *Construction loans.* Generally provided by commercial banks, life insurance companies, and credit companies, construction loans usually have interest rates that float with the prime rate. The loan typically covers the entire development cost and is tied to the ability of the developer to obtain permanent financing.

+ *Combined construction and term loans.* These combined loans are packaged to appeal to developers who do not wish to share equity with a money partner who is providing debt financing. Lenders generally require guarantees for cost overruns and operating deficits, and the developer usually must provide equity for at least 10 percent of the project. Terms for these loans run between five and seven years, while interest rates float with prime, have a fixing option, or involve a cap percentage. Ordinarily, these loans carry a minimum prepayment penalty to stimulate refinancing; also, if a hotel operator is a joint venture partner, lenders usually require that incentive management fees be subordinated to the debt service.

+ *Term and bullet loans.* Term and bullet (limited-term and limited-amortization, with the balance due at completion of the term) loans usually function as interim financing vehicles to cover cost overruns or operating deficits. Interest rates vary within the range of one to four points over prime. The loans generally run from three to five years in length and take a subordinate position to the primary financing instruments.

Developers most frequently use short- to intermediate-term loans when a project involves a high risk, when permanent financing does not cover the entire development cost, or when sharing equity is not desirable.

The eight major long-term debt instruments include:

+ *Convertible mortgages.* The developer receives 100 percent of the project's development cost, control of the property for a period of time (usually 10 years), and a loan at or below the market rate. The lender receives a fixed interest return, participates in 10 to 50 percent of the cash flow

---

[1] Conducted by Laventhol & Horwath.

after debt service, and receives the right to convert the mortgage into 50 percent of the equity at an agreed-upon conversion date. Insurance companies, pension funds, and foreign trusts represent the primary sources for convertible mortgages.

+ *Land sale leasebacks and leasehold loans.* The developer generally sells the land to the lender at market value and then leases it back at a low rate (10 to 13 percent of the land value, or 3 to 4 percent of gross room sales) for 40 to 50 years. The developer must also pay out a percentage of future cash flows and a share of the property's appreciation. This method provides long-term capital appreciation to the lender (usually an insurance company or a pension fund) and a tax-deductible land lease expense to the developer.

+ *Permanent loans with no lender ownership.* Most permanent loans without lender ownership involve some lender participation in futures. Participation is normally based on gross sales, cash flow after debt service, shared appreciation of the property, or some combination of all three; revenue participation specifically is based on sales or on a percentage of sales over a base or stabilized year. Loan principal amounts depend on a debt coverage ratio of 1.10 to 1.35 times the projected cash flow before debt service. These loans run from five to 10 years in length, are amortized over 25 to 30 years with a series of call provisions generally beginning in the tenth year, and carry high prepayment penalties. Insurance companies, pension funds (through separate accounts), and some commercial banks are the principal providers of these loans.

+ *Permanent loans with lender ownership.* Currently one of the more popular financing methods, the permanent loan with lender ownership (equity partner) usually serves the project with 100 percent financing of the development cost; a fixed, below-market interest rate; and a fully amortized loan (15 to 32 years) with a 15-year call. The lender—an insurance company, a pension fund separate account, a private or public pension fund, or a foreign trust—provides 40 to 70 percent of the equity. The lender also forms a joint venture with the developer and with any hotel operating company involved. Distribution of the cash flow to each equity partner may either be cumulative (10 to 12 percent of the lender's equity base) or noncumulative (9 to 11 percent of the lender's equity base). Ordinarily, the lender will assign to the developer the assumption of all cost overruns, to the joint venture the assumption of all operating deficits, and to itself a share in the residuals upon sale or refinancing.

+ *Mortgages with a kicker.* This financing method provides the developer with a loan at market or below-market rate, having a long term or an extra-long term. The maximum loan depends on coverage, and the kicker takes the form of a percentage of future cash flows (10 to 50 percent), part of the residuals, or both of these options.

88

◆ *Industrial Revenue Bonds (IRBs).* These bonds represent perhaps the most commonly used public financing mechanisms for lodging projects. Most projects that are successful in attracting IRBs involve an experienced developer, a hotel operating company, a good location, and the satisfaction of a community's development objectives. IRBs are generally amortized over 25 to 30 years, with a fixed or variable interest rate, and the loan principal typically covers 40 to 100 percent of a project's cost.

◆ *Urban Development Action Grants (UDAGs).* UDAGs serve to bridge a many-layered debt structure for medium-sized properties in urban redevelopment areas. Provided by the federal government for qualified projects in qualified cities, UDAGs have low fixed interest rates (3 to 12 percent) and a repayment schedule that defers payments until sufficient cash flow becomes available.

◆ *Wraparound mortgages (wraps).* Generally provided by sellers or credit companies, these mortgages entail a fixed rate on the underlying wrap mortgages, plus a share of the residuals, a kicker, or both.

◆ *Other long-term debt instruments.* Other such instruments include seller financings, exchanges, second mortgages, and standby mortgages. These debt instruments are primarily used when other, more favorable, financing methods will not cover all development costs, operating deficits, cost overruns, or land assembly costs.

The three major equity structures used to finance hotel development are: (1) joint ventures; (2) limited partnerships; and (3) all-equity packages:

◆ *Joint ventures (JVs).* A joint venture typically involves a developer, a lender, and, in most cases, an operator—although most lenders prefer the developer and operator to form their own joint venture before entering into a joint venture with the lender. Most JVs bring together "equals"—a developer who is neither larger nor smaller than the operator, and a lender who requires some assurance that the project will succeed under the terms of the joint venture. Division of equity and sharing of revenues and appreciation are determined by the cash and the imputed value of the services of each JV partner, and by each partner's investment objectives. When structuring a joint venture, the partners must clarify the payout priorities and the conditions governing buyout or sale of a partner's interest.

◆ *Limited partnerships.* Private offerings of limited partnerships have represented a major option for equity financing of smaller to medium-sized lodging facilities. The success of these partnerships principally ensues from the high cost of public offerings and from investors' desire to take advantage of recent tax legislation. Because each partnership arises from different sets of assumptions, objectives, and products, no standard formulas exist for structuring a limited partnership. Generally, however, the

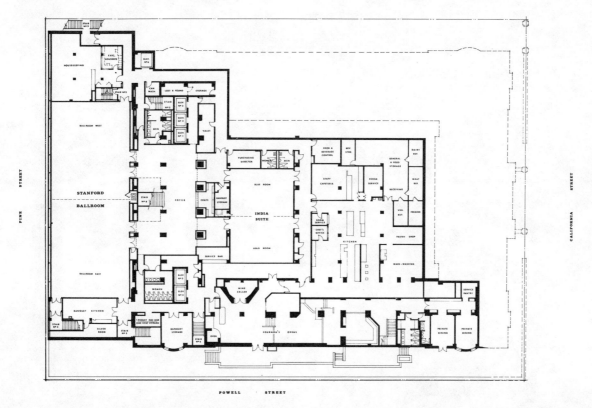

The lower-level floor plan for the Stanford Court Hotel in San Francisco, which, when developed, was a joint venture among A. Cal Rossi and Associates, the Royal Street Development Corporation, and Stancourt Corporation, a wholly owned subsidiary of UAL, Inc.

general partner puts the deal together, receives a 5 to 15 percent development fee for that effort, collects an on-going development fee based on a percentage of revenues, and obtains a percentage of the net cash flow as a partner. The limited partners each receive a major portion of the depreciation benefits and tax credits, a preferential return on investment, and a prorated share of the remaining cash flow and sales proceeds.

◆ *All-equity financing.* When interest rates are high and opportunities to obtain debt financing are limited, all-equity financings offer an alternative solution. All-equity financings entail either a joint venture (developer and lender), a public or private limited partnership, or a single entity (a large insurance company, a developer, or a hotel operator). With few exceptions, all-equity financings are an intermediate step, either until more favorable debt financing becomes available or until the property can be sold.

A project team's ability to select the proper financing method depends on its experience and on its understanding of the dynamic characteristics of those financing mechanisms available to it. Financing conditions change almost daily, and successful developers and operators of lodging properties are those who are able to analyze, interpret, and predict trends in the equity and debt financing markets. Today, developers and operators commonly turn to specialists in the hotel finance field for an explication of a project's financing alternatives and a program for obtaining the best financing package.

PREPARING A LOAN PACKAGE

All hotel lenders, parties to limited partnerships and joint ventures, buyers, and sellers of lodging properties require certain documents and reports. Although the type of documentation and level of information required varies significantly with the case, lenders usually call for the following principal documents before initiating a project's financing:

◆ A transmittal letter to the lender from the project team that clearly states the loan amount requested.

◆ A formal feasibility study prepared by a nationally recognized hotel consulting firm.

◆ A rendering of the proposed project, a preliminary site plan, and general design specifications.

The Lucayan Beach Hotel in Freeport, Bahamas.

- A cash flow statement that indicates the cash available for debt service and that identifies the first expected stabilized year of operation.

- A preliminary projection of the project's overall cost estimate.

- A copy of any agreement or letter of understanding with a hotel operating company.

- A copy of any franchise agreement.

- Resumes and financial statements of the project's owners and developers.

- A copy of the deed, title policy, or lease agreement for the site.

- Copies of all documents such as legal agreements, other leases, constraints, and easements that affect the site or project.

- Any environmental impact statements or reports needed before the site may be developed.

- Descriptions and photographs of similar projects developed by the project's proposed developer and operator.

- A one-page fact sheet that describes the project, its size, its type of ownership and management, and its operating, locational, and design characteristics.

These documents should be organized and presented in a professionally prepared folder, binder, or booklet. Lenders do not want glossy documents that largely contain "filler" information, or brochures in which the project's characteristics and requirements are difficult to locate.

CRITERIA FOR EVALUATING THE FINANCING PACKAGE

Developers, investors, and operators differ widely in their investment objectives and in their criteria for deciding their involvements in a lodging project. The three most common criteria, and a few others, used to judge a project's viability are:

- *The internal rate of return (IRR) hurdle rate.* The IRR hurdle rate is that level of return on investment that the developer, investor, and operator determine independently is the minimum acceptable blend of equity and debt cost of capital rate. Currently, pretax IRR hurdle rates range from 15 to 22 percent for freestanding hotels, and 13 to 20 percent for hotels in mixed-use projects. When determining the IRR, evaluators should define

cash flows as cash available after all operating expenses, property taxes, insurance, reserves for replacement, and incentive management fees are deducted, but before debt service.

- *Debt service coverage.* Lenders generally rate debt service coverage as the most appropriate indication of a project's ability to secure debt financing. Lenders typically use the project's first stabilized year of cash flow (the third year for most hotel projects and the fifth year for most resort projects) as a basis. Cash flow in this context means cash flow available after all operating expenses, property taxes, insurance, and reserve for replacement are deducted. Today, acceptable coverage ratios range from 1.05 to 1.50, with most lenders agreeing that a 1.25 to 1.35 debt coverage is preferred. In the opinion of most lenders, hotels present more risk than do office or retail projects with their guaranteed cash flows.

- *Loan-to-value.* As a rule, a lender is prevented from making loans on properties whose appraised real estate value exceeds the amount of the loan. Lenders want the developer to share in the development risk; thus, they evaluate the developer's equity commitment when determining a loan package's viability.

- *Other evaluative criteria.* Some lenders, developers, and investors use cash-on-cash return, the payback period, net present value, or return on equity as guides to an expected return on investment.

In turn, the primary data required to evaluate a project's return on investment are:

- An estimate of the overall development cost.

- Estimated productive life of the project, or hypothetical date of a "forced" sale.

- Income and cash flow projections.

Formulas for and descriptions of each evaluative method may be found in most real estate finance books, or can be explained by experienced hotel operators, developers, and consultants.

The hotel development process cannot work without financing. This chapter has discussed the sources and methods of hotel financing. No standard formulas or methodologies exist that can guarantee project funding. Nor do only one or two sources avail themselves for debt or equity financing. Implicit in this chapter is the belief that in order to obtain financing for a lodging property, the project team will need to be creative, tenacious, and flexible. The fundamentals of financing are not new; rather, the ways in which they are packaged and used are new and constantly changing. Securing long-term financing for lodging properties will challenge hotel developers. The future can be promising, however, for those who take advantage of the various sources and methods of financing.

How To Finance That Unworkable Deal

Many developers of hotels today find themselves stymied by the apparent imbalance of low economic returns and high costs. "Hotels just don't pencil out like office buildings," complain those developers who confront the three-year average stabilization period for new hotel projects, and the financing premiums required by lending institutions. (To compensate for market volatility and operating risk, lenders today frequently charge high interest rates and stipulate equity positions for themselves in the projects.)

How do new hotels get developed and financed? In recent years, resourceful developers have devised a variety of techniques. Most notable have been institutional partnerships, leasehold financings, and equity syndications. And it is no coincidence that hotels have been the most common beneficiaries of UDAG funds. Hotels match the UDAG program's principal criteria: providing jobs, guaranteeing private sector financial leverage, and being unworkable without the UDAG money.

Consider John Doe, a developer who owns a suburban site at the intersection of two major highways. He is currently completing the surrounding project, a mixed-use development of mid-rise office buildings and some strip community retail. Everyone advises him that the site is ideal for a hotel. His hotel consultants concur and give him a report that looks positive: a 200-room deluxe hotel could achieve a stabilized occupancy rate of 77 percent four years after opening (at 60 percent), and could obtain a $60-per-night average room rate, expressed in constant uninflated dollars. When the consultants inflate the projected cash flows from operations at 6 percent annually, they come up with the following amounts:

Year	Amount
1986	$1,057,000
1987	1,431,000
1988	1,700,000
1989	1,902,000
1990	2,230,000
1991	2,363,000
1992	2,505,000
1993	2,655,000

Meanwhile, Doe's architects advise him that this facility will cost approximately $11 million to construct, including all the hard costs and most of the soft costs. By adding the $1 million that the land parcel is worth, now that the other development is nearing completion, and now that the utility improvements have been provided, the total estimated cost becomes $12,000,000, or $60,000 per room. Because the conventional wisdom holds that a hotel should cost about $1,000 per room for every $1 of projected average room rate, the $60,000 cost per room confirms the $60 average rate ($60 × $1,000 × 200 rooms = $12,000,000).

SAVINGS INSTITUTION

When the developer visits a local savings institution with which he has done business for years, the lending institution informs him that it can offer 25-year, fixed-rate mortgages at 13½ percent interest.

After reviewing the consultants' and architects' projections, the lending officer does some quick calculations and states that she is willing to lend the developer $7,840,000 nonrecourse, or $9.8 million if he can guarantee the top $1,960,000 personally. Only one point would be charged.

As the developer and his financial consultant review these numbers, they analyze them; the consultant puts the information into his computer and displays the results. (See Figure 5–1.) He explains that, based on the projections, the total project costs will be $12.34 million and not $12 million, after providing for other fees and for $162,000 of working capital for the hotel's operations. While the occupancy rate grows slowly from its opening level of 60 percent in 1986, the lending institution will be worried about cash flow coverage on its loan during the early years. In 1987, the operating cash flow will be $1,431,000, which, after providing for replacement reserves of $112,000, leaves $1,319,000 available for debt service.

This $1.319 million only supports $7,840,000 of debt when the institution applies its 1.2:1 coverage ratio to the 13½ percent, 25-year mortgage constant. Even with the debt service of $1,105,000, the developer will have an after–debt service cash flow loss of $28,000 ($1,085,000 less $1,057,000) in 1986—a loss that will somehow have to be funded.

The later years look better, after the operations mature and the cash flow increases with the rise in occupancy. The startup period presents the greatest difficulty. Even so, the adjusted rate of return, making some assumptions for selling the property in 1994, remains only 17.4 percent—better than the rate of the loan, but not enough to compensate for the risk and for the amount of the developer's own cash that will have to be contributed.

If the developer takes the lender's second alternative, the $9.8 million recourse loan (Figure 5–2), the picture brightens. Now the developer need only put up $2.55 million initially, $450,000 to cover the after–debt service cash flow shortfall in 1986, and $75,000 in 1987. His outlay will total $3,075,000, and the adjusted rate of return will become 21.05 percent. The higher loan amount means that the institution is willing to compute its coverage on the 1988 cash flow at a lower ratio (1.1:1). Thus, it will want a guarantee that the developer will make up two years of the shortfall and will assume the risk of the lower coverage on behalf of the lending institution.

INSURANCE COMPANY

The financial consultant now asks Doe to consider, as a third alternative, the way in which he financed his office buildings. An insurance company gave him a mortgage at a below-market rate in exchange for 50 percent of the ownership. In the present case, for example, the insurance company, which is investing pension fund monies, would be willing to negotiate a purchase of the land for the $1 million price, and then to lease it back to the developer at 10 percent per year; it would advance a nonrecourse mortgage at 11 percent for 25 years, to finance only the improvements, in exchange for 50 percent of the deal.

If the developer takes these terms, he will now be able to get an $8.625 million loan and $1 million from the sale of the land. His initial cash equity contribution will be reduced to $2.775 million. But the positive cash flow will not begin until 1987, the second year of operation. Additionally, the developer will need to fund the $100,000 land lease payment in 1985 and the cash flow shortfall ($175,000) in 1986. Thus, his total contribution will come to $3.05 million.

Under this arrangement, when the hotel achieves a positive cash flow, the developer will receive a non-cumulative, 10 percent priority return on the total $3.05 million. And at the sale of the property, he will get back his equity investment before the remaining proceeds are split.

The overall return is still not exceptional, at 17.12 percent. (See Figure 5–3.) And the developer will still have to fund any cash shortfalls. In the first year, this situation might be tolerable, but it would grow in seriousness if the projected occupancies and room rates failed to materialize. With this deal, the developer still takes the downside risk.

From the lender's point of view, the deal makes sense. The insurance company gets its 11 percent mortgage interest, plus 10 percent on the land lease, although the cash flow kicker and the proceeds upon sale, combined with the permanent loan point, bring its final return to 14.14 percent. Thus, the lender's yield is 64 basis points better than the one achieved in the previous example.

If the insurance company were to advance additional funds in the form of a 14.5 percent second mortgage, this second trust would require the developer's guarantee. (See Figure 5–4.) In this case, the lender would be willing to commit a total of $11,055,000 ($8.625 million first trust, plus $2.43 million second trust) in debt financing, plus the $1 million for the land. The equity contribution would be only $345,000.

But the project would now be more highly leveraged, and although the increased debt is attractive, the developer would find himself in a negative cash flow position for the first three years and personally on the hook for the second mortgage forever. He would need an additional $825,000 to cover these shortfalls. In fact, covering these shortfalls constitutes yet another form of equity contribution, which brings the total requirement here to $1,170,000.

In practice, if the developer failed to keep up the contributions, the insurance company would probably make the additional contributions and simply add them to the second mortgage balance, to be paid later. But if this eventuality occurred often enough, the lender would foreclose on the second trust, and the developer would lose his position entirely. In effect, the developer would have built the hotel for the insurance company.

Moreover, two other considerations exist: 1) the second mortgage balloons in 10 years, and 2) because the insurance company is now a partner, the developer will need permission to sell or refinance. And the lender will insist on a right of first refusal. These considerations could serve to weaken the developer's position if, say, performance failed to meet projections.

Nevertheless, Doe could expect a higher return. If he can pay the projected shortfalls, and if the project does as well as the hotel consultants predict, or better, he will earn 27.21 percent on his investment.

This insurance company is a sophisticated lender; it knows, on the one hand, the upside potential of hotels and, on the other hand, the means of protecting its own position on the downside. Beyond the contract rates (10 percent on the land lease, 11 percent on the first mortgage, and 14.5 percent on the second mortgage), it also receives substantial benefits if the project performs as projected. Thus, its total investment realizes either a 14.14 percent adjusted rate of return (Figure 5–3) or a 13.48 percent rate of return (Figure 5–4).

Note that although the lender receives 14.5 percent on its second mortgage, its return here does not exceed its return in the first alternative. This is because it has converted some of its kicker position into the fixed-rate second trust. Although the lender's return is lower, its position is more secure because the developer has made a guarantee, and because it knows the developer will be better able to meet his obligations.

Without question, the deal now looks better, and, with the second insurance-company option, the deal may be practicable. But John Doe will still have to take all the risk.

SYNDICATION

The financial consultant has, however, overlooked an important component of these deals—the tax benefits. Under the alternatives discussed, the tax benefits are there, but the consultant has assumed that the developer could fully use them. Hotels do involve a substantial amount of personal property that qualifies for investment tax credits and that may also be depreciated for tax purposes over five years.

But the insurance company is investing money on behalf of pension funds, which are tax-exempt institutions, and the developer is already well sheltered by other projects. Inability to use the tax benefits reduces the returns that the consultant calculated for the developer's position. Hence, considering that neither party to the deal so far can use the benefits, selling them to yet other investors becomes attractive. And because, under the contemplated structure, the land would be owned by the insurance company's client, the pension fund, the tax leverage would already be favorable.

The financial consultant alters the insurance-company deals slightly in his projections. He leaves both deals in place (Figures 5–3 and 5–4), except that the developer's position in each deal is now occupied by a limited partnership of which the developer is the general partner. This arrangement may be structured so that the economic returns to the developer take the form of various fees for services, incentive compensation for performance, or both. The limited partners have no voice in the management of the property, get their investments back in cash on a priority basis over the life of the partnership, and are allocated 99 percent both of the taxable income (as distinct from the cash flow) and of the losses.

The developer sells limited partnership interests to outside investors, principally high-tax-bracket individuals seeking tax shelters. Their benefits will arise principally out of the depreciation of the property, the use of allowable investment tax credits, and the deductibility of interest. They will pay for their limited partnership positions over a five-year pay-in period in order to lessen the amount of their investment up front, to increase their tax leverage, and ultimately to improve their use of the tax benefits of the property.

The consultant generates two limited-partnership alternatives. Under the first alternative (Figure 5–5), the investors would contribute $2,550,000 over five years. These proceeds would be used to fund the projected cash flow shortfalls. In effect, then, the developer would use the limited partners' contributions instead of his own equity, and the limited partners would assume the downside risk. In exchange, they would be entitled to the tax benefits, which, in the 50 percent tax bracket, would be worth $2,578,000 to them over the seven-year loss period. Therefore, they would have no cumulative risk, unless the lender foreclosed.

Additionally, on a cash flow basis, after the insurance company's returns are deducted as interest, and after certain supervisory fees are paid out to the developer, the limited partners would be entitled to an 8 percent, noncumulative preferred return on their invested capital. Then the developer would receive an incentive management fee. At the sale of the property (liquidation of the partnership), the limited partners would also be given a distribution of 60 percent of the net proceeds after receiving a priority return of the $3,050,000 to which the developer was originally entitled. (See Figure 5–3.) If the property should not perform as projected, of course, their returns would be sacrificed and not the developer's. He would not guarantee them anything.

With this alternative, the insurance company's position remains the same as in Figure 5–3. The total adjusted rate of return to the limited partners, imputing their tax benefits at 50 percent, would be 16.19 percent. The developer is in for no cash and no risk, and he receives modest general partner management fees equal to $50,000 per year. He is also entitled to 40 percent of the 50 percent he originally negotiated with the insurance company, an amount projected at $1,617,000 before taxes.

Under the second alternative, the one involving the second mortgage and the guarantee (Figure 5–6), the developer will "need" less equity. Thus, he can either sell the same amount to the partnership and keep the difference for himself, or, because of the additional leverage, price the equity more aggressively and give the investors a better overall return. This would provide a "deeper" shelter for them, a riskier and more highly leveraged one.

There is a drawback to this second plan, however. The limited partners are called limited because, by law, their liability must be limited to the amount of their contributions. Therefore, the general partner must assume all liability for the second mortgage. He cannot transfer this risk to them.

Under this second alternative, the developer has no money in the deal and may bank projected cash flows of $100,000 per year in the form of general partner fees. The limited partners prefer this option because their tax benefits and cash distributions, less their equity pay-ins, now result in a higher adjusted rate of return of 16.69 percent. And because the pay-ins have been structured to result in at least a 2:1 write-off ratio on an after-tax basis, the limited partners do not have any money in the deal, after taxes, beginning in the third year. Finally, with this alternative, the developer's net return from the sale of the property at the end of the partnership approximates $1 million.

The insurance company, whose position essentially remains the same, is happier, too. The cash the developer raises from the limited partners is, in effect, a reserve fund that cushions against the risk of foreclosure.

Reviewing the situation under the projected conditions, the financial consultant's computer produces the following table:

Projected Performance

Figure	Developer's Cumulative Investment	Developer's Adjusted Rate of Return (in percent)	Lender's Total Adjusted Rate of Return (in percent)	Limited Partner's Adjusted Rate of Return (in percent)
5–1	$4,528,000	17.4	13.5	—
5–2	$3,075,000	21.1	13.5	—
5–3	$3,050,000	17.1	14.1	—
5–4	$1,170,000	27.2	13.5	—
5–5	-0-	inf.	14.1	16.2
5–6	-0-	inf.	13.5	16.7

The financial consultant then constructs a downside sensitivity analysis, that is, one showing the returns if the project's performance (operating cash flow) falls 15 percent below projections. The computer produces this table:

Projected Performance Less 15 Percent

Figure	Developer's Cumulative Investment	Developer's Adjusted Rate of Return (in percent)	Lender's Total Adjusted Rate of Return (in percent)	Limited Partner's Adjusted Rate of Return (in percent)
5–1	$4,775,000	16.44	—	—
5–2	$3,630,000	19.00	—	—
5–3	$3,400,000	15.80	13.62	—
5–4	$1,995,000	21.84	13.01	—
5–5	$2,550,000	—	13.62	15.81
5–6	$ 500,000	—	13.01	16.30

According to this table, if John Doe has only $1 million net worth, both he and the project could be ruined under the alternatives shown in Figures 5–3 and 5–4. And because his contribution is too high to start with in Figures 5–1 and 5–2, he could not even begin to implement one of these plans. Under the arrangements shown in Figures 5–5 and 5–6,

however, no one would lose, although no one would succeed outstandingly. The limited partners would still receive some of their returns, namely, those from the tax benefits.

The financial consultant then constructs an upside sensitivity analysis—one showing the returns if the project's performance exceeds projections by 15 percent. The computer printout shows:

Projected Performance Plus 15 Percent

Figure	Developer's Cumulative Investment	Developer's Adjusted Rate of Return (in percent)	Lender's Total Adjusted Rate of Return (in percent)	Limited Partner's Adjusted Rate of Return (in percent)
5–1	$4,675,000	18.19	—	—
5–2	$3,075,000	21.95	—	—
5–3	$3,050,000	17.81	14.66	—
5–4	$1,170,000	27.96	13.95	—
5–5	—	—	14.66	16.95 (16.19)
5–6	—	—	13.95	17.23 (16.69)

According to this table, the developer's upside returns would be almost as high under Figures 5–5 and 5–6 as under Figures 5–3 and 5–4, while he would carry little of the downside risk. Although the financing options shown in figures 5–5 and 5–6, then, do seem to offer several advantages, it will still likely be a perplexed John Doe who leaves the consultant's office en route to making his decision. He—and other prospective hotel developers—have a complex financing picture with which to acquaint themselves before plunging into a lodging project.

FIGURE 5-1

DEVELOPER NONRECOURSE

Proposed 200-Room Hotel, Projected Statement of Cash Flow, 1984–1993
(in thousands)

Sources	1984	1985	1986	1987	1988	1989	1990	1991	1992	1993	Total
Cash Flow from Operations	0	0	1,057	1,431	1,700	1,902	2,230	2,363	2,505	2,655	15,843
Add Developer Contribution	4,500	0	175								4,675
Add Construction Loan	7,840										7,840
Add Permanent Mtg			7,840								7,840
Add Swing Loan											0
Working Capital Balance	0	162	162	162	200	200	200	200	200	200	1,685
Total Sources	12,340	162	9,234	1,593	1,900	2,102	2,430	2,563	2,705	2,855	37,884
Applications											
Acquisition—Land	1,000										1,000
Acquisition—Building	0										0
Improvements—Real	9,000										9,000
Improvements—Personal	2,000										2,000
Point—Construction Loan	78										78
Point—Perm Mtg			78								78
Point—Swing Loan	0										0
Tax Advice	50										50
Organization Cost	50										50
Syndication Professional											0
Selling Commissions											0
Pay Off Construction Loan			7,840								7,840
Debt Service of Perm Mtg			1,105	1,105	1,105	1,105	1,105	1,105	1,105	1,105	8,840
Interest on Swing Loan											0
Swing Loan Amortization											0
Asset Replacements			48	112	188	204	226	240	254	269	1,540
Working Capital Balance	162	162	162	200	200	200	200	200	200	200	1,885
Total Applications	12,340	162	9,234	1,417	1,493	1,509	1,531	1,545	1,559	1,574	32,363
Cash Flow	0	0	0	176	407	593	899	1,019	1,146	1,281	5,521

Projected Statement of Taxable Income, 1984–1993
(in thousands)

	1984	1985	1986	1987	1988	1989	1990	1991	1992	1993	Total
Cash Flow from Operations			1,057	1,431	1,700	1,902	2,230	2,363	2,505	2,655	15,843
Tax Advice	50										50
Interest Exp—1st Mtg			1,056	1,050	1,044	1,036	1,027	1,017	1,005	992	8,228
Interest Exp—Swing											0
Amortization	13	13	13	13	13	3	3	3	3	3	81
Depreciation	0	0	1,388	1,367	1,288	1,232	1,180	702	728	745	8,629
Total Expenses	63	13	2,457	2,430	2,345	2,271	2,210	1,722	1,736	1,740	16,988
Taxable Income	(63)	(13)	(1,400)	(999)	(645)	(369)	20	641	769	915	(1,145)

Projected Statement of Net Benefits, 1984–1993
(in thousands)

	1984	1985	1986	1987	1988	1989	1990	1991	1992	1993	Total
Developer Contribution	4,500	0	175	0	0	0					4,675
Taxable Loss	(63)	(13)	(1,400)	(999)	(645)	(369)	20	641	769	915	(1,145)
Tax Savings at 50%	32	7	700	500	322	184	(10)	(320)	(384)	(458)	572
Add: Investment Tax Credit			163	7	11	12	14	14	15	16	252
Add: Cash Distributions	0	0	0	176	407	593	899	1,019	1,146	1,281	5,521
Total Benefits	32	7	863	682	741	790	902	713	777	840	6,346
Net Benefit	(4,468)	7	688	682	741	790	902	713	777	840	1,671
Cumulative Net Benefit	(4,468)	(4,462)	(3,774)	(3,092)	(2,351)	(1,560)	(658)	54	831	1,671	

FIGURE 5-1 (CONT'D)

DEVELOPER NONRECOURSE

Footnote Information

Acquisition Date .... January 1, 1984
Placed in Service .... January 1, 1986
Number of Rooms 200
Acquisition Cost ..... $12,000,000 (includes land, building, and improvements)
Per Room Cost $60,000
Per Room Realty $50,000
Per Room Personal $10,000

Summary of Financing Information, Note 1

Amount 7,840
Interest Rate 11.25%
Amortization Period .... 25 Years

Calculation of Mortgage Amount

1987 Cash Flow from Operations	1,431	
Less: Asset Replacement	112	
Available for Debt Service	1,319	
Available, Based on 1.2:1 DSC	1,099	1,199
Amount of Mtg, Based on 13.5%, 25 Years	7,843	8,556
Used if Nonrecourse	7,840	
Used if Recourse	8,550 (based on 1.1:1 DSC)	

Calculation of Adjusted Rate of Return

Year	Investment	Benefits	Side Fund Interest	Side Fund Balance
1984	4,500	32	0	32
1985	0	7	3	41
1986	175	863	3	907
1987	0	682	73	1,662
1988	0	741	133	2,536
1989	0	790	203	3,529
1990		902	282	4,713
1991		713	377	5,803
1992		777	464	7,044
1993		840	564	8,447
1994		14,001	676	23,124

	4,650
Side Fund Interest	8.00%
Adjusted Rate of Return	17.40%

Calculation of 1-1-94 Sale
(in thousands)

Gross Rental Income	2,655
Less: Operating Exp	
Real Estate Taxes	
Management Fee	
Net Income Before Debt Service	2,655
Sales Price, Based on 11%	26,554
Less Disposition Cost—5%	1,328
Net Sales Price	25,226
Less Mtg Balance	7,228
Cash Available	17,998
Available	17,998
Total LP Cash	17,998
LP Tax upon Sale	
Contrib	4,675
Income (Loss)	(1,145)
Cash Flow	5,521
Cash upon Sale	17,998
Taxable Gain	19,990
Total Tax @ 20%	3,998 (ignoring recapture)
Net After-Tax Cash	14,001

Depreciation Schedule
(in thousands)

	Basis	1984	1985	1986	1987	1988	1989	1990	1991	1992	1993	Total
Real Property	9,000			1,080	900	810	720	630	540	540	540	5,760
Personal Property	2,000			300	440	420	420	420				2,000
Asset Replacement—Real				1	3	6	9	13	17	21	26	95
Asset Replacement—Personal				7	24	52	83	117	145	167	179	774
Total Depreciation		0	0	1,388	1,367	1,288	1,232	1,180	702	728	745	8,629
Amortization Schedule												
Points—1st Mtg		3	3	3	3	3	3	3	3	3	3	30
Points—Swing												0
Organization Cost		10	10	10	10	10						50
Total Amortization		13	13	13	13	13	3	3	3	3	3	80

Asset Replacement Assumptions

Real Property	25.00%
Personal Property	75.00%

FIGURE 5-2

DEVELOPER RECOURSE

Proposed 200-Room Hotel, Projected Statement of Cash Flow, 1984–1993
(in thousands)

Sources	1984	1985	1986	1987	1988	1989	1990	1991	1992	1993	Total
Cash Flow from Operations	0	0	1,057	1,431	1,700	1,902	2,230	2,363	2,505	2,655	15,843
Add Developer Contribution	2,550	0	450	75							3,075
Add Construction Loan	9,800										9,800
Add Permanent Mortgage			9,800								9,800
Add Swing Loan											0
Working Capital Balance	0	152	152	132	144	200	200	200	200	200	1,580
Total Sources	12,350	152	11,459	1,638	1,844	2,102	2,430	2,563	2,705	2,855	40,098
Applications											
Acquisition—Land	1,000										1,000
Acquisition—Building	0										0
Improvements—Real	9,000										9,000
Improvements—Personal	2,000										2,000
Point—Construction Loan	98										98
Point—Perm Mtg			98								98
Point—Swing Loan	0										0
Tax Advice	50										50
Organization Cost	50										50
Syndication Professional											0
Selling Commissions											0
Pay Off Construction Loan			9,800								9,800
Debt Service of Perm Mtg			1,381	1,381	1,381	1,381	1,381	1,381	1,381	1,381	11,050
Interest on Swing Loan											0
Swing Loan Amortization											0
Asset Replacements			48	112	188	204	226	240	254	269	1,540
Working Capital Balance	152	152	132	144	200	200	200	200	200	200	1,780
Total Applications	12,350	152	11,459	1,638	1,769	1,785	1,807	1,821	1,835	1,850	36,466
Cash Flow	0	0	0	0	75	317	622	743	870	1,005	3,632

Projected Statement of Taxable Income, 1984–1993
(in thousands)

	1984	1985	1986	1987	1988	1989	1990	1991	1992	1993	Total
Cash Flow from Operations			1,057	1,431	1,700	1,902	2,230	2,363	2,505	2,655	15,843
Tax Advice	50										50
Interest Exp—1st Mtg			1,320	1,313	1,305	1,295	1,284	1,271	1,257	1,240	10,285
Interest Exp—Swing											0
Amortization	14	14	14	14	14	4	4	4	4	4	90
Depreciation	0	0	1,388	1,367	1,288	1,232	1,180	702	728	745	8,629
Total Expenses	64	14	2,722	2,694	2,606	2,531	2,467	1,977	1,989	1,989	19,053
Taxable Income	(64)	(14)	(1,665)	(1,263)	(906)	(629)	(238)	386	517	667	(3,210)

Projected Statement of Net Benefits, 1984–1993
(in thousands)

	1984	1985	1986	1987	1988	1989	1990	1991	1992	1993	Total
Developer Contribution	2,550	0	450	75	0	0					3,075
Taxable Loss	(64)	(14)	(1,665)	(1,263)	(906)	(629)	(238)	386	517	667	(3,210)
Tax Savings at 50%	32	7	833	631	453	314	119	(193)	(258)	(333)	1,605
Add: Investment Tax Credit			163	7	11	12	14	14	15	16	252
Add: Cash Distributions	0	0	0	0	75	317	622	743	870	1,005	3,632
Total Benefits	32	7	996	638	540	644	755	564	627	688	5,489
Net Benefit	(2,518)	7	546	563	540	644	755	564	627	688	2,414
Cumulative Net Benefit	(2,518)	(2,511)	(1,966)	(1,402)	(863)	(219)	536	1,100	1,727	2,414	

FIGURE 5-2 (CONT'D)

DEVELOPER RECOURSE

Footnote Information

Acquisition Date	January 1, 1984
Placed in Service	January 1, 1986
Number of Rooms	200
Acquisition Cost	$12,000,000 (includes land, building, and improvements)
Per Room Cost	$60,000
Per Room Realty	$50,000
Per Room Personal	$10,000

Summary of Financing Information, Note 1

Amount	9,800
Interest Rate	13.5%
Amortization Period	25 Years

Calculation of Mortgage Amount

1988 Cash Flow from Operations	1,700	
Less: Asset Replacement	188	
Available for Debt Service	1,512	
Available, Based on 1.2:1 DSC	1,260	1,375
Amount of Mtg, Based on 13.5%, 25 Years	8,996	9,814
Used if Nonrecourse	8,000	
Used if Recourse		9,800 (based on 1.1:1 DSC)

Calculation of Adjusted Rate of Return

Year	Investment	Benefits	Side Fund Interest	Side Fund Balance
1984	2,550	32	0	32
1985	0	7	3	41
1986	450	996	3	1,040
1987	75	638	83	1,762
1988	0	540	141	2,442
1989	0	644	195	3,281
1990		755	263	4,299
1991		564	344	5,206
1992		627	417	6,250
1993		688	500	7,438
1994		12,200	595	20,232

2,995

Side Fund Interest	8.00%
Adjusted Rate of Return	21.05%

Calculation of 1-1-94 Sale
(in thousands)

Gross Rental Income	2,655
Less: Operating Exp	
Real Estate Taxes	
Management Fee	
Net Income Before Debt Service	2,655
Sales Price, Based on 11%	26,554
Less Disposition Cost—5%	1,328
Net Sales Price	25,226
Less Mtg Balance	9,035
Cash Available	16,191
Available	16,191
Total LP Cash	16,191
LP Tax upon Sale	
Contrib	3,075
Income (Loss)	(3,210)
Cash Flow	3,632
Cash upon Sale	16,191
Taxable Gain	19,958
Total Tax @ 20%	3,992 (ignoring recapture)
Net After-Tax Cash	12,200

Depreciation Schedule
(in thousands)

	Basis	1984	1985	1986	1987	1988	1989	1990	1991	1992	1993	Total
Real Property	9,000			1,080	900	810	720	630	540	540	540	5,760
Personal Property	2,000			300	440	420	420	420				2,000
Asset Replacement—Real				1	3	6	9	13	17	21	26	95
Asset Replacement—Personal				7	24	52	83	117	145	167	179	774
Total Depreciation		0	0	1,388	1,367	1,288	1,232	1,180	702	728	745	8,629
Amortization Schedule												
Points—1st Mtg		4	4	4	4	4	4	4	4	4	4	40
Points—Swing												0
Organization Cost		10	10	10	10	10						50
Total Amortization		14	14	14	14	14	4	4	4	4	4	90

Asset Replacement Assumptions

Real Property	25.00%
Personal Property	75.00%

FIGURE 5-3

11 PERCENT NONRECOURSE MORTGAGE WITH A 50 PERCENT KICKER

Proposed 200-Room Hotel, Projected Statement of Cash Flow, 1984–1993
(in thousands)

Sources	1984	1985	1986	1987	1988	1989	1990	1991	1992	1993	Total
Cash Flow from Operations	0	0	1,057	1,431	1,700	1,902	2,230	2,363	2,505	2,655	15,843
Add Developer Contribution	2,775	100	175								3,050
Add Construction Loan	8,625										8,625
Add Permanent Mtg			8,625								8,625
Add Land Sale	1,000										
Working Capital Balance	0	114	114	97	200	200	200	200	200	200	1,525
Total Sources	12,400	214	9,971	1,528	1,900	2,102	2,430	2,563	2,705	2,855	38,668

Applications	1984	1985	1986	1987	1988	1989	1990	1991	1992	1993	Total
Acquisition—Land	1,000										1,000
Improvements—Real	9,000										9,000
Improvements—Personal	2,000										2,000
Point—Construction Loan	86										86
Point—Perm Mtg			86								86
Tax Advice	50										50
Organization Cost	50										50
Pay Off Construction Loan			8,625								8,625
Debt Service of Perm Mtg			1,014	1,014	1,014	1,014	1,014	1,014	1,014	1,014	8,115
Land Lease	100	100	100	100	100	100	100	100	100	100	1,000
Asset Replacements			48	112	188	204	226	240	254	269	1,540
Working Capital Balance	114	114	97	200	200	200	200	200	200	200	1,725
Total Applications	12,400	214	9,971	1,427	1,502	1,518	1,540	1,554	1,568	1,584	33,278
Cash Flow	0	0	0	101	398	584	889	1,009	1,137	1,272	5,390
Priority Return on Equity				101	305	305	305	305	305	305	0
Balance				0	93	279	584	704	832	967	5,390
Addit. Interest—Bank 50% CF	0	0	0	0	46	139	292	352	416	483	2,695
Cash Flow	0	0	0	101	351	444	597	657	721	788	2,695

Projected Statement of Taxable Income, 1984–1993
(in thousands)

	1984	1985	1986	1987	1988	1989	1990	1991	1992	1993	Total
Cash Flow from Operations			1,057	1,431	1,700	1,902	2,230	2,363	2,505	2,655	15,843
Tax Advice	50										50
Interest Exp—1st Mtg			949	942	934	925	915	904	892	878	7,337
Additional Interest			0	0	46	139	292	352	416	483	1,730
Land Lease	100	100	100	100	100	100	100	100	100	100	1,000
Amortization	13	13	13	13	13	3	3	3	3	3	80
Depreciation	0	0	1,388	1,367	1,288	1,232	1,180	702	728	745	8,629
Total Expenses	163	113	2,450	2,422	2,381	2,399	2,490	2,062	2,139	2,209	18,829
Taxable Income	(163)	(113)	(1,393)	(991)	(681)	(497)	(260)	302	366	446	(2,986)

Projected Statement of Net Benefits, 1984–1993
(in thousands)

	1984	1985	1986	1987	1988	1989	1990	1991	1992	1993	Total
Developer Contribution	2,775	100	175	0	0	0					3,050
Taxable Loss	(163)	(113)	(1,393)	(991)	(681)	(497)	(260)	302	366	446	(2,986)
Tax Savings at 50%	82	57	697	495	341	249	130	(151)	(183)	(223)	1,493
Add: Investment Tax Credit			160	7	11	12	14	14	15	16	250
Add: Cash Distributions	0	0	0	101	351	444	597	657	721	788	3,661
Total Benefits	82	57	857	603	703	705	741	521	553	582	5,403
Net Benefit	(2,693)	(43)	682	603	703	705	741	521	553	582	2,353
Cumulative Net Benefit	(2,693)	(2,737)	(2,055)	(1,452)	(748)	(43)	698	1,219	1,772	2,353	

FIGURE 5-3 (CONT'D)

11 PERCENT NONRECOURSE MORTGAGE WITH A 50 PERCENT KICKER

Footnote Information

Acquisition Date .... July 1, 1984
Placed in Service .... January 1, 1986
Number of Units 200
Acquisition Cost ..... $12,000,000 (includes land, building, and improvements)
Per Unit $60,000

Summary of Financing Information, Note 1

Amount 8,625
Interest Rate 11.00%
Amortization Period .... 25 Years

Calculation of Mortgage Amount

1987 Cash Flow from Operations	1,431	
Less: Land Lease	100	
Less: Asset Replacement	112	
Available for Debt Service	1,219	
Available, Based on 1.2:1 DSC	1,016	1,108
Amount of Mtg, Based on 11.0%, 25 Years	8,628	9,413
Used if Nonrecourse	8,625	
Used if Recourse	10,150	

Calculation of Adjusted Rate of Return

A) Developer

Year	Investment	Benefits	Side Fund Interest	Side Fund Balance
1984	2,775	82	0	82
1985	100	57	7	145
1986	175	857	12	1,013
1987	0	603	81	1,698
1988	0	703	136	2,537
1989	0	705	203	3,445
1990		741	276	4,462
1991		521	357	5,339
1992		553	427	6,319
1993		582	506	7,407
1994		6,653	593	14,652

3,018

Side Fund Interest	8.00%
Adjusted Rate of Return	17.12%

B) Pension Fund

Year	Investment	Pretax Benefits	Interest	Balance
1984	1,000	100	0	100
1985		100	8	208
1986	8,625	1,201	17	1,425
1987		1,114	114	2,654
1988		1,161	212	4,027
1989		1,254	322	5,603
1990		1,406	448	7,458
1991		1,467	597	9,521
1992		1,530	762	11,813
1993		1,598	945	14,356
1994		16,011	1,148	31,516

8,395

Side Fund Interest	8.00%
Adjusted Rate of Return	14.14%

Calculation of 1-1-94 Sale
(in thousands)

Gross Rental Income	2,655
Less: Operating Exp Real Estate Taxes Management Fee	
Net Income Before Debt Service	2,655
Sales Price, Based on 10%	26,554
Less Disposition Cost—5%	1,328
Net Sales Price	25,226
Less Mtg Balance	7,846
Less Land Acquisition	2,000
Cash Available	15,380
Less Dev Equity	3,050
Balance	12,330
Additional Interest—50%	6,165
Total Dev Cash	9,215
Tax upon Sale	
Contrib	3,050
Income (Loss)	(2,986)
Cash Flow	3,661
Cash upon Sale	9,215
Taxable Gain	12,812
Total Tax @ 20%	2,562 (ignoring recapture)
Net Cash	6,653

FIGURE 5-3 (CONT'D)

11 PERCENT NONRECOURSE MORTGAGE WITH A 50 PERCENT KICKER

Depreciation Schedule
(in thousands)

	Basis	1984	1985	1986	1987	1988	1989	1990	1991	1992	1993	Total
Real Property	9,000			1,080	900	810	720	630	540	540	540	5,760
Personal Property	2,000			300	440	420	420	420				2,000
Asset Replacement—Real				1	3	6	9	13	17	21	26	95
Asset Replacement—Personal				7	24	52	83	117	145	167	179	774
Total Depreciation		0	0	1,388	1,367	1,288	1,232	1,180	702	728	745	3,409
Amortization Schedule												
Points—1st Mtg		3	3	3	3	3	3	3	3	3	3	30
Organization Cost		10	10	10	10	10						50
Total Amortization		13	13	13	13	13	3	3	3	3	3	80

Mortgage Amortization
(in thousands)

Year	Payment	Interest	Principal	New Outstanding
				8,625
1986	1,014	949	66	8,559
1987	1,014	942	73	8,486
1988	1,014	934	81	8,406
1989	1,014	925	90	8,316
1990	1,014	915	100	8,216
1991	1,014	904	111	8,105
1992	1,014	892	123	7,983
1993	1,014	878	136	7,846
1994	1,014	863	151	7,695
1995	1,014	846	168	7,527

FIGURE 5-4

11 PERCENT NONRECOURSE MORTGAGE WITH A 14.5 PERCENT SECOND MORTGAGE AND A 50 PERCENT KICKER

Proposed 200-Room Hotel, Projected Statement of Cash Flow, 1984–1993
(in thousands)

Sources	1984	1985	1986	1987	1988	1989	1990	1991	1992	1993	Total
Cash Flow from Operations	0	0	1,057	1,431	1,700	1,902	2,230	2,363	2,505	2,655	15,843
Add Developer Contribution	345	100	575	150							1,170
Add Construction Loan	11,055										11,055
Add Permanent Mtg			8,625								8,625
Add 2nd Mtg			2,430								2,430
Add Land Sale	1,000										1,000
Working Capital Balance	0	89	89	86	78	114	200	200	200	200	1,257
Total Sources	12,400	189	12,776	1,667	1,778	2,016	2,430	2,563	2,705	2,855	41,380

Applications	1984	1985	1986	1987	1988	1989	1990	1991	1992	1993	Total
Acquisition—Land	1,000										1,000
Improvements—Real	9,000										9,000
Improvements—Personal	2,000										2,000
Point—Construction Loan	111										111
Point—Perm Mtgs			111								111
Tax Advice	50										50
Organization Cost	50										50
Pay Off Construction Loan			11,055								11,055
Debt Service of Perm Mtg			1,014	1,014	1,014	1,014	1,014	1,014	1,014	1,014	8,115
Debt Service of 2nd Mtg			362	362	362	362	362	362	362	362	2,899
Land Lease	100	100	100	100	100	100	100	100	100	100	1,000
Asset Replacements			48	112	188	204	226	240	254	269	1,540
Working Capital Balance	89	89	86	78	114	200	200	200	200	200	1,457
Total Applications	12,400	189	12,776	1,667	1,778	1,880	1,903	1,916	1,931	1,946	38,387
Cash Flow	0	0	0	0	0	135	527	647	774	910	2,993
Priority on Equity	0	0	0	0	0	117	117	117	117	117	117
Balance	0	0	0	0	0	18	410	530	657	793	2,876
Additional Interest—Bank 50% CF	0	0	0	0	0	9	205	265	329	396	1,497
Cash Flow	0	0	0	0	0	126	322	382	446	513	1,497

Projected Statement of Taxable Income, 1984–1993
(in thousands)

	1984	1985	1986	1987	1988	1989	1990	1991	1992	1993	Total
Cash Flow from Operations			1,057	1,431	1,700	1,902	2,230	2,363	2,505	2,655	15,843
Tax Advice	50										50
Interest Exp—1st Mtg			949	942	934	925	915	904	892	878	7,337
Additional Interest			0	0	0	9	205	265	329	396	1,204
Interest Exp—2nd Mtg			352	350	348	346	343	341	337	333	2,750
Land Lease	100	100	100	100	100	100	100	100	100	100	1,000
Amortization	14	14	14	14	14	4	4	4	4	4	90
Depreciation	0	0	1,388	1,367	1,288	1,232	1,180	702	728	745	8,629
Total Expenses	164	114	2,803	2,773	2,684	2,616	2,747	2,316	2,390	2,457	21,064
Taxable Income	(164)	(114)	(1,746)	(1,342)	(984)	(714)	(518)	47	115	199	(5,221)

Projected Statement of Net Benefits, 1984–1993
(in thousands)

	1984	1985	1986	1987	1988	1989	1990	1991	1992	1993	Total
Developer Contribution	345	100	575	150	0	0					1,170
Taxable Loss	(164)	(114)	(1,746)	(1,342)	(984)	(714)	(518)	47	115	199	(5,221)
Tax Savings at 50%	82	57	873	671	492	357	259	(24)	(58)	(99)	2,610
Add: Investment Tax Credit			160	7	11	12	14	14	15	16	250
Add: Cash Distributions	0	0	0	0	0	126	322	382	446	513	1,789
Total Benefits	82	57	1,033	678	503	495	594	373	403	430	4,649
Net Benefit	(263)	(43)	458	528	503	495	594	373	403	430	3,479
Cumulative Net Benefit	(263)	(306)	152	680	1,183	1,679	2,273	2,646	3,049	3,479	

FIGURE 5-4 (CONT'D)

11 PERCENT NONRECOURSE MORTGAGE WITH A 14.5 PERCENT SECOND MORTGAGE AND A 50 PERCENT KICKER

Footnote Information

Acquisition Date	July 1, 1984
Placed in Service	January 1, 1986
Number of Units	200
Acquisition Cost	$12,000,000 (includes land, building, and improvements)
Per Unit	$60,000

Summary of Financing Information

	Note 1	Note 2
Amount	8,625	2,430
Interest Rate	11.00%	14.50%
Amortization Period	25 Years	25 Years
Status	Nonrecourse	Recourse

Calculation of First Mortgage Amount

1987 Cash Flow from Operations	1,431
Less: Land Lease	100
Less: Asset Replacement	112
Available for Debt Service	1,219
Available, Based on 1.2:1 DSC	1,016
Amount of Mtg, Based on 11.0%, 25 Years	8,628
Used	8,625 if nonrecourse

Calculation of Second Mortgage Amount

1988 Cash Flow from Operations	1,700
Less: 1st Mtg Payment	1,014
Less: Land Lease	100
Less: Asset Replacement	188
Available for Debt Service	398
Available, Based on 1.1:1 DSC	362
Amount of Mtg, Based on 14.5%, 25 Years	2,427
Used	2,430

Calculation of 1-1-94 Sale
(in thousands)

Gross Rental Income	2,655
Less: Operating Exp	
Real Estate Taxes	
Management Fee	
Net Income Before Debt Service	2,655
Sales Price, Based on 10%	26,554
Less Disposition Cost—5%	1,328
Net Sales Price	25,226
Less Mtg Balance	7,846
Less 2nd Mtg	2,282
Less Land Acq	2,000
Cash Available	13,098
Less Dev Equity	1,170
Balance	11,928
50% Share to Dev	5,964
Total Dev Cash	7,134
Tax upon Sale	
Contrib	1,170
Income (Loss)	(5,221)
Cash Flow	1,789
Cash upon Sale	7,134
Taxable Gain	12,974
Total Tax @ 20%	2,595 (ignoring recapture)
Net Cash	4,539

Calculation of Adjusted Rate of Return

A) Developer

Year	Investment	Benefits	Side Fund Interest	Side Fund Balance
1984	345	82	0	82
1985	100	57	7	146
1986	575	1,033	12	1,191
1987	150	678	95	1,963
1988	0	503	157	2,624
1989	0	495	210	3,329
1990		594	266	4,190
1991		373	335	4,898
1992		403	392	5,693
1993		430	455	6,578
1994		4,539	526	11,644

1,050

Side Fund Interest	8.00%
Adjusted Rate of Return	27.21%

B) Pension Fund

Year	Investment	Pretax Benefits	Interest	Balance
1984	1,000	100	0	100
1985		100	8	208
1986	11,055	1,587	17	1,812
1987		1,477	145	3,434
1988		1,477	275	5,185
1989		1,486	415	7,086
1990		1,682	567	9,334
1991		1,742	747	11,823
1992		1,805	946	14,574
1993		1,873	1,166	17,613
1994		18,092	1,409	37,114

10,478

Side Fund Interest	8.00%
Adjusted Rate of Return	13.48%

FIGURE 5-4 (CONT'D)

11 PERCENT NONRECOURSE MORTGAGE WITH A 14.5 PERCENT SECOND MORTGAGE AND A 50 PERCENT KICKER

	Basis	1984	1985	1986	1987	1988	1989	1990	1991	1992	1993	Total
				Depreciation Schedule (in thousands)								
Real Property	9,000			1,080	900	810	720	630	540	540	540	5,760
Personal Property	2,000			300	440	420	420	420				2,000
Asset Replacement—Real				1	3	6	9	13	17	21	26	95
Asset Replacement—Personal				7	24	52	83	117	145	167	179	774
Total Depreciation		0	0	1,388	1,367	1,288	1,232	1,180	702	728	745	3,409
Amortization Schedule												
Points—1st Mtg		4	4	4	4	4	4	4	4	4	4	40
Organization Cost		10	10	10	10	10						50
Total Amortization		14	14	14	14	14	4	4	4	4	4	90

Mortgage Amortization
(in thousands)

Year	Payment	Interest	Principal	New Outstanding
				8,625
1986	1,014	949	66	8,559
1987	1,014	942	73	8,486
1988	1,014	934	81	8,406
1989	1,014	925	90	8,316
1990	1,014	915	100	8,216
1991	1,014	904	111	8,105
1992	1,014	892	123	7,983
1993	1,014	878	136	7,846
1994	1,014	863	151	7,695
1995	1,014	846	168	7,527

FIGURE 5-5

SYNDICATION WITH AN 11 PERCENT NONRECOURSE MORTGAGE AND A 50 PERCENT KICKER

Proposed 200-Room Hotel, Projected Statement of Cash Flow, 1984–1993
(in thousands)

Sources	1984	1985	1986	1987	1988	1989	1990	1991	1992	1993	Total
Cash Flow from Operations	0	0	1,057	1,431	1,700	1,902	2,230	2,363	2,505	2,655	15,843
Add Limited Partner Contrib	400	500	650	600	400						2,550
Swing Loan	3,000										3,000
Add Construction Loan	8,625										8,625
Add Permanent Mortgage			8,625								8,625
Add Second Mortgage						2,200					2,200
Add Land Sale	1,000										1,000
Working Capital Balance	0	45	5	23	39	54	134	200	200	200	900
Total Sources	13,025	545	10,337	2,054	2,139	4,156	2,364	2,563	2,705	2,855	42,743
Applications											
Acquisition—Land	1,000										1,000
Improvements—Real	9,000										9,000
Improvements—Personal	2,000										2,000
Point—Construction Loan	86										86
Point—Perm Mtgs			86								86
Tax Advice	50										50
Organization Cost	50										50
Syndication Professional	50										50
Selling Commission	204										204
Management Fee	50	50	50	50	51	57	67	71	75	80	601
Pay Off Construction Loan			8,625								8,625
Debt Service of Perm Mtg			1,014	1,014	1,014	1,014	1,014	1,014	1,014	1,014	8,115
Debt Service of 2nd Mtg						308	308	308	308	308	1,539
Swing Loan Interest	390	390	390	338	286	0	0	0			1,794
Swing Loan Amortization				400	400	2,200					3,000
Land Lease	100	100	100	100	100	100	100	100	100	·100	1,000
Asset Replacements			48	112	188	204	226	240	254	269	1,540
Working Capital Balance	45	5	23	39	54	134	200	200	200	200	1,100
Total Applications	13,025	545	10,337	2,054	2,093	4,017	1,915	1,933	1,951	1,971	39,840
Cash Flow	0	0	0	0	46	139	449	631	754	884	2,903
Modified Cash Flow—Pension	−100	−100	−105	204	398	584	889	1,009	1,137	1,272	5,188
Priority Return on Equity				204	305	305	305	305	305	305	2,034
Balance				0	93	279	584	704	832	967	3,459
Additional Interest	0	0	0	0	46	139	292	352	416	483	1,730
Balance of Dist CF	0	0	0	0	(0)	(0)	156	279	338	401	1,174
LP Priority 8%	0	0	0	0	(0)	(0)	156	204	204	204	768
Balance	0	0	0	0	0	0	0	75	134	197	406
Incentive Management—30%	0	0	0	0	0	0	0	22	40	59	122
Distributed Cash Flow	0	0	0	0	0	0	0	52	94	138	2,135
Total LP Cash	0	0	0	0	0	0	156	256	297	341	

Projected Statement of Taxable Income, 1984–1993
(in thousands)

	1984	1985	1986	1987	1988	1989	1990	1991	1992	1993	Total
Cash Flow from Operations			1,057	1,431	1,700	1,902	2,230	2,363	2,505	2,655	15,843
Tax Advice	50										50
Management Fee	50	50	50	50	51	57	67	71	75	80	601
Incentive Management Fee	0	0	0	0	0	0	0	22	40	59	122
Interest Exp—1st Mtg			949	942	934	925	915	904	892	878	7,337
Additional Interest	0	0	0	0	46	139	292	352	416	483	1,730
Interest Exp—2nd Mtg						295	295	293	291	288	1,461
Land Lease	100	100	100	100	100	100	100	100	100	100	1,000
Amortization	13	13	13	13	13	3	3	3	3	3	80
Depreciation	0	0	1,388	1,367	1,288	1,232	1,180	702	728	745	8,629
Total Expenses	213	163	2,500	2,472	2,432	2,751	2,851	2,448	2,545	2,636	21,013
Taxable Income	(213)	(163)	(1,443)	(1,041)	(732)	(849)	(622)	(84)	(40)	19	(5,169)

FIGURE 5-5 (CONT'D)

SYNDICATION WITH AN 11 PERCENT NONRECOURSE MORTGAGE AND A 50 PERCENT KICKER

Projected Statement of Net Benefits, 1984–1993
(in thousands)

	1984	1985	1986	1987	1988	1989	1990	1991	1992	1993	Total
Limited Partner Contribution	400	500	650	600	400	0					2,550
Taxable Loss	(211)	(162)	(1,429)	(1,030)	(725)	(841)	(616)	(84)	(39)	19	(5,118)
Tax Savings at 50%	106	81	714	515	363	420	308	42	20	(9)	2,559
Add: Investment Tax Credit			161	7	11	12	13	14	15	16	250
Add: Cash Distributions	0	0	0	0	(0)	(0)	156	256	297	341	1,049
Total Benefits	106	81	876	522	373	432	478	312	332	347	3,858
Net Benefit	(294)	(419)	226	(78)	(27)	432	478	312	332	347	1,308
Cumulative Net Benefit	(294)	(713)	(488)	(566)	(592)	(160)	317	629	961	1,308	

Footnote Information

Acquisition Date	July 1, 1984
Placed in Service	January 1, 1986
Number of Units	200
Acquisition Cost	$12,000,000 (includes land, building, and improvements)
Per Unit	$60,000

Summary of Financing Information

	Note 1	Note 2
Amount	8,625	0
Interest Rate	10.00%	13.50%
Amortization Period	25 Years	25 Years
Status	Nonrecourse	Recourse

Calculation of Mortgage Amount

1987 Cash Flow from Operations	1,431	
Less: Land Lease	100	
Less: Asset Replacement	112	
Available for Debt Service	1,219	
Available, Based on 1.2:1 DSC	1,016	1,108
Amount of Mtg, Based on 11.0%, 25 Years	8,628	9,413
Used	8,625 if nonrecourse	
Used	9,410 recourse	

Depreciation Schedule
(in thousands)

	Basis	1984	1985	1986	1987	1988	1989	1990	1991	1992	1993	Total
Real Property	9,000			1,080	900	810	720	630	540	540	540	5,760
Personal Property	2,000			300	440	420	420	420				2,000
Asset Replacement—Real				1	3	6	9	13	17	21	26	95
Asset Replacement—Personal				7	24	52	83	117	145	167	179	774
Total Depreciation		0	0	1,388	1,367	1,288	1,232	1,180	702	728	745	3,409
Amortization Schedule												
Points—1st Mtg		3	3	3	3	3	3	3	3	3	3	30
Organization Cost		10	10	10	10	10						50
Total Amortization		13	13	13	13	13	3	3	3	3	3	80

Mortgage Amortization
(in thousands)

Year	Payment	Interest	Principal	New Outstanding
				8,625
1986	1,014	949	66	8,559
1987	1,014	942	73	8,486
1988	1,014	934	81	8,406
1989	1,014	925	90	8,316
1990	1,014	915	100	8,216
1991	1,014	904	111	8,105
1992	1,014	892	123	7,983
1993	1,014	878	136	7,846
1994	1,014	863	151	7,695
1995	1,014	846	168	7,527

Asset Replacement Assumptions

Real Property	25.00%
Personal Property	75.00%

FIGURE 5-5 (CONT'D)

SYNDICATION WITH AN 11 PERCENT NONRECOURSE
MORTGAGE AND A 50 PERCENT KICKER

Calculation of Adjusted Rate of Return

A) Limited Partner

Year	Investment	Benefits	Side Fund Interest	Side Fund Balance
1984	400	106	0	106
1985	500	81	8	195
1986	650	876	16	1,086
1987	600	522	87	1,695
1988	400	373	136	2,204
1989	0	432	176	2,813
1990		478	225	3,515
1991		312	281	4,108
1992		332	329	4,768
1993		347	381	5,497
1994		3,884	440	9,820

2,191

Side Fund Interest	8.00%
Adjusted Rate of Return	16.19%

B) Pension Fund

Year	Investment	Pretax Benefits	Interest	Balance
1984	1,000	100	0	100
1985		100	8	208
1986	8,625	1,201	17	1,425
1987		1,114	114	2,654
1988		1,161	212	4,027
1989		1,254	322	5,603
1990		1,406	448	7,458
1991		1,467	597	9,521
1992		1,530	762	11,813
1993		1,598	945	14,356
1994		16,011	1,148	31,516

8,395

Side Fund Interest	8.00%
Adjusted Rate of Return	14.14%

Calculation of 1-1-94 Sale
(in thousands)

Gross Rental Income	2,655
Less: Operating Exp	
Real Estate Taxes	
Management Fee	
Net Income Before Debt Service	2,655
Sales Price, Based on 10%	26,554
Less Disposition Cost—5%	1,328
Net Sales Price	25,226
Less Mtg Balance	7,846
Less Land Acq	2,000
Cash Available	15,380
Less LP Priority	3,050
Balance	12,330
Additional Interest—50%	6,165
Balance	6,165
Less 2nd Mtg	2,122
Balance	4,043
GP 40%	1,617
LP 60%	2,709
Total LP Cash	5,759
Total GP Cash	1,617

Tax upon Sale	LP	GP
Contrib	2,550	0
Income (Loss)	(5,118)	−52
Cash Flow	1,049	21
Cash upon Sale	5,759	1,617
Taxable Gain	9,375	1,690
Total Tax @ 20%	1,875	338
Net Cash	3,884	1,279

Developer's Statement of After-Tax Benefits
(in thousands)

	1984	1985	1986	1987	1988	1989	1990	1991	1992	1993	Total
Management Fee	50	50	50	50	51	57	67	71	75	80	601
Incentive Management—30%	0	0	0	0	0	0	0	22	40	59	122
1% of Cash Flow	0	0	0	0	0	0	0	1	1	1	3
Presale Cash	50	50	50	50	51	57	67	94	116	140	725
Taxable Income—Fees	50	50	50	50	51	57	67	93	115	139	722
1% of Partnership Income	(2)	(2)	(14)	(10)	(7)	(8)	(6)	(1)	(0)	0	(52)
Tax Income—Transaction	48	48	36	40	44	49	61	92	115	139	671
Tax Cost—30%	(14)	(15)	(11)	(12)	(13)	(15)	(18)	(28)	(34)	(42)	(201)
ITC from Partnership	0	0	2	0	0	0	0	0	0	0	3
Tax Savings	−14	−15	−9	−12	−13	−14	−18	−28	−34	−42	−198
After-Tax Win before Sale	36	35	41	38	38	43	49	66	82	99	527
Win from Sale										1,279	1,279
NPV @ 12% of Win before Sale	299										
NPV @ 12% of Win after Sale	760										

FIGURE 5-6

SYNDICATION WITH AN 11 PERCENT NONRECOURSE MORTGAGE, A 14.5 PERCENT SECOND MORTGAGE, AND A 50 PERCENT KICKER

Proposed 200-Room Hotel, Projected Statement of Cash Flow, 1984–1993
(in thousands)

Sources	1984	1985	1986	1987	1988	1989	1990	1991	1992	1993	Total
Cash Flow from Operations	0	0	1,057	1,431	1,700	1,902	2,230	2,363	2,505	2,655	15,843
Add Limited Partner Contrib	350	350	400	500	500	400					2,500
Swing Loan	400		500								900
Add Construction Loan	11,055										11,055
Add Permanent Mortgage			8,625								8,625
Add Second Mortgage			2,430								2,430
Add Land Sale	1,000										1,000
Working Capital Balance	0	142	240	258	266	269	200	200	200	200	1,976
Total Sources	**12,805**	**492**	**13,252**	**2,189**	**2,466**	**2,571**	**2,430**	**2,563**	**2,705**	**2,855**	**44,329**
Applications											
Acquisition—Land	1,000										1,000
Improvements—Real	9,000										9,000
Improvements—Personal	2,000										2,000
Point—Construction Loan	111										111
Point—Perm Mtgs			111								111
Tax Advice	50										50
Organization Cost	50										50
Syndication Professional	50										50
Selling Commission	200										200
Management Fee	50	100	100	100	100	57	67	71	75	80	800
Pay Off Construction Loan		11,055									11,055
Debt Service of Perm Mtg			1,014	1,014	1,014	1,014	1,014	1,014	1,014	1,014	8,115
Debt Service of 2nd Mtg			362	362	362	362	362	362	362	362	2,898
Swing Loan Interest	52	52	104	85	33	0	0	0			325
Swing Loan Amortization			100	150	400	250					900
Land Lease	100	100	100	100	100	100	100	100	100	100	1,000
Asset Replacements			48	112	188	204	226	240	254	269	1,540
Working Capital Balance	142	240	258	266	269	200	200	200	200	200	2,176
Total Applications	**12,805**	**492**	**13,252**	**2,189**	**2,466**	**2,187**	**1,970**	**1,987**	**2,006**	**2,025**	**41,380**
Cash Flow	**0**	**0**	**0**	**0**	**0**	**384**	**460**	**576**	**699**	**830**	**2,949**
Modified Cash Flow—Pension	−100	−100	−468	−158	36	222	527	647	775	910	2,290
Priority Return on Equity				117	117	117	117	117	117	117	819
Balance						105	410	530	658	793	2,495
Additional Interest	0	0	0	0	0	52	205	265	329	396	1,247
Balance of Dist. CF	0	0	0	0	0	331	255	311	371	434	1,702
LP Priority 8%	0	0	0	0	0	200	200	200	200	200	1,000
Balance	0	0	0	0	0	131	55	111	171	234	702
Incentive Management—30%	0	0	0	0	0	39	17	33	51	70	211
Distributed Cash Flow	0	0	0	0	0	92	39	78	119	164	1,949
Total LP Cash	**0**	**0**	**0**	**0**	**0**	**291**	**238**	**277**	**318**	**362**	

Projected Statement of Taxable Income, 1984–1993
(in thousands)

	1984	1985	1986	1987	1988	1989	1990	1991	1992	1993	Total
Cash Flow from Operations			1,057	1,431	1,700	1,902	2,230	2,363	2,505	2,655	15,843
Tax Advice	50										50
Management Fee	50	100	100	100	100	57	67	71	75	80	800
Incentive Management Fee	0	0	0	0	0	39	17	33	51	70	211
Interest Exp—1st Mtg			949	942	934	925	915	904	892	878	7,337
Additional Interest	0	0	0	0	0	52	205	265	329	396	1,247
Interest Exp—2nd Mtg			352	350	348	346	343	341	337	333	2,750
Land Lease	100	100	100	100	100	100	100	100	100	100	1,000
Amortization	14	14	14	14	14	4	4	4	4	4	90
Depreciation	0	0	1,388	1,367	1,288	1,232	1,180	702	728	745	8,629
Total Expenses	**214**	**214**	**2,903**	**2,873**	**2,784**	**2,756**	**2,830**	**2,421**	**2,516**	**2,606**	**22,117**
Taxable Income	**(214)**	**(214)**	**(1,846)**	**(1,442)**	**(1,084)**	**(854)**	**(601)**	**(58)**	**(11)**	**49**	**(6,274)**

FIGURE 5-6 (CONT'D)

SYNDICATION WITH AN 11 PERCENT NONRECOURSE MORTGAGE, A 14.5 PERCENT SECOND MORTGAGE, AND A 50 PERCENT KICKER

Projected Statement of Net Benefits, 1984–1993
(in thousands)

	1984	1985	1986	1987	1988	1989	1990	1991	1992	1993	Total
Limited Partner Contribution	350	350	400	500	500	400					2,500
Taxable Loss	(212)	(212)	(1,828)	(1,427)	(1,073)	(845)	(595)	(57)	(11)	49	(6,211)
Tax Savings at 50%	106	106	914	714	537	423	297	28	5	(24)	3,106
Add: Investment Tax Credit			161	7	11	12	13	14	15	16	250
Add: Cash Distributions	0	0	0	0	0	291	238	277	318	362	1,486
Total Benefits	106	106	1,075	720	548	726	549	320	339	353	4,842
Net Benefit	(244)	(244)	675	220	48	326	549	320	339	353	2,342
Cumulative Net Benefit	(244)	(488)	187	408	455	781	1,330	1,650	1,988	2,342	

Calculation of Adjusted Rate of Return

A) Limited Partner

Year	Investment	Benefits	Side Fund Interest	Side Fund Balance
1984	350	106	0	106
1985	350	106	8	221
1986	400	1,075	18	1,314
1987	500	720	105	2,139
1988	500	548	171	2,858
1989	400	726	229	3,812
1990		549	305	4,666
1991		320	373	5,359
1992		339	429	6,126
1993		353	490	6,970
1994		2,089	558	9,617

2,054

Side Fund Interest	8.00%
Adjusted Rate of Return	16.69%

B) Pension Fund

Year	Investment	Pretax Benefits	Interest	Balance
1984	1,000	100	0	100
1985		100	8	208
1986	11,055	1,225	17	1,450
1987		1,114	116	2,680
1988		1,114	214	4,009
1989		1,167	321	5,496
1990		1,319	440	7,255
1991		1,379	580	9,215
1992		1,443	737	11,396
1993		1,511	912	13,818
1994		15,810	1,105	30,734

10,478

Side Fund Interest	8.00%
Adjusted Rate of Return	11.36%

Calculation of Second Mortgage Amount

1988 Cash Flow from Operations	1,700
Less: 1st Mtg Payment	1,014
Less: Land Lease	100
Less: Asset Replacement	188
Available for Debt Service	398
Available, Based on 1.1:1 DSC	362
Amount of Mtg, Based on 14.5%, 25 Years	2,428
Used	2,430

Calculation of 1-1-94 Sale
(in thousands)

	LP	GP
Gross Rental Income	2,655	
Less: Operating Exp Real Estate Taxes Management Fee		
Net Income Before Debt Service	2,655	
Sales Price, Based on 10%	26,554	
Less Disposition Cost—5%	1,328	
Net Sales Price	25,226	
Less Mtg Balance	7,846	
Less 2nd Mtg	2,282	
Less Land Acq	2,000	
Cash Available	13,098	
Less LP Priority	1,170	
Balance	11,928	
Additional Interest—50%	5,964	
Balance	5,964	
Balance	3,682	
Less Remaining Priority	1,330	
Balance	2,352	
GP 40%	941	
LP 60%	1,411	
Total LP Cash	3,911	
Total GP Cash		941
Tax upon Sale	LP	GP
Contrib	2,500	0
Income (Loss)	(6,211)	−63
Cash Flow	1,486	19
Cash upon Sale	3,911	941
Taxable Gain	9,109	1,023
Total Tax @ 20%	1,822	205
Net Cash	2,089	736

FIGURE 5-6 (CONT'D)

SYNDICATION WITH AN 11 PERCENT NONRECOURSE MORTGAGE, A 14.5 PERCENT SECOND MORTGAGE, AND A 50 PERCENT KICKER

Footnote Information		Summary of Financing Information		
			Note 1	Note 2
Acquisition Date . . . . July 1, 1984		Amount	8,625	2,430
Placed in Service . . . . January 1, 1986		Interest Rate	11.00%	14.50%
Number of Units 200		Amortization Period	25 Years	25 Years
Acquisition Cost . . . . . $12,000,000 (includes land, building, and improvements)		Status	Nonrecourse	Recourse
Per Unit $60,000				

Depreciation Schedule
(in thousands)

	Basis	1984	1985	1986	1987	1988	1989	1990	1991	1992	1993	Total
Real Property	9,000			1,080	900	810	720	630	540	540	540	5,760
Personal Property	2,000			300	440	420	420	420				2,000
Asset Replacement—Real				1	3	6	9	13	17	21	26	95
Asset Replacement—Personal				7	24	52	83	117	145	167	179	774
Total Depreciation		0	0	1,388	1,367	1,288	1,232	1,180	702	728	745	3,409
Amortization Schedule												
Points—1st Mtg		4	4	4	4	4	4	4	4	4	4	40
Organization Cost		10	10	10	10	10						50
Total Amortization		14	14	14	14	14	4	4	4	4	4	90

Mortgage Amortization
(in thousands)

Year	Payment	Interest	Principal	New Outstanding
				8,625
1986	1,014	949	66	8,559
1987	1,014	942	73	8,486
1988	1,014	934	81	8,406
1989	1,014	925	90	8,316
1990	1,014	915	100	8,216
1991	1,014	904	111	8,105
1992	1,014	892	123	7,983
1993	1,014	878	136	7,846
1994	1,014	863	151	7,695
1995	1,014	846	168	7,527

Asset Replacement Assumptions

Real Property	25.00%
Personal Property	75.00%

Developer's Statement of After-Tax Benefits
(in thousands)

	1984	1985	1986	1987	1988	1989	1990	1991	1992	1993	Total
Management Fee	50	100	100	100	100	57	67	71	75	80	800
Incentive Management—30%	0	0	0	0	0	39	17	33	51	70	211
1% of Cash Flow	0	0	0	0	0	1	0	1	1	2	5
Presale Cash	50	100	100	100	100	97	84	105	128	151	1,015
Taxable Income—Fees	50	100	100	100	100	96	83	104	126	150	1,010
1% of Partnership Income	(2)	(2)	(18)	(14)	(11)	(9)	(6)	(1)	(0)	0	(63)
Tax Income—Transaction	48	98	82	86	89	88	77	104	126	150	947
Tax Cost—30%	(14)	(29)	(24)	(26)	(27)	(26)	(23)	(31)	(38)	(45)	(284)
ITC from Partnership	0	0	2	0	0	0	0	0	0	0	3
Tax Savings	−14	−29	−23	−26	−27	−26	−23	−31	−38	−45	−281
After-Tax Win before Sale	36	71	77	74	73	71	61	74	90	106	734
Win from Sale										736	736
NPV @ 12% of Win before Sale	439										
NPV @ 12% of Win after Sale	705										

TRENDS IN HOTEL DEVELOPMENT

CHAPTER SIX

Almost every change in American society has been reflected in the lodging industry. As the economy has expanded, the small room at a country inn has been transformed into the high-rise suite with a computer console. Hotel owners no longer need to hire boys to grab the reins of a traveler's horse, but they still have most of the same problems of the colonial innkeeper: they must find customers and keep them coming back. They must give good value and make an acceptable profit.

It has sometimes been difficult for the lodging industry to meet these objectives during the past few years. Cyclical economic downturns, unpredictable fuel prices, and the resultant changes in patterns of travel have forced a variety of industry adjustments. Although some of these changes have been as simple as providing a separate floor for women executives, others have required fundamental alterations in the way lodging properties are conceived and financed. Modern hoteliers need to know far more today than the mere cost per room of a facility. They must be sensitive to changes in the economy as a whole. They must be able to use the services of bankers and real estate agents, as well as of designers and color consultants.

The recent downturn in the world economy has caused major changes in hotel development. The accelerated pace of hotel building in the middle to late 1970s has given way to a complex development process that depends heavily on chain affiliation and on innovative financing. The challenge of the 1980s for developers, investors, and operators of lodging properties is to strike a proper balance between diversification and specialization, risk and opportunity.

Dale Carnegie once defined business as "a tightrope act with no net." Anyone involved in the hotel industry will encounter a difficult set of problems, but overcoming these problems can lead to success, profits, and knowledge that may be applied to other real estate ventures. The successful hotel developer of the 1980s will be sensitive to shifting market needs and will strive to provide tailored services and quality management. Developers, investors, and operators of lodging properties who are willing to take risks and to recognize opportunities will be able to maintain leadership positions in a dramatically expanding industry.

SUPPLY AND DEMAND

In 1982, the U.S. lodging industry comprised approximately 2.5 million rooms, generated total sales of $29.3 billion, employed 1.2 million people, and served over 250 million guests. Today, nearly 1.8 million rooms are less than 20 years old, while the net growth in available rooms has averaged only 1.2 percent annually since 1958 and the net growth in demand (as measured by occupied rooms) has amounted to only 1.1 percent annually. Despite declines in occupancy levels since the late 1940s, when overall occupancies were 95 percent, the lodging industry has remained fairly profitable. Hoteliers have been able to maintain increases in total revenues by offsetting declines in occupancy with increases in room rates, food and beverage prices, and fees for supportive services.

The U.S. lodging industry has experienced two periods of major growth. The first occurred from 1920 to 1929, when nearly 500,000 rooms were added, raising the available capacity to over 1.5 million rooms. The second period began in the late 1950s in response to the large number of new household formations, the completion of the interstate highway system, and an increase in vacation travel patterns. The second growth period, which was interrupted by the oil embargo from 1975 to 1978 and by high interest rates from 1980 to 1981, has continued.

The current construction rate of new hotel rooms (about 100,000 per year) will likely decline during the next 10 years. Projections for the decade between 1982 and 1992 hold that the number of available rooms will increase at an average annual rate of 1.8 percent per year, while the average number of occupied rooms will grow at a rate of 2 percent per year. Thus, the current low occupancy rate (in historical terms), which was 64.6 percent for the lodging industry in 1982, should improve between 1982 and 1992 as the excess rooms are absorbed. This increase, however, will probably be slow in developing because some U.S. markets are currently overbuilt and will therefore take a few years to achieve the higher occupancy levels. (Figure 6–1 shows the average annual increase in guest rooms since 1959.)

Data on the number of new rooms added since 1960 appears in Figure 6–2. Based on a projected annual increase of 100,000 new guest rooms and on the probable refurbishing of between 175,000 and 200,000 guest rooms, the lodging industry should require approximately $7.5 billion annually (in 1983 dollars) to fund these improvements over the next decade.

Several circumstances affect the level of demand for lodging facilities. These include employment and overall economic conditions, the level of discretionary income, and the need for face-to-face meetings to conduct business. During periods of economic uncertainty, business travel is one of the first items to be reduced as a cost-saving measure. Similarly, consumers more frequently spend their holidays and vacations closer to home. Resorts and budget hotels suffer the most during recessions, while lodging facilities in strategic urban or suburban locations typically fare better during these periods.

Lodging properties that have served as major anchors for many downtown revitalization programs and as focal points for recreation destinations are now enjoying slow to moderate growth. But for all hotels, the ability to obtain financing for new construction will determine future growth. Lodging is an ongoing business, requiring a day-to-day effort to maximize revenues. A hotel developer not only must design a building but also must create a self-supporting business operation. Thus, the financing and development of hotels require creativity and insight.

MAJOR INFLUENCES ON HOTEL DEVELOPMENT

The long-term development potential for lodging properties in the United States will depend on several emerging trends:

◆ By 1990, about 60 percent of U.S. women will have joined the work force. The continued rise of the two-income family (currently 50 percent of all households) and the declining size of the American household (2.8 in 1983) will create greater demand for quality leisure products and services. During the 1980s, the two-income family will likely seek vacation packages for extended weekends and for full weeks to a variety of recreation destinations. This expanding consumer group is a well-informed and sophisticated market. Whether rafting on the Colorado River or playing golf in Hawaii, two-income families will expect quality and personalized treatment.

During periods of economic certainty, consumers will more readily spend their holidays and vacations away from home.

The Hyatt Regency/Capitol Hill aims at business travelers but also tries to lure both vacationers and local residents.

No longer will a vacationer return to the same hotel yearly. A lodging property will need to prove itself to a changing and discerning market.

◆ By 1990, two-thirds of all U.S. households will contain no children under the age of 15 years. Also by then, more than one-third of all Americans will be 50 years old or older. Already by 1980, more than 50 percent of American households had only one or two persons. As the population ages and as the household size shrinks, a large new market segment will form, having a good deal of leisure time, a desire to participate in activities with individuals of equal age, and the economic means to enjoy long-deferred pleasures.

◆ The elderly market, the fastest growing market segment in the United States, spends an average of 7.3 nights away from home per trip—60 percent longer than the average for other travelers. This market also travels farther per trip, is twice as likely to travel on a group program, and prefers sightseeing and entertainment to active recre-

ational activities. The astute hotelier will realize that these older guests cannot be targeted as a homogeneous group. They will have varying interests and physical capacities; for instance, many will not be satisfied with only card games and shuffleboard. They will seek organized recreational experiences that offer a variety of individual choices.

◆ If current trends persist, the top U.S. travel destinations will be California, Texas, Florida, New York, and Pennsylvania.

◆ Teleconferencing, which will probably be present in 1,000 of the 8,000 largest commercial hotels by the end of 1984, has not so far curtailed travel of business meeting attendees. It will primarily be used to enhance business communications and to expand a hotel's marketability. During the next decade, teleconferencing will not deter travel or the use of lodging facilities.

◆ Many analysts in the 1960s predicted increased leisure time for the typical U.S. worker. This prediction has not proven true. Workers, in many cases out of necessity, have chosen to work more hours to increase their incomes, rather than to take time off from work. When this trend is combined with that toward the rising number of two-income households, the proximity, the cost, and the quality of vacation lodging become paramount. The vision of a world in which robots do the work while society focuses on recreation has not been realized. The robots have appeared, but they are controlled by workers with fixed vacation schedules.

◆ The economic environment of America in the 1980s will shape consumer patterns of travel and leisure expenditure. During times of strong economic growth (over 3 percent annual growth in the GNP) and of low inflation, individuals will take more trips, travel farther, and show less price sensitivity. During periods of weak economic growth (less than 1 percent annual growth in the GNP), however, people will take fewer vacation trips, will travel

FIGURE 6-1

AVERAGE ANNUAL INCREASE IN GUEST ROOMS

	Available*	Occupied
1959–1969	1.1%	1.2%
1969–1979	.5	2.2
1979–1982	2.8	(.6)
1982–1992 (projected)	1.8	2.0
1959–1992	1.3	1.6

*Net of those rooms removed from inventory for various reasons.
Source: Laventhol & Horwath, based on U.S. Department of Commerce statistics.

FIGURE 6-2

SUMMARY OF GUEST ROOMS ADDED, 1960–1982

1960–1969	1,058,152
1970–1979	860,382
1980–1982	320,039
	2,238,573

Source: Laventhol & Horwath, based on U.S. Department of Commerce statistics.

closer to home, and will demand more value at a lower cost. Without economic growth, tourism, travel, and the use of lodging facilities will decline.

◆ According to the U.S. Census Bureau, by the year 2000, the three most populous states in the country will be California, Texas, and Florida. This population shift to the Sunbelt will correspond to a shift by U.S. industry to these areas. Consequently, new lodging opportunities will arise in these high-growth areas. In the past, many lodging facilities needed to emphasize "ideal climate" as their strongest selling point. In the future, they will have to market year-round recreational activities with a wide spectrum of consumer alternatives.

◆ Foreign travel to the United States will probably suffer a decline during the first half of the 1980s and will not increase during the second half, unless the strength of the U.S. dollar on the world's capital markets decreases sharply.

◆ During the 1980s, the amount of time an individual spends at home engaged in a leisure activity will continue to grow.

◆ The construction and expansion of convention and conference center facilities throughout the country will continue until the mid- to late 1980s, as it has over the past five years. Communities will thus compete increasingly for the lucrative convention market.

◆ Businesses have traditionally been located in urban centers. In the future, new commercial centers will be shifted to suburban areas closer to the workers' homes. The recently expanding high-tech industries will follow this pattern, basing their choices of locations on land availability, cost, and proximity to major educational institutions. The lodging industry must respond to this change. It must establish and expand its facilities in these emerging areas.

◆ Because many first-time buyers cannot afford the traditional primary homes, they will buy timeshares in recreational properties, thus increasing timeshare ownership. Timesharing will also serve as an alternative for those primary homeowners who cannot buy vacation homes by themselves. The growing complexity of the timeshare industry will eventually cause expanded government regulation.

Powell Place on Nob Hill in San Francisco offers 28 suites, ranging from efficiencies to one-bedroom units, with garden patios on the ground level. Originally constructed around 1912, the building has been converted to timeshare ownership. Sales began in February 1981, and by December of that year, about 700 weeks (out of a total of 1,400) had sold at $8 million gross.

◆ The single most important influence on the lodging industry in the 1980s will continue to be the economy. A strong economy will generate more expenditure on travel and leisure. It is impossible to predict the future economic and political climate, but most analysts foresee persisting federal budget deficits and no acute drop in interest rates. This strongly suggests that at least the financing of a hotel will continue to be a challenging proposition.

FUTURE TRENDS

The lodging industry will continue to grow and to adapt to shifting socioeconomic and consumer expenditure patterns. Perceptive developers will be quick to change their operational strategies and the design of their units in response to the commitment by the major lodging chains and operating companies to maintain and increase their own market shares and to diversify their product lines; the rising cost of land, construction, furnishings, and preopening expenses; the changing profile of group and individual travelers; the high cost of financing hotel development; and the accelerating trend toward mixed-use developments. Some of these phenomena—and many others only briefly discussed in this and other chapters—deserve closer attention, with an eye to the future of hotel development.

PRODUCT DIVERSIFICATION

During the past few years, several of the largest U.S. lodging chains have diversified their product types to penetrate new market segments, to increase their market shares, and to respond to specialized demands from their guests. For example, Quality Inns announced in May 1981 that it was creating two distinct new lodging chains within its system, with each of its total of three chains targeted at a separate market segment. The three chains—Comfort Inns (appealing to value-conscious guests); Quality Inns (appealing to commercial and middle-income pleasure travelers); and Quality Royale (appealing to business executives, upper-income professionals, and affluent vacationers)—now offer distinct choices to travel planners and guests. This successful diversification enabled Quality Inns to pursue its aggressive expansion program for the 1980s.

Other lodging chains have promptly followed this example. Ramada Hotels introduced its first Ramada Renaissance hotel in Colorado to provide "the new dimension of quiet elegance and personal service required by today's more discerning travelers." Renaissance properties, according to Juergen Bartels, former president of Ramada's hospitality division, embody a response to the "growing number of two-income families . . . who travel for an experience" and who expect quality facilities and amenities. By 1985, Ramada expects to have more than 40 Renaissance properties in operation.

Trusthouse Forte, Ltd., encompasses about 300 properties worldwide. Approximately one-third of these are classified as "inns," or smaller, modestly priced establishments. In 1982, the chain opened its Excelsior Hotel in Tulsa, Oklahoma, in response both to the rapid growth of the Sunbelt, and to the demands of the commercial and meetings market, with its desire for deluxe accommodations at competitive prices. Currently, Trusthouse Forte is converting some of its TraveLodge properties into another, separate Viscount brand.

The Marriott Corporation, consistently among the industry leaders in occupancy rates and in profitability, has embarked upon an expansion program by which it expects to double its guest room inventory between 1983 and 1986. Marriott has diversified into "hotels," "inns," "resorts," and the new "courtyards" (moderately priced facilities). The chain now offers airport, downtown, and suburban locations, as well as convention hotels and a newly developing network of international properties. Specifically to supply the needs of two distinct market subsegments, Marriott has created Club Marquis, a membership in which entitles commercial travelers to a wide range of additional services and benefits, and the International Welcome Service, a hospitality program for foreign business travelers.

Holiday Inns' expansion and diversification program primarily aims to capture a broader middle-market cross section. To appeal to the high end of the middle-market segment, Holiday Inns inaugurated Crowne Plaza (50 units projected by 1988) and Embassy Suite properties. In December 1983, the 21-unit Granada Royale Hometels system became a part of the Embassy Suites division, thereby enhancing the new division's appeal. Also positioned in the middle of the market is Holiday Inns' gaming division, Harrah's. To round out its program of diversification, Holiday Inns intends to open its first of a chain of budget hotels, Hampton Inns, in June 1984 and to have opened 300 Hampton Inns by 1986.

A Comfort Inn in Raleigh, North Carolina.

117

With 1,750 properties now, Holiday Inns expects to have an annual cash flow of nearly $1 billion by the 1990s and to continue developing and acquiring new hotels aggressively. Having divested itself of Trailways Bus Lines, Delta Steamship Lines, and other subsidiaries, Holiday Inns will emphasize those products and services that appeal to specific growing market segments and that compete minimally with the existing core of its lodging business. According to James Schorr, president of Holiday Inns' hotels group, "Holiday Inns wants to own the middle of the market."

Several other lodging chains engaged in product diversification are:

✦ Radisson Hotels ("plazas," "hotels," "inns," and "resorts," all carrying the Radisson name).

✦ Intercontinental Hotels (Intercontinental Hotels and Forum Hotels).

✦ Hospitality International (Master Host Inns, Red Carpet Inns, and Scottish Inns).

Throughout the 1980s, the movement toward diversification should accelerate as each of the principal lodging chains seeks to maintain or enhance its market share. The high cost of land, the unavailability of franchises in many markets, and the demand for specific new products will continue to spur this development trend.

THE INCREASE IN FRANCHISE OPPORTUNITIES

Competition will grow as the quality of hotel rooms continues to increase, and as the overall U.S. lodging market stabilizes. Because major funding sources more and more frequently require chain affiliation as a condition of financing, independent hotels will find themselves forced to acquire a "brand name." Consequently, franchised lodging properties can only multiply. The boom in franchises principally arises from:

✦ The aggressive expansion and growth programs of the big American hotel chains.

✦ The desire by foreign-based lodging firms to expand into the U.S. market.

✦ A greater emphasis on downtown, airport, corporate park, university, and hospital settings.

✦ A perceived need for affiliation with a large national chain or operating company in order to benefit from advantages such as international reservation systems.

✦ The growth in secondary market areas, where land and construction costs are lower and where financing through local banks is easier to obtain.

Franchising will remain a popular development vehicle for existing and new hotels. Best Western Vice President Frank Hansen states that Best Western has felt a slowdown in the primary market areas and a boom in the secondary markets. In entering a new secondary market successfully, in competing effectively for guests, and in getting financing, independents are having difficulties, Hansen says. They are turning to a brand name to ease these difficulties. Days Inns, for instance, illustrate the impact that franchise affiliation may have on financing. The Days Inns franchise development division successfully secured $60 million in Industrial Revenue Bond financing in 1982, thereby easing financing burdens on behalf of a number of its new franchisees.

During the present decade, as marketing costs continue to rise, as dependence on computerized reservation systems grows, and as financing becomes more difficult to obtain, franchise units will significantly rise in number. Recently, several franchisees have even begun to develop their own brand names: AIRCOA with its Clarion Hotels; Servico with Royce Hotels; Lincoln Properties with Summit Hotels; and W.B. Johnson with Monarch Hotels.

THE SUNBELT GROWTH CORRIDOR

Most lodging chains, operating companies, and lenders will maintain their development focus on the Sunbelt region. Chains such as Marriott, Radisson, Holiday Inns, Ramada, Quality Inns, Trusthouse Forte, Ltd., Sheraton, and several others have opened or are opening new properties in the Sunbelt. Although some markets in this region are by now overbuilt, economic projections for the region still foresee a healthy pace exceeding that of sites in the Midwest or Northeast. The sustained travel volume to many of the Sunbelt states signifies a continuing opportunity for hotel developers, operators, and chains.

THE UPGRADING AND DIVERSIFICATION OF PRODUCTS AND SERVICES

During the 1980s, chain and independent hotels alike are expected to undergo extensive refurbishing and upgrading, and to add new in-room and overall hotel services. Approximately 1.6 million hotel rooms are over 10 years old, and the furnishings and fixtures in many such rooms will soon need upgrading. New services and guest room amenities will become requirements if a hotel is to remain competitive. Within this decade, guests will see most of the following innovations take hold:

✦ Later in this decade, many hotels with 100 or more rooms will install a sophisticated call-accounting system. Because several telecommunications firms now offer these systems, a handful of these firms will likely surface as the industry leaders in quality, service, and price.

Approximately 1.6 million hotel rooms are over 10 years old and will soon need upgrading. The 721-room Mayflower, a Stouffer hotel on Connecticut Avenue in Washington, D.C., is undergoing a major renovation at a cost of $72 million.

✦ The accelerated evolution of computers and of computer-based technology will show up in new applications across the lodging industry. Before 1990, this enhancement of operational capabilities will involve widely used cost-saving systems for energy control, security, registration, reservations, payroll, communications, inventory control, and guest services. Many hotels will also provide in-room computers that can project video games, stock market quotations, news reports, and recreation guides. For guests, computers will not only form a link with a hotel's many departments, but with travel agents, airlines, car rental agencies, and local entertainment centers.

✦ To provide frequent guests with added benefits, several chains will initiate "guest clubs." These clubs (e.g., Marriott's Club Marquis or Sheraton Towers) will offer frequent travelers added personal services such as travel arrangements, private lounges, complimentary copies of *The Wall Street Journal,* access to the hotel's limousine service, secretarial assistance, and use of microcomputers. In addition, members will receive price discounts and travel incentives—much as in the current airline mileage bonus systems.

✦ Cable television systems and in-room movies will probably become virtual necessities in the late 1980s. The lodging industry already buys over 500,000 television sets annually. As guests become more accustomed to cable services in their homes, they will expect to see similar systems in their hotels.

✦ During this decade, several properties will design and offer guests such considerations as nonsmoking rooms or floors, women-only lounges or floors, family areas apart from those for commercial travelers, and other market segment–specific areas.

✦ Custom amenities will become more widespread during the 1980s. Guest room provisions such as bathrobes, mouthwash, disposable razors, high-quality soaps, daily newspapers, toiletries, and many other items will not only show up in luxury properties but also in budget hotels. As guests become more sophisticated in their expectations, so, too, will hoteliers in their standards. Hotelkeepers will use these amenities as advertising vehicles and as enhancements to their product differentiation efforts.

119

Clearly, all of these new services and product additions arise from three industry preoccupations. They focus on quality, on tailored services, and on careful differentiation of properties according to market segment served.

RETIREMENT INNS

The retirement-age population represents the fastest growing market segment in the country today. By the year 2000, thirty million people will be 65 years old or older. In the future, hotel developers will use their design capabilities and operational expertise to develop retirement housing: old and poorly performing hotels will lead other facilities in undergoing this conversion, particularly in overbuilt lodging markets. The guaranteed occupancy and income for these properties will attract the eye of the financial community and will thus stimulate development. By 1990, several of the large U.S. lodging chains will likely have diversified to include this type of product.

INTERNATIONAL HOTEL DEVELOPMENT

Despite the difficulties in developing American hotels outside this country, leading U.S. chains will continue to expand into foreign markets. By reinforcing their reputations abroad, these chains will simultaneously extend the marketability of their domestic properties. The Marriott Corporation, for example, has reported that the number of international guests booking Marriott hotels in the United States rose 60 percent in 1981 and 1982 as a result of the growth and acceptance of Marriott properties abroad. During the next decade, development of international hotels by U.S. firms will likely focus on Europe, on the Pacific Rim countries, and on selected areas in Latin America.

Meanwhile, within the United States, leading European lodging companies will step up their own development of hotels. Emphasizing "the European touch," these firms will introduce during the 1980s a number of deluxe and luxury lodging properties. The comparative stability of the U.S. economy, and foreign firms' perception of ample development opportunities throughout America will serve as the primary motivations for investment.

DOWNSIZING

During the next decade, lodging chains will probably reduce the size of their new and remodeled hotel rooms in order to increase the density of buildable units, as well as to reduce development costs and operating expenses. New or remodeled hotel rooms may well be reduced by 15 to 20 percent from current industry standards. By the 1990s, it is even likely that lodging facilities offering "miniaccommodations" will appear near transportation and entertainment centers. These small facilities will offer units (about 100 square feet in size) consisting of a bed, a chair, and a communications/entertainment console; bathroom facilities will be centrally located and shared by several units. On the other hand, the market for certain older properties built, for example, in the 1920s may be repositioned as these older hotels expand their smaller rooms.

Downsizing may pertain not only to room size but also to hotel size. Two small hotels offering personalized service are The Canterbury (99 suites) and the Hotel Tabard Inn (40 rooms).

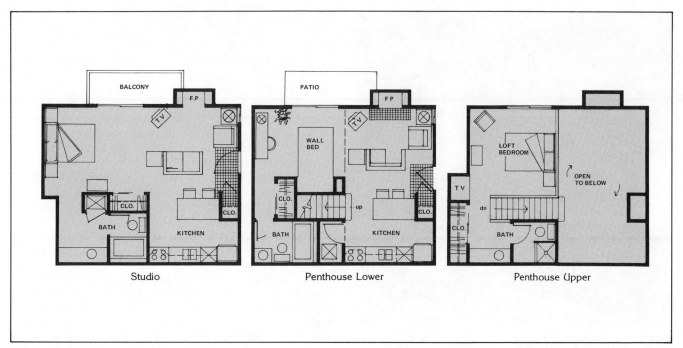

Floor plan for a typical Brock Residence Inn.

Brock Residence Inns exemplify the residential all-suite concept.

THE ALL-SUITE CONCEPT

Pioneered in 1969 by Granada Royale Hometels and later adopted by other chains, including the Brock Hotel Corporation and Brookhollow Inns, the all-suite concept focuses on guest room facilities and on "free" services (no-tipping policy, complimentary breakfast or cocktails, etc.). All-suite hotel guest rooms typically look like small modern condominium units. Rooms are larger than normal and have a living/dining area separated from the sleeping area. These hotels charge higher room rates than do conventional hotels in comparable markets. Because these facilities are dis-

tinctive, they are not bound by locational constraints and have become increasingly attractive to meeting planners and to travelers looking for something different. While the concept varies widely from property to property, all-suite hotels may be urban, suburban, or residential in type.

Granada Royale Hometels, for instance, characteristically use a Spanish architectural style, average 200 to 300 units surrounding an enclosed and skylighted atrium, allot from 500 to 600 square feet to living and sleeping space for guests, and cost from $13 to 30 million to develop. Each Granada Royale Hometel features meeting space as well as high-quality guest room appointments.

While personalized service is a hallmark of the all-suite hotel, most operators also emphasize quality and suburban location. In the 1980s, the development of this kind of facility should increase.

FINANCING

During the 1980s, the financing of lodging properties will change dramatically. Syndications, limited partnerships, developers, and operating companies will be the major sources for equity financing, while insurance companies, pension funds, banks, and savings and loan associations will function as the primary sources for debt financing. During the first half of the 1980s, it will be easier to raise equity than to obtain debt financing. Lenders and investors will be more selective as to the properties they acquire or develop. The independent lodging property will increasingly give way to the chain-affiliated property. Hotels will continue to be viewed as a business and real estate venture, and, as a result, will be required to prove feasibility before receiving a financing commitment.

Hoteliers of the future will need a particularly comprehensive knowledge of their guests' identities, needs, and preferences.

PERSONALIZED GUEST SERVICES

During the 1980s, as the technology for information storage and recall grows more sophisticated, guest services will grow more personalized. It will not be uncommon for a hotel guest in the future to be greeted, not only by a hello, but by a specific question about his or her trip (" . . . and how was your flight from Omaha to Chicago today?"), or his or her last stay at the hotel, for example. Hotel operators will find it easy to generate a profile of each guest, identifying his or her preferences for restaurants, entertainment, transportation, size and type of room, use of hotel guest facilities, and numerous other data that will help the hotelier to provide a personal touch for that guest.

In many ways, lodging represents the ultimate service industry. Not only does it offer its market the basic commodities of food and housing, but it can also provide computer hookups, cable television entertainment, and many of the other resources of the electronic age. Facts and figures about the lodging industry can help in anticipating future trends, but data are no substitute for a hotelier's instincts about customers' needs.

A successful hotelier's operation bears an indefinable atmosphere of success that derives from quality management and careful planning. The responsiveness of a courteous bellhop or the solicitousness of a restaurant waitress, for instance, together help to create this atmosphere. The staff of an effective hotel knows how to handle both a simple billing problem and a complex convention.

An analysis of a successful hotel operation will show that meticulous planning occurred before even the first blueprints appeared. The developers, investors, and operators of successful hotels have, by definition, responded to shifting economic trends and reacted to the needs for product and service differentiation. Historically, the lodging industry has been one of the leading indices of economic growth. As the U.S. economy emerges from its downturn, those members of the industry who have anticipated the resulting changes in travel patterns and been receptive to new ideas will lead a rapidly expanding field.

Hoteliers of the future will require a close knowledge of who their guests are and will be, what their guests desire in products and services, and why their guests select one hotel over another. Lodging properties of the future must remain competitive for a minimum of 10 years. To accomplish this, their developers and operators must be responsive, perceptive, and innovative. As the hotel industry approaches the 1990s, development opportunities are plentiful for those who can recognize and respond to them.

CASE STUDIES

CHAPTER SEVEN

SHERATON GRANDE

Chain Luxury Hotel ✦ Los Angeles, California

The Sheraton Grande—with 13 stories, 487 rooms, and about 518,000 square feet—is a luxury hotel consisting of 10 floors of guest rooms, a floor housing both offices and guest rooms, another devoted to convention facilities, a ground-level public and retail area, ample space allotted to hotel support services, four 200-seat movie theatres, and one basement-level parking garage with 132 spaces. The complex also contains a four-story, 50,000-square-foot office building. The hotel stands on the west side of Figueroa Street between Third and Fourth Streets in downtown Los Angeles.

The Sheraton Grande has the facilities, amenities, and staff to be rated a five-star hotel and to attract those discriminating domestic and international business and pleasure travelers who wish luxury accommodations in a downtown location. Sheraton expects fewer and smaller groups to book here than normally book into a 487-room hotel because of the size of the meeting facilities and the property's image of "class, not mass."

The site comprises a strategic parcel of 3.78 acres in the Bunker Hill Urban Renewal Project. It lies on the western edge of Bunker Hill, along the Harbor Freeway and at the hub of international and commercial centers. Immediately adjacent to the site are the existing World Trade Center, Union Bank Square, and the 1,400-room Westin Bonaventure Hotel. Within a short walking distance are Security Pacific National Bank, Atlantic Richfield Plaza, the Music Center, Dorothy Chandler Pavilion, Little Tokyo, and Bunker Hill Towers condominiums. Other landmarks, to be tied to the site by a projected pedestrian walkway and people mover system, include the Convention Center and federal, state, county, and municipal offices. The Hyatt Regency, Biltmore Hotel, and Hilton Otari are also close neighbors.

The 3,000-square-foot Lobby Lounge seats 75 persons.

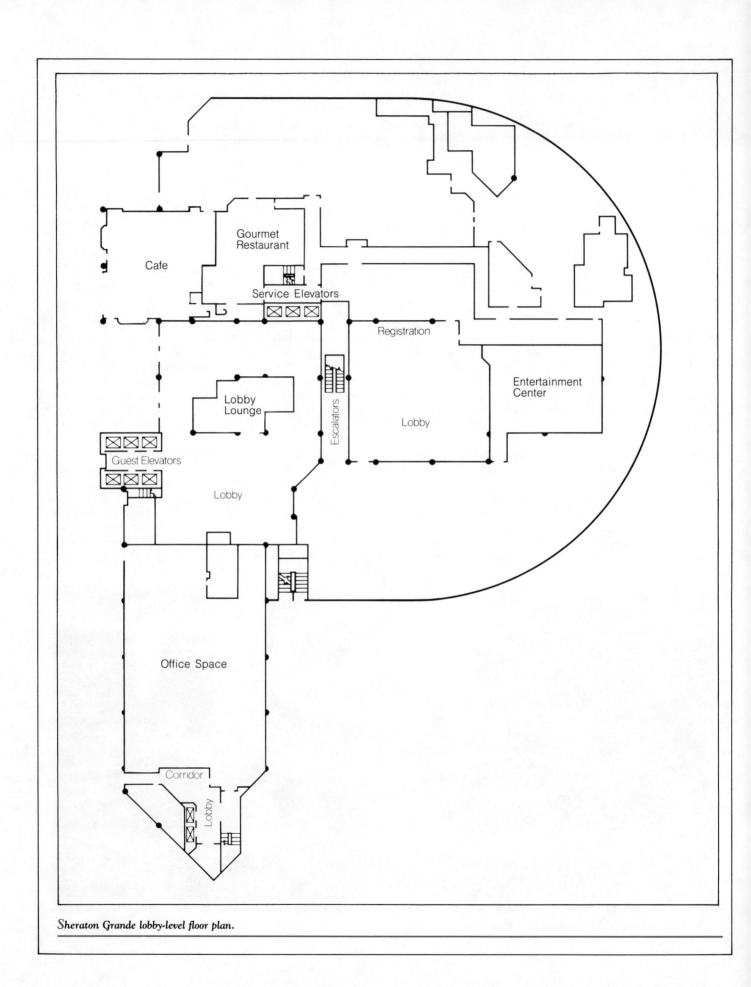

Cafe

Gourmet
Restaurant

Service Elevators

Registration

Lobby
Lounge

Escalators

Entertainment
Center

Lobby

Guest Elevators

Lobby

Office Space

Corridor

Lobby

Sheraton Grande lobby-level floor plan.

THE PLANNING AND DEVELOPMENT PROCESS

MAT Associates undertook the development in April, 1976, under an agreement with the Community Redevelopment Agency (CRA) of the city of Los Angeles. The Sheraton Corporation, MAT Associates, and Metropolitan Life Insurance Company organized among themselves a joint venture partnership. Their proposed architectural design had to be reviewed and approved by the CRA because of the strict criteria applied to the Bunker Hill redevelopment area, namely, a building height restriction of 168 feet, limited ingress/egress for hotel traffic from Figueroa Street, parking requirements, energy and life safety requirements, and landscaping provisions. After several years of design modifications and negotiations, the CRA approved a mixed-use facility with a 487-room hotel as the focal point; a 50,000-square-foot, four-story office building; and a four-screen movie theatre. The CRA, owner of the land, conveyed the 3.78-acre site to the joint venture partnership in December 1980. Construction commenced shortly thereafter.

The lead construction lender was Manufacturers Hanover Trust Company of New York. A California bank also participated as a partner by taking one-half of the required construction loan. With this aid, the facility was completed in October 1983 and fully operational by the middle of that month. Permanent financing came from the New York State Employees Retirement System, with equity contributions from the joint venture partnership.

DESIGN

The design of the 13-story structure, with its mirrored glass sheath in the shape of a parallelogram, won the first award of the Southern California chapter of the American Institute of Architects. The structure offers elegance in a contemporary setting. The landscaping, an integral part of the hotel environment, uses palm trees reminiscent of early California that provide the arriving guest with a serene yet stately, welcoming first impression. The outdoor/indoor Cafe enhances the blend of the urban environment with the tranquil parklike setting.

The guest rooms are designed and furnished as residential minisuites. They each contain 380 square feet and bathrooms finished in marble.

MARKETING

The Sheraton Grande Hotel caters to the luxury market. No facility that appealed to this market existed in downtown Los Angeles or in Bunker Hill before the Sheraton Grande opened. This market has three distinct segments:

◆ Top-level domestic and international executives from commercial, governmental, and industrial concerns.

◆ Upper-echelon domestic and international pleasure travelers using Los Angeles as a destination or as an in-transit stopover point.

◆ Small conferences and group meetings of commercial and industrial organizations.

The quality level of the Sheraton Grande places it in competition with such luxury properties as the Beverly Wilshire Hotel, the Beverly Hilton Hotel, L'Ermitage, and the Century Plaza Hotel, all in the Beverly Hills/Westwood/Century City area. For the top-level executive or commercial traveler who demands to be in the latter, more western area, the Sheraton Grande will only represent an alternative. For the traveler of this class who needs to stay in the center city, however, the Sheraton Grande will be the only world-class luxury hotel in the desired location.

The Sheraton Grande will not discount rooms as do most convention and commercial hotels. Thus, the average room rates will more closely approximate the published rates than do those of most hotel operations. Current room rates are:

One person:	$ 90.00 to $125.00
Two persons:	$105.00 to $140.00
Suites:	$155.00 to $550.00

The hotel retains a staff of 11 marketing professionals who contact corporate travel planners, conference planners, and travel agents, and who work with Sheraton's worldwide network of marketing personnel to direct the discriminating traveler to the property.

The Tango Lounge, with 4,000 square feet, will accommodate 200 patrons.

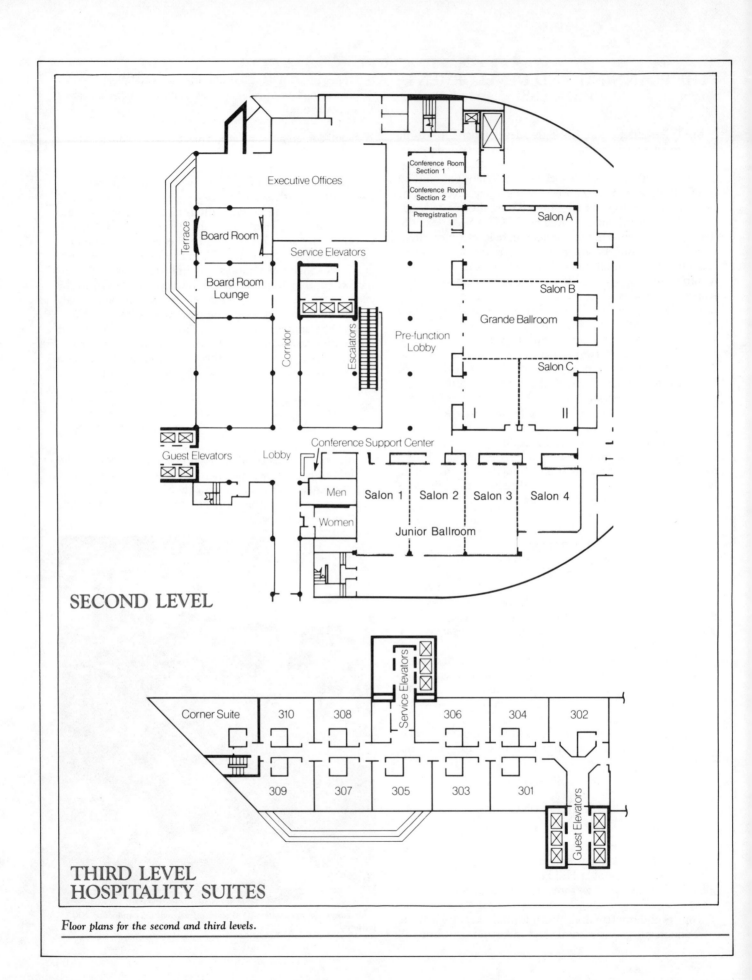

SECOND LEVEL

- Executive Offices
- Conference Room Section 1
- Conference Room Section 2
- Preregistration
- Salon A
- Terrace
- Board Room
- Service Elevators
- Salon B
- Board Room Lounge
- Grande Ballroom
- Corridor
- Pre-function Lobby
- Escalators
- Salon C
- I
- II
- Guest Elevators
- Lobby
- Conference Support Center
- Men
- Women
- Salon 1
- Salon 2
- Salon 3
- Salon 4
- Junior Ballroom

THIRD LEVEL HOSPITALITY SUITES

- Corner Suite
- 310
- 308
- Service Elevators
- 306
- 304
- 302
- 309
- 307
- 305
- 303
- 301
- Guest Elevators

Floor plans for the second and third levels.

PROJECT DATA

Land Use Information
Site Area: 3.78 acres
Total Rooms: 533 room modules
487 saleable rooms
Parking Spaces: 132 in a subbasement structure

Food & Beverage Facilities

Name	Number of Square Feet	Number of Seats	Decor
"Back Porch"	3,150	175	Contemporary Casual Cafe
"Ravel"	3,000	103	Elegant French
"Lobby Lounge"	3,000	75	Atrium
"Tango Lounge"	4,000	200	Contemporary Art

Recreational Facilities
Outdoor swimming pool.
Gift and sundry shop, florist, and hairstylist.
Use of six outdoor tennis courts.
Four 200-seat, first-run movie theatres.

Economic Information

Total investment	$66,000,000
Total investment per guest room	$ 135,500
Equity (percent of total investment)	24.25%
Financed (percent of total investment)	75.75%
	100.00%

Developer: MAT Associates
Chicago, Illinois

Architecture: Maxwell Starkman AIA & Associates
Beverly Hills, California

Landscape Architecture: The SWA Group
Laguna Beach, California

Management: The Sheraton Corporation
Boston, Massachusetts

The 13-story structure in the shape of a parallelogram won the first award of the Southern California chapter of the American Institute of Architects.

THE QUEEN ANNE

Independent Luxury Hotel ✦ San Francisco, California

When asked to name one of their favorite U.S. cities, most people mention San Francisco, and with good reason. The topography and the temperate climate, the fine restaurants, the cable cars, the architecture (new and old), the nearby resort areas such as Lake Tahoe, the national parks, and the wine country, all combine to make San Francisco a favorite tourist and convention city. In fact, San Francisco's largest employer is now tourism and related industries.

San Francisco has developed a reputation as a center for high technology and as a financial center, especially with the Far East. Consequently, the Bay Area attracts not only tourists but also business travelers. Housing them apparently does not pose a problem; in 1982, the Bay Area had more than 25,000 hotel rooms in 150 hotels, and well over half of these were in the city of San Francisco itself.[1]

One of San Francisco's newest hotels is not actually so new. The Queen Anne—a 49-room guest house with a four-star rating from the *Mobil Travel Guide*—started life as a girls' school. It is located outside of downtown, between Nihonmachi (Japan Town) and the residential neighborhood of Pacific Heights. Through the imaginative efforts of the K.R.V. Company of Columbus, Ohio, it was saved from demolition, and, after a year-long renovation, it opened as The Queen Anne in April 1981.

The building was constructed originally as Mary Lake's School for Girls. James G. Fair, one of the "kings" of the Nevada Comstock Lode, built it in 1890. Even for the day, when Victorian architecture was more the rule than the exception, the school was hailed for its design.

---

[1] Source of data: Real Estate Research Corporation.

The 1890-vintage building now housing The Queen Anne Hotel was constructed originally as Mary Lake's School for Girls.

A parlor, adjacent to the lobby, was fashioned out of the former school gymnasium.

In 1899, however, the school closed, and an elite turn-of-the-century men's club, The Cosmos, bought the building. The structure survived the great earthquake of 1906 and barely escaped the fire resulting from the earthquake when it was checked at Van Ness Avenue, some three blocks east of the site. After the catastrophe, this area, west of the downtown, became one of the few parts of San Francisco where urban activities and business could be continued almost as usual. This did not, however, prevent the aftermath of the fire from starting a swift decline for this neighborhood. Mel Scott writes in *The San Francisco Bay Area: A Metropolis in Perspective,*

> The clamor for dwelling space was so great that property owners quickly converted their homes into boarding-houses, even fitting up basements, attics, and storage rooms as bedrooms. Apartment houses, hastily enlarged, became commercial hotels. To meet the demand for commercial space, numerous householders raised their dwellings and built stores underneath them. Stores, restaurants, and workshops opened for business in basements. Industries, too, invaded the area, carrying on noisy and often dangerous operations next door to single-family homes or multifamily structures.

The building changed hands again in the 1920s when the Episcopal Diocese of San Francisco purchased it. Under its new ownership, the structure became the Girls Friendly Society Lodge and housed young working women. After World War II, the Diocese sold the building, and it became one of the city's many smaller hotels catering to newcomers. As the years passed, and as subsequent owners showed no interest in reviving the former school, the building deteriorated further and eventually closed.

THE DEVELOPMENT PROCESS

In 1980, the K.R.V. Company purchased the property and gave it its new identity. The K.R.V. Company—owned and operated by general partners James D. Klingbeil, Eugene S. Rosenfeld, and Jerome W. Vogel—has as its primary development objective the acquisition and renovation of existing properties such as The Queen Anne.

Unlike major hotels, which usually undergo a two-and-one-half- to three-year lag between initial design and completion, The Queen Anne, because it was a renovation, opened a year after acquisition. Occupancy rates steadily increased from about 9 percent in January 1982 to 60 percent a year later—this, in a city with such landmark hotels for competition as the Mark Hopkins, the Huntington, the St. Francis, and the Stanford Court. (The overall occupancy rate for San Francisco hotels currently stands at about 75 percent.) An occupancy level over 70 percent represents the break-even point for The Queen Anne.

The K.R.V Company opted to manage the new hotel itself. According to K.R.V., hiring a major management company to run The Queen Anne would have launched the hotel faster, but large companies used to handling 400-room hotels might have had difficulties in dealing with such a small property. Running a small hotel requires a high level of flexibility and openness to change.

The Queen Anne is indicative of a trend in hotel development. Having generally satisfied the current demand for large luxury and convention hotels, developers are shifting to mid-sized projects and to hotels that carve out distinctive niches for themselves. The small independent hotel focusing on personalized service occupies one such niche. The developers of The Queen Anne believe that a resurgence of small hotels with an emphasis on service is occurring. They claim that the whole philosophy of hotel management hinges on individuals offering service to other individuals. Even the major chains are moving in this direction. In fact, letters from guests at The Queen Anne invariably mention the attentive service of the staff, which now numbers 18 full- and parttime employees.

THE SITE

The Queen Anne sits on a 9,660-square-foot lot at the corner of Sutter and Octavia Streets in a stable residential neighborhood. The building itself contains 27,160 gross square feet, exclusive of attic and basement. Twelve parking spaces, free to registered guests, are leased from a surface lot across the street from the hotel; street parking is also available. The two closest hotels to The Queen Anne—the 156-

room Westin Miyako and the 125-room Kyoto Inn—are located in Japan Town.

Although location is generally of prime importance to the national chain hotels, it has not been a prime factor in the success of The Queen Anne. The hotel compensates for its location in a residential section by offering superior service and by emphasizing in its marketing efforts that a stay at The Queen Anne is like no other. In fact, a project as small as The Queen Anne would not have been possible downtown, given the higher land prices there and the fact that the building itself would have been out of scale.

Because the project stands in a specially controlled renewal area, exterior modifications were minimal and subject to the approval of the local redevelopment agency. The architectural style today remains Queen Anne Victorian, with a gabled roofline, shingle insets, and a rounded turret. Exterior painting costs came to $54,000. Repairs were made to the roof, and a canopy was installed over the front door.

RENOVATION

Meticulous attention to detail shows itself throughout the 49-room, four-story structure. The guest rooms, ranging in size between 204 and 696 square feet, each contain English and American antiques. Each room is individually papered or painted, and several rooms have bay-window dining alcoves. Two of the rooms are equipped for the handicapped.

Wood floors employing intricate wood inlay patterns, as well as walls and staircases of solid wood, grace the public spaces. New partitioning, ceilings, floors, bathrooms, and electrical service were installed, as well as a hydraulic elevator (oversized for handicapped users), a sprinkler system in the public areas, smoke detectors, and individually con-

A *rendering of The Queen Anne.*

trolled baseboard heaters. A parlor, adjacent to the lobby, was fashioned out of the former school gymnasium.

By far the most difficult hurdle was the plumbing; the old rooming-house guest spaces had to be enlarged to accommodate modern bathrooms and then soundproofed. Moreover, the developer restored all of the fireplaces to working condition. Construction costs amounted to nearly $1.4 million, with soft costs adding another $718,471 to the total project cost. The cost per room was $56,543, including purchase price and furnishings. Architects for the renovation were from Group 4 Architecture, Research, & Planning of South San Francisco; Gateway Cities Construction of San Francisco was the contractor.

Completed in early 1983 at a cost of $100,000, The Queen Anne Centre, an executive meeting facility, is located on the first floor. The 935-square-foot salon, which features a fireplace and wood paneling, accommodates 65 persons in theater seats, or up to 85 persons for receptions. The Boardroom (250 square feet) and The Library (293 square feet, with fireplace) will hold 10 and 12 persons respectively. The Queen Anne Centre occupies space that originally served as the school's main dining room and pantry, although all dining events at the Centre are catered by outside firms.

The K.R.V. Company purchased the property for $700,000. It obtained a purchase money mortgage on the property for $180,000 at 8 percent; the remaining financing takes the form of a three-year Westinghouse credit loan for $2,750,000, at two points over prime. Actual ownership of the hotel vests in The Queen Anne Hotel Company, an Ohio limited partnership owned by K.R.V. Most of the accounting for the project is therefore done in Columbus.

MARKETING

While the initial marketing of The Queen Anne had been fairly low-key—it had been referred to as a bed and breakfast

The 293-square-foot Library will hold 12 persons comfortably.

The Queen Anne is located in a residential neighborhood, a few blocks from Japan Town, the focal point of which is the Japanese Cultural and Trade Center. The Trade Center comprises the Westin Miyako Hotel, the San Francisco headquarters for Japan's consulate, a peace pagoda, a theater, commercial and retail space, and an 800-car public garage. Other commercial and retail shops have sprung up on the streets surrounding the center.

inn—it rose well beyond that image. The Queen Anne now aims its marketing at the senior-level corporate traveler and at the independent tourist who travels first-class. The Queen Anne's competition comes from Nob Hill hotels such as the Huntington, the Clift, the Stanford Court, and the Mark Hopkins, and not from timeshare or condotel properties.

Guests of The Queen Anne are entitled to all services of the house, which include a complimentary continental breakfast with morning newspaper; afternoon tea or sherry in the parlor; and courtesy limousine service one way from the hotel to the San Francisco financial district and Union Square, available from 8:00 A.M. to 9:00 A.M., Monday through Friday, by previous appointment.

Most of the room rates, which begin at $80, fall below the market level for the city, in part because of the hotel's location and in part because they are based on a maximum of two people to a room. In fact, in June 1981, shortly after The Queen Anne opened, room rates from a sample of four-star hotels in San Francisco[2] were $104 for a single room and over $120 for a double room. This compares with an average room rate of $55 for all U.S. hotel rooms in 1981.

For the corporate traveler, there is The Queen Anne Society, an executive guest program. Members of the society, currently 38 firms, receive a special corporate room rate of $85 for a medium or deluxe room. In addition to the normal services of the hotel, the member companies of the society have complimentary use of The Boardroom, when it is available, and may make free local telephone calls.

Much of the marketing for The Queen Anne from 1981 to 1983 consisted of publicizing the hotel and its location at trade shows and elsewhere. An "800" telephone number for reservations has helped in obtaining bookings. Once a prospective guest has arrived, however, the property simply "sells itself."

---

[2] As reported by the Real Estate Research Corporation in *Real Estate Report.*

PROJECT DATA

Guest Room Mix

Room Type	Number	Daily Rate[1]
Standard[2]	15	$ 80
Medium	12	$105
Medium with Fireplace[3]	3	$125
Deluxe	14	$140
Suites (One Bedroom)	3	$185
Suite (Two Bedroom)	1	$250
	48[4]	

Economic Information

Acquisition Cost $700,000

Hard Costs

General conditions	$ 297,431
Site work and demolition	63,406
Concrete (structural)	807
Carpentry	235,330
Roof repairs, sealants, insulation	21,854
Glazing (storm windows)	36,571
Finishes	262,885
Specialties	6,704
Elevators	74,902
Plumbing, HVAC, sprinklers	195,672
Electrical	156,600
Total Hard Costs	**$1,352,162**

Soft Costs

Financing fees	32,000
Legal, title, & closing fees	11,128
Advertising & promotion	19,556
Furniture, fixtures, & equipment[5]	370,594
Management & overhead	14,000
Architectural & engineering	14,466
Interest	200,104
Taxes	3,142
Insurance	22,710
Utilities	7,217
Accounting	1,097
Contingency & travel	22,457
Total Soft Costs	**$ 718,471**
Total Project Cost[6]	**$2,770,633**

Projected Statement of Income & Expenses

	1983	1984
Income		
Occupancy percentage	73%	80%
Average room rate	$82	$90
Room revenues	$1,071,000	$1,288,000
Expenses		
Payroll	$285,000	$290,000
Payroll taxes	29,000	29,000
Room expenses	24,000	26,000
Commissions—4 percent	43,000	52,000
Food & beverage	30,000	33,000
Telephone—net of revenues	8,000	9,000
Administrative & general	55,000	60,000
Sales & marketing	50,000	50,000
Repairs & maintenance	20,000	22,000
Utilities	30,000	33,000
Taxes & licenses	40,000	44,000
Insurance	40,000	40,000
Total	**$654,000**	**$688,000**
Direct House Profit	**$417,000**	**$600,000**
Debt Service	**$367,000**	**$370,000**
Net Income	**$50,000**	**$230,000**

Developer: K.R.V. Company
Columbus, Ohio

Architect: Group 4 Architecture, Research, & Planning
South San Francisco, California

Notes
[1]The daily rate is based on up to two people in a room. There is no charge for children 12 years or younger when in the same room with an adult.
[2]Room 417 rents for $65 per night.
[3]Nine rooms have wood-burning fireplaces, three in the medium category, six in the deluxe category.
[4]With the two-bedroom suite rented separately, the total would be 49.
[5]This figure is 13.4 percent of the total project cost.
[6]Does not include The Queen Anne Centre.

Buena Vista Palace

Independent Resort Hotel ✦ Lake Buena Vista, Florida

In Lake Buena Vista, Florida, the Buena Vista Palace stands within Walt Disney World Village, the host community developed inside Walt Disney World as one component of a master plan to create a total destination resort.

Walt Disney World is the primary generator of visitor activity in the greater Orlando area. It is also the largest attraction in the country, encompassing 27,000 acres, or 43 square miles, only a fraction of which has been developed. In addition to Walt Disney World Village, it includes:

✦ The Magic Kingdom;
✦ River Country;
✦ Fort Wilderness;
✦ EPCOT (Experimental Prototype Community of Tomorrow), with two theme areas, Future World and World Showcase; and
✦ Three Disney hotels offering other recreational facilities.

Since the opening of the Magic Kingdom in October 1971, Orlando has been transformed from just one of several popular winter resorts into the leading tourist destination in the state. A major airport has been constructed, and area highways have been expanded and improved to accommodate the ever-growing traffic volume.

Walt Disney World Village stands approximately 18 miles southwest of Orlando, at the intersection of Interstate 4 and State Road 535, in the eastern section of Walt Disney World. For a number of years, Walt Disney World Village was called Lake Buena Vista. However, for marketing purposes, in the early 1980s, Walt Disney World officials changed the name to reflect more closely the Village's affiliation with Disney World.

The preview center at the Village was the first facility there to be opened to the public. Before the Magic Kingdom welcomed its first visitor, tourists were able to obtain an idea of what Walt Disney World would offer.

The design of the Buena Vista Palace suggests a medieval castle. With four triangular towers, the tallest of which has 27 stories, the Palace is the tallest hotel in Central Florida.

By 1983, Walt Disney World Village had grown substantially and embraced a variety of land uses:

◆ The Hotel Plaza, including the Buena Vista Palace, the 396-room Royal Plaza, the 322-room Howard Johnson's, the 613-room Dutch Inn, the 325-room TraveLodge Tower, and the 816-room Hilton.

◆ The Walt Disney World Shopping Village, with approximately 73,000 square feet given over to 29 shops and five restaurants.

◆ The Lake Buena Vista Club, consisting of an 18-hole championship golf course, tennis courts, restaurant, and lounge.

◆ The Villa Sections, comprising the Vacation, Treehouse, Fairway, and Club Lake Villas with a total of 550 units, as well as the Walt Disney World Conference Center.

◆ The Sun Bank Building, a five-story, 106,000-square-foot office building.

◆ The Empress Lilly Riverboat, containing three restaurants and two lounges.

Continued expansion of Walt Disney World Village is projected, although the specific facilities to be built and the timing of construction will be determined by market demand, by the capital requirements of various projects, and by Disney's development priorities. New development at Walt Disney World Village will likely include:

◆ Additional hotel rooms to accommodate the increased demand following the opening of EPCOT in late 1982.

◆ An expansion of the Walt Disney World Shopping Village around the lake near the Empress Lilly Riverboat (approximately 40,000 square feet of New Orleans–themed, upper-tier retail space, plus a 600-room hotel).

◆ Additional villa clusters devoted to tennis, equestrian activities, and boating.

◆ A monorail system to connect Walt Disney World Village with the Magic Kingdom and EPCOT Center.

Walt Disney World Village is not only convenient to the Magic Kingdom and EPCOT, the two leading tourist attractions in the state of Florida; it is also within five miles of Sea World, a 135-acre marine life park (the third most popular attraction in Florida), and of the Orange County Convention/Civic Center (325,000 square feet of meeting and exhibition space that opened in early 1983). Furthermore, Circus World, the world's only circus-centered amusement park, lies approximately 10 miles southwest of Walt Disney World Village, while the Kennedy Space Center and Cypress Gardens are within 50 miles—a convenient day trip.

THE SITE

The Buena Vista Palace, less than a mile from the entrance to Walt Disney World Village, stands just west of the Dutch Inn at the corner of Buena Vista Drive and Hotel Plaza Boulevard, and across the street from the Walt Disney World Shopping Village.

The site is an irregularly shaped but essentially flat parcel consisting of about 32 acres. A frontage of approximately 1,337 feet follows the north side of Buena Vista Drive and extends northeast to the shoreline of Lake Buena Vista. A 900-foot-long lagoon divides the site into two tracts. The hotel and its parking facilities occupy the larger tract, while the remaining acreage, reached by a bridge, offers recreational amenities. The lagoon connects Lake Buena Vista with the lake on which Walt Disney World Shopping Village is sited.

The parcel—zoned for commercial use, including lodging, food and beverage service, tourist services, merchandising establishments, financial and professional offices, and health facilities—required no zoning change. The commercial zoning designation, however, stipulates that a minimum of 30 percent of the total area of the site must remain open space.

This location offers easy access from Interstate 4, the main traffic artery through the greater Orlando area, and from the Florida Turnpike and the Beeline Expressway, two other primary routes through Orlando.

From all standpoints, the Buena Vista Palace occupies an excellent site. With a location in prestigious Walt Disney World Village, the hotel is well placed to capture the room demand generated by tourists and convention or meeting delegates. Walt Disney World Village is a well-planned, prospering community that provides high-quality surroundings for the hotel. The Village's excellent reputation, as well

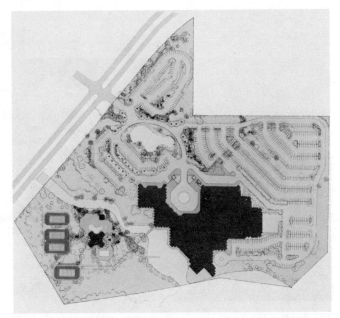

Site plan for the Buena Vista Palace.

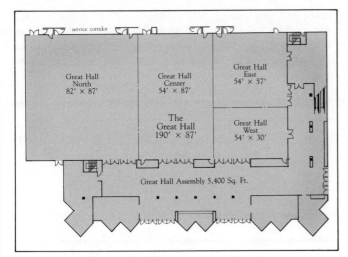

Floor plan for the first-floor meeting rooms.

as the control that Disney exerts over existing and future tenants through ground leases, will ensure that the high-quality environment prevails.

THE PLANNING AND DEVELOPMENT PROCESS

Shimberg, Kennedy and Frost, Inc. (SKF) of Tampa, owners and managers of apartment projects, office buildings, and hotels, acquired the 396-room Hotel Royal Plaza in December 1975. The Royal Plaza was one of the four original hotels in the Walt Disney World Village Hotel Plaza, operated under a ground lease with Disney. In 1979, SKF began examining the potential of obtaining additional land for the expansion of the Royal Plaza. Discussions with Disney representatives, however, led to the conclusion that developing a new hotel represented a preferable option to enlarging the Royal Plaza.

In early 1980, SKF and Lake Buena Vista Communities, Inc., a subsidiary of Walt Disney Productions, agreed on a hotel site that was then set aside for SKF's eventual use. On December 11, 1980, a ground lease was drawn up that had an initial term of 50 years beginning on the completion date of the building, and a renewal option for an additional 25 years at the same terms.

Construction of the project began in January 1981, and the hotel opened on March 1, 1983. While the number of available guest rooms at opening was 99, more rooms were added to the inventory every several days through mid-June 1983.

The original design program contemplated 600 guest rooms with about the same amount of meeting space as is now included. As construction estimates came in, however, the developer concluded that the cost per room with 600 rooms would be too high. Consequently, a revised design program increased the number of guest rooms to 870 room modules (844 keys), bringing the cost per room down to a manageable level.

DESIGN

Rising 27 stories, the Buena Vista Palace is the tallest hotel in Central Florida, as well as the first new hotel in the Walt Disney World Hotel Plaza since the Magic Kingdom opened in 1971. The hotel's design suggests a medieval castle and consists of four triangular towers faced with reflective glass. The towers include the 27-story main tower; two atrium towers, one of five stories and the other of 14 stories; and an eight-story courtyard tower. Balcony rails and sliding doors occur at different angles so that the towers shimmer as the sun moves. Waterfalls, fountains, plants, and tapestries accent the Palace's unusual architectural concept.

Guests enter the lobby from a semi-enclosed entrance court that is framed with castlelike turrets and approached via an elevated semicircular driveway. This entrance opens onto the third floor of the main tower, which houses the front desk, lobby, meeting rooms, and administrative offices. When large groups register, management has the option of registering them on the first floor, where most of the service areas of the hotel are found, including two restaurants, a night club, the main ballroom, the exhibition hall, retail shops, a game room, and the in-house laundry. This technique for keeping group and convention guests separated from individuals and families means that the hotel may cater effectively to both market segments simultaneously.

Guest room corridors are single-loaded, with rooms opening onto either central atriums or hallways. The unusual shapes of the guest rooms afford views of the lake or lagoon. In addition, many rooms offer an excellent view of EPCOT.

A steel and wooden bridge spans the lagoon and connects the hotel structure with a variety of recreational amenities,

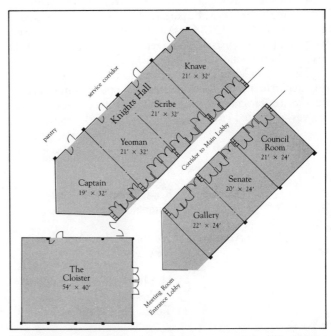

Floor plan for the main tower's third-floor meeting rooms. The third floor also houses the front desk, the lobby, and administrative offices.

among them two swimming pools, four lighted tennis courts, a whirlpool bath, and a sauna. The main swimming pool lies half undercover to protect swimmers from inclement weather, and a poolside snack bar and liquor bar are provided. Guests may operate motor and paddleboats on Lake Buena Vista and can also play golf on the three Disney 18-hole championship courses. The Buena Vista Palace will reserve tee times up to a year in advance—an exclusive privilege both of the Disney-owned hotels and of those properties located in the Hotel Plaza.

Because of the project's location within the Village, the design of the Buena Vista Palace had to be approved by the landlord, Lake Buena Vista Communities, Inc. (WED Enterprises, Disney Productions' design group, reviewed the design approval application on behalf of the landlord.) Reedy Creek Improvement District, the governing authority for Lake Buena Vista, also had approval authority on design specifications, as well as the power to issue building permits. This tight control on the quality of the environment ensures the future value of existing and new projects, with an eye to the synergistic effect of neighboring projects on each other.

MARKETING

The targeted market for the Buena Vista Palace is a mix of convention/meeting business and tourists, projected to approximate 55 percent groups and 45 percent tourists. About 90 percent of the hotel's guests will likely be domestic travelers.

Through its association with Walt Disney World, the hotel benefits from the considerable advantage of the Disney Central Reservation System. It also gains access to Disney amenities such as shops, restaurants, golf, marina facilities, and complimentary transportation to and from the Magic Kingdom and EPCOT. These advantages, plus the extensive facilities the hotel itself offers, represent important assets in the marketing effort.

The Buena Vista Palace employs 15 people in its marketing department. Well before the hotel opened, an extensive marketing program began. It then involved—and still involves—targeted group sales solicitation in the association,

corporate, insurance, and incentive travel markets; in the retail and wholesale travel agent markets; and through airline reservation systems, both domestic and international. Professional publicity and advertising campaigns, plus promotional materials and activities, support these efforts. The hotel also receives exposure through Walt Disney World's marketing program, with which it shares cooperative marketing agreements.

EXPERIENCE GAINED

✦ For a project as large as this one, be certain to retain both an on-site architect and a project manager representing the owner.

✦ A development team must designate one person to make timely decisions. Relying on committees, with the resulting frequent indecision, is more costly than making no decision at all, when the "interest clock" and the "architect's clock" are both running. Contractors lose their timing if delays occur. Constructing a building of this size, after all, resembles assembling a huge puzzle.

✦ Experienced hotel management people must be involved in design decisions. A hotel cannot simply be aesthetically pleasing; it must also succeed from an operational standpoint.

✦ Build model rooms to test the workability of layouts and of furniture, and to aid in decisions regarding interior decoration.

✦ As a general rule, in easing decisions regarding, e.g., kitchens and laundries, equipment consultants are not as effective as are well-recommended suppliers with proven track records.

✦ A good furniture, fixtures, and equipment purchasing company can save a developer large sums of money. Effective coordination between purchasing and installation will ensure that items arrive as needed.

Developer:	Royal Palace Hotel Associates Tampa, Florida	*Joint Venture Partners:*	The Equitable Life Assurance Society of the United States New York, New York
Architect:	Welton Becket Associates New York, New York		Buena Vista Investment Fund, Ltd. Tampa, Florida
	McElvy Jenniswein Stefany Howard Tampa, Florida	*Hotel Operator:*	BVP Management Associates Tampa, Florida

PROJECT DATA

Guest Room Mix	Rooms	Keys
Queen/Queen	546	546
Queen/Queen/Studio	120	120
King	5	5
King/Studio	133	133
Suites	66	40
	870	844

Food & Beverage Facilities	Number of Seats	Size (Square Feet)[3]
"Arthur's 27" (top-floor, premier restaurant)	160	6,181
"The Outback Restaurant"	185[1]	5,436
"The Laughing Kooka-burra" Night Club	200	3,730
"Watercress Cafe" (open 24 hours)	307[2]	7,633
"Lobby Lounge"	84	–
Pool Bar	–	–
Pool Snack Bar	–	–
Game Room Snack Bar	–	–
Total	936	

Meeting & Exhibition Space	Banquet Seats	Meeting Seats[4]	Size (Square Feet)
Ballroom	1,450	2,050	16,530
Prefunction Area			4,800
14 Meeting Rooms	500	725	6,450
Exhibition Hall			26,520
	1,950	2,775	54,300

Parking	Number of Spaces
On-Grade	806
Handicapped	17
Valet	85
Total	908

Total Spaces per Key: 1.08.

Building Space Description	Gross Square Feet
Guest Rooms	327,850
Lobby Space and Corridors	188,475
Restaurants and Lounges	22,980
Convention, Meeting, and Banquet	54,300
Retail	5,975
Back-of-House	55,750
Mechanical Space	34,670
Total	690,000

Economic Information

Site: 32 acres; 50-year ground lease with a renewal option for an additional 25 years at same terms.

Economic Investment	Amount	Percentage
Site preparation	$ 3,000,000	3.49%
Building construction	53,500,000	62.21
Fees (legal, architectural, interior design, etc.)	4,000,000	4.65
Financing costs, insurance, and taxes during construction	10,000,000	11.63
Furniture, fixtures, and equipment	11,500,000	13.37
Operating equipment[5]	1,500,000	1.74
Preopening expenses	2,000,000	2.33
Working capital	500,000	.58
Total investment	$86,000,000	100.0%

Total investment per guest room	$ 98,850	

Financing

Equity—13%
  Construction financing: Equitable Life Assurance Society of the United States

Debt—87%
  Permanent financing: AEtna Life & Casualty

Notes

[1]Excludes additional 60 seats outside.
[2]Excludes additional 70 seats outside.
[3]Excludes kitchen/storage space.
[4]Theatre style.
[5]China, glassware, silver, linen, kitchen utensils, and other items with a short useful life not classified in furniture, fixtures, and equipment.

SCANTICON-PRINCETON

Executive Conference Center ✦ Princeton, New Jersey

The Princeton Forrestal Center is a 1,604-acre, university-owned, multiuse office and research park located in Princeton, New Jersey. The project, which is being developed on Princeton University land, contains over 50 businesses, foundations, and research institutions; the 300-room Scanticon-Princeton Executive Conference Center and Hotel; and residential clusters of townhouses, duplexes, and garden apartments. Today, over 3,500 employees work in the park, and over 500 people live in the residential area, which will contain 412 units when completed.

BACKGROUND ON THE FORRESTAL CENTER

Princeton University assembled the site in the early 1970s, when the university became concerned with protecting the environment of its James Forrestal Research Campus,

an 850-acre area acquired in 1950 from the Rockefeller Medical Institute. In 1972, a study, which evaluated the university's future land needs and the probable impact of inevitable regional growth on the university's surroundings, found that the land around the James Forrestal Research Campus was one of the few remaining large undeveloped sites in the heavily developed corridor between New York and Philadelphia. It offered an ideal location for private industry, with good access to cities, natural beauty, the prestige of an internationally known university, and the amenities of a college town. The strategy of developing a multiple-use center around the James Forrestal Research Campus allowed the university to safeguard its surroundings and to set the standard for development in the area, while also earning a return on investment for its endowment funds. The university engaged K.S. Sweet Associates to manage the development and operation of the Forrestal Center, thereby gaining experienced and capable direction without day-to-day university involvement.

Scanticon-Princeton is the largest single Danish investment in the United States and the first Danish-owned hotel in this country.

The 300-room executive conference center is situated on a 25-acre site.

The strategy has succeeded. The site has been developed with buildings of architectural distinction set in landscaped areas and against a backdrop of 500 acres of protected woodlands. Forrestal Center contributes a steadily growing sum of money to the university's operating budget each year. Eventually, this income should exceed $1 million annually.

The land developer, Princeton University, has provided all roadways, underground utilities, and water and sewer systems to individual sites. Lots range from five to 275 acres in size. Builder/developers have leased most of the sites, usually for 50-year terms.

The residential uses cluster between the university's main campus and the center of the site, overlooking Lake Carnegie. Princeton Landing, which occupies a parcel sold to the housing developer, offers garden apartments, duplexes, and townhouses linked by pedestrian walkways to a clubhouse and recreational facility.

The central part of the site accommodates three major complexes: the existing Forrestal Research Campus, the Princeton Plasma Physics Laboratories, and the Robert Wood Johnson Foundation. A belt of natural woodlands, bisecting the site from north to south, separates these uses from the new office/research complexes and the Scanticon-Princeton Executive Conference Center and Hotel. The latter developments concentrate along the principal access roads crossing the east and south parts of the site.

The street system within the site consists primarily of a single arterial loop. College Road East provides the principal entrance from U.S. 1 and was constructed in stages by the university. It intersects a newly constructed bypass, Scudders Mill Road, which loops back to U.S. 1 south of the main entrance.

A master stormwater drainage system ensures proper management of the quality and quantity of stormwater runoff at the site. The system emphasizes the use of natural drainage swales rather than of piped drainage wherever possible. The governing bodies having jurisdiction over stormwater management in the region fully reviewed and approved the drainage plan.

DEVELOPMENT CONTROLS

All land was rezoned for planned multiuse development (PMUD) under the provisions of the Plainsboro Township ordinance, which requires not less than three acres of common open space for every 10 acres of land devoted to office/research/retail uses, and one acre of common open space for every eight units of housing. The master development plan for Forrestal Center contains a detailed set of design and development criteria that in many cases are more stringent than the PMUD requirements. The criteria cover the usual items, such as building mass, location, exterior appearance, parking and service, signs, lighting, and drainage, as well as prevention of environmental disruption during construction and preservation of existing trees. The design guidelines provide detailed drawings to demonstrate tree preservation techniques, and require "substantive proposals for effecting energy conservation."

SCANTICON

Opened at a cost of nearly $36 million, the Scanticon-Princeton Executive Conference Center and Hotel is the largest single Danish investment in the United States and the first Danish-owned hotel facility in this country. The concept for Scanticon-Princeton—a focus on meetings first and accommodations second, coupled with a skilled and dedicated conference center staff—was actually born more than 15 years ago in Aarhus, Denmark's second largest city,

The architecture blends with the site, which is heavily wooded with mature trees.

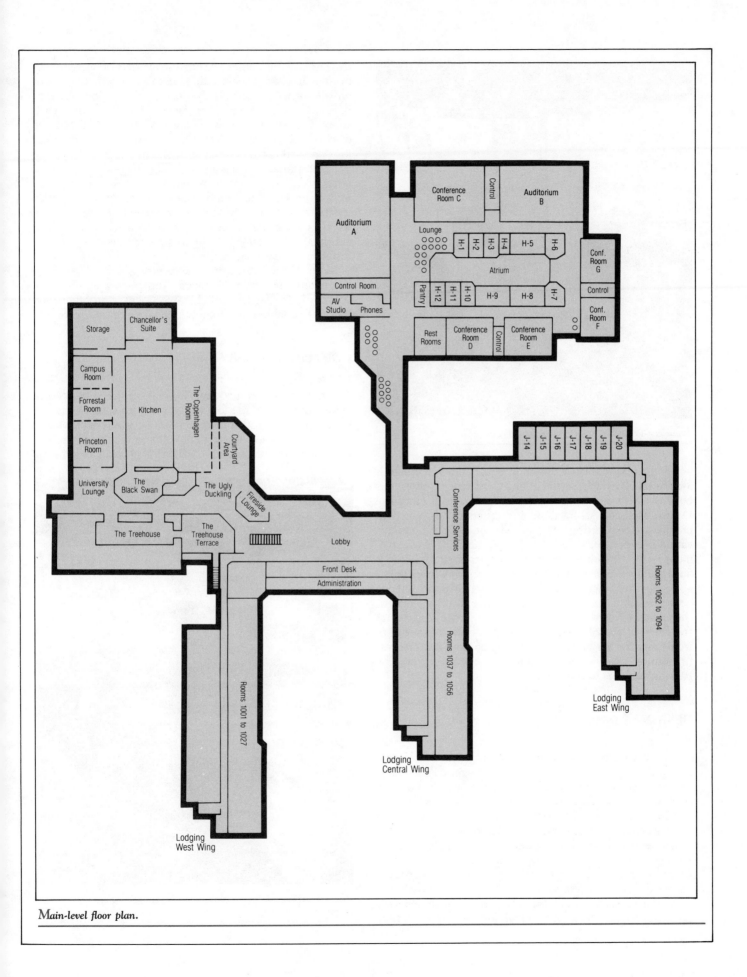

Auditorium
A

Conference
Room C

Control

Auditorium
B

Lounge

Conf.
Room
G

H-1 H-2 H-3 H-4 H-5 H-6

Control Room

Atrium

Control

AV
Studio

Phones

Pantry

H-12 H-11 H-10 H-9 H-8 H-7

Conf.
Room
F

Rest
Rooms

Conference
Room
D

Control

Conference
Room
E

Storage

Chancellor's
Suite

Campus
Room

Forrestal
Room

Kitchen

The
Copenhagen
Room

J-14 J-15 J-16 J-17 J-18 J-19 J-20

Princeton
Room

Courtyard
Area

University
Lounge

The
Black Swan

The Ugly
Duckling

Fireside
Lounge

Conference Services

Rooms 1062 to 1094

The Treehouse

The
Treehouse
Terrace

Lobby

Rooms 1037 to 1056

Lodging
East Wing

Front Desk

Administration

Rooms 1001 to 1027

Lodging
Central Wing

Lodging
West Wing

Main-level floor plan.

Scanticon-Princeton has three wings of guest rooms.

where the first Scanticon was built. Scanticon, which stands for Scandinavian Management and Conference Center, was built as a joint venture of the Danish Engineers' Society, the Danish Medical Association, and others. They aimed to provide an ideal setting for advanced training and communication of expertise, skills, and ideas in the fields of management, science, technology, and administration. The search for a site for the first American Scanticon took three years.

Scanticon-Princeton is a 300-room executive conference center on 25 acres. Constructed in three distinct sections, the Center reflects its intent in its design. To make meetings the focus of activity but to enhance the visitor's sense of wellbeing, the design team employed luxurious guest rooms, fine dining areas, lounges, and recreational amenities. The parking facilities accommodate 450 cars.

DESIGN

The architecture focuses on blending with the 25-acre site, which is heavily wooded with mature trees. Reached by an enclosed walkway from the lobby, the one-level conference section is a world apart from Scanticon's living, dining, and recreation areas. The 26 meeting rooms, surrounding a quiet garden courtyard, range in size from 135 to 4,956 square feet and will house groups of up to 330 persons. Airflow, lighting, sound, seating, ceiling height, and visibility of the speaker and of audiovisuals, all constituted serious design considerations.

At the opposite end of the lobby are three restaurants, private banquet rooms, and cocktail lounges, which occupy

two levels of the Center and provide a variety of surroundings from casual to sophisticated. These rooms, which look out on the scenery, take full advantage of the Center's setting.

Scanticon has three wings of guest rooms and suites, each stretching into the woods. The wings, three stories tall, are reached by elevator or by open staircase from the lobby. They join up with corridors that skirt the lobby.

Recreational facilities abound. The 91-foot indoor swimming pool has an uninterrupted vista of the outdoors. A well-equipped health club includes a treadmill, a uniflex sports trainer, and Dynavit computerized bicycles. In the woods are jogging trails and four lighted tennis courts. A whirlpool, two saunas, and two game rooms complete the roster of recreational facilities.

More than 80 percent of the furniture and accessories at Scanticon came from Denmark, and custom designs were commissioned for the china, table linens, and other such items. The fabrics are notably rich in color and texture.

CONFERENCE SERVICES

Scanticon-Princeton offers special services. Its technicians can produce the following: artwork for flipcharts and signs, multicolored transparencies, special effects slides, color or black and white photography, videotape productions, and audio recordings. Scanticon also makes available

Twenty-six meeting rooms answer the needs of Scanticon's group clientele.

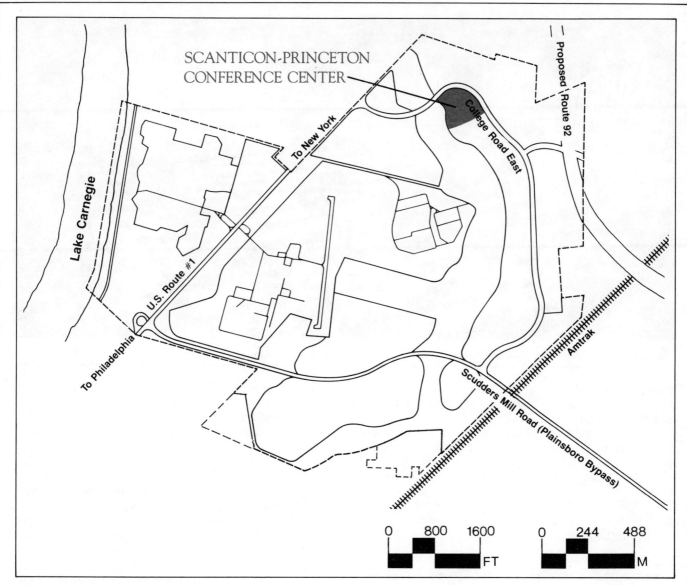

SCANTICON-PRINCETON
CONFERENCE CENTER

College Road East

Proposed Route 92

To New York

Lake Carnegie

U.S. Route #1

To Philadelphia

Amtrak

Scudders Mill Road (Plainsboro Bypass)

| 0 | 800 | 1600 | FT |

| 0 | 244 | 488 | M |

Site plan for the Forrestal Center.

Scanticon-Princeton's meeting rooms will handle groups of as few as eight persons to as many as 330 persons.

photocopying and secretarial services, closed-circuit color television, varied audiovisual equipment, and simultaneous interpretation facilities.

Scanticon assigns a conference service coordinator to each meeting. The coordinator works with the client in planning and actually administering the conference and is the client's liaison with all service departments in the Center.

FINANCING

Scanticon International initiated this project, while a joint venture between Scanticon and Total Development Associates handled the development and construction. The project benefited from 100 percent financing furnished by the New York branch of Privatbanken A/S of Copenhagen.

MARKETING

Although the prime market area for Scanticon-Princeton is the region between Washington and Boston, the Center's location is accessible enough that its managers estimate that fully one-fifth of its business will come from foreign sources.

For corporate clients, Scanticon can handle management, training, and sales meetings. For associations, Scanticon specializes in management and training meetings. Currently, 60 to 70 percent of the Center's business arises from executive conference bookings obtained through sales of 24-hour conference packages. The other 30 to 40 percent comprises transient lodging business and local food and beverage sales.

The estimated market mix of guests in 1983 was:

Commercial travelers	25%
In-house conference groups	65
Tourists	10
	100%

The marketing department at Scanticon employs 13 persons. Five sales managers oversee direct sales efforts in eight geographic locations in the northeast corridor. Regular promotions through radio, television, professional journals, mailing lists, and travel agents constitute the yearly marketing plan.

Preopening marketing of this project began 20 months before opening. Brochures were printed and distributed. The preopening marketing effort enabled Scanticon to book a substantial amount of conference business before the facility opened.

EXPERIENCE GAINED

◆ During construction, the local community was kept informed through newspaper stories and advertisements of what Scanticon was and what the Scanticon facility would mean to the local economy. This proved to be a valuable policy.

◆ Interior construction schedules had to be tightly adhered to, because much of the furniture, fixtures, and equipment came from Europe. In fact, Scanticon moved its corporate headquarters from Denmark to Princeton so that the organization could have daily contact with local officials, tradespeople, and residents.

PROJECT DATA

Land Use Information
Site Area:	25 acres
Number of Rooms:	300
Floor Area Ratio (FAR):	.25
Parking Spaces:	450
Parking Index:	1.5 spaces per guest room

Land Use Plan

	Developable (acres)	Open Space (acres)	Total (acres)	Percent
Residential	93.8	112.9	206.7	13%
Commercial	28.0	3.0	31.0	2
Office/Research/ Conference Center	582.6	272.0	854.6	53
Forrestal Research Campus	277.0	83.0	360.0	23
Right-of-Way	—	—	151.4	9
			1,603.7	100%

Guest Room Mix

Room Type	Number of Rooms	Size (Square Feet)
Single	289	350–400
Suite	11	650
	300	

Food & Beverage Facilities

Name	Size (Square Feet)	Number of Seats
"Copenhagen Room"	4,600	230
"The Ugly Duckling"	1,660	40
"The Black Swan"	1,450	62
"Treehouse Lounge"	1,500	35
"Fireside Lounge"	600	15
"Tivoli Gardens"	5,100	225
"Tivoli Bar"	4,000	60
"Princeton Forrestal Campus Room"	4,400	230

Developer:	Total Development Associates New York, New York
Architecture/ Interior Design:	Friis & Moltke, Inc. Princeton, New Jersey

Meeting Space

Name	Capacity	Size (Square Feet)
Auditorium A	330–theater 230–classroom	4,956
Auditorium B	224–theater 165–classroom	2,996
Conference Room C	165–theater 120–classroom	2,432
Conference Room D	66–theater 48–classroom	1,200
Conference Room E	66–theater 48–classroom	1,184
Conference Room F	36–theater 28–classroom	868
Conference Room G	44–theater 32–classroom	950
Breakout Rooms (19)	8-20 persons	135 to 425

Economic Information
Land Rent	$ 1,640,000
Site Improvement Cost	$ 1,430,000
Construction Cost	$22,460,000
Fees	$ 1,750,000
Furniture, Fixtures, & Equipment	$ 5,130,000
Operating Equipment (china, glass, silver, linen, kitchen utensils)[1]	$ 400,000
Preopening Expenses	$ 2,000,000
Working Capital	$ 1,000,000
Total	$35,810,000

Total per Guest Room: $119,366

Operating Data

Year	Annual Average Occupancy (percent)	Annual Average Room Rent
1982	60	$ 79.00
1983	63	$ 85.00
1984[2]	66	$ 90.00
1985[2]	70	$ 95.00
1986[2]	73	$100.00

Notes
[1] Items with a short useful life.
[2] Projected.

Landscape Architecture:	Lane & Carruth, P.C. Pleasantville, New York
Management:	Scanticon International Princeton, New Jersey

HOLIDAY INN

Suburban Company-Owned Hotel ✦ Nashville, Tennessee

A twin-tower, high-rise hotel of contemporary design became the Nashville area's eighth Holiday Inn in March 1981. Holiday Inns intended the 14-story, 394-room, company-owned facility to appeal to vacationing families and to business travelers alike. To this end, the structure incorporates a six-story, glass-enclosed Holidome with recreational facilities geared to children and adults.

The Inn is located in the northeast section of Nashville, a quadrant heavily traveled by tourists because it contains the Grand Ole Opry, the Hermitage, Opryland, and the Opryland Hotel. All of these attractions are within a radius of two miles from the hotel.

The site is also two miles from the Nashville airport, five miles from downtown, and within one-half mile of an industrial park that is considered one of the best and most diversified in Nashville.

The Nashville Holiday Inn at Briley Parkway is near Opryland and the Grand Ole Opry.

153

THE SITE

The hotel is located at the intersection of Elm Hill Pike and Briley Parkway, a position that provides it with direct access to the airport and to Interstates 40, 24, and 65.

The flat, 5.27-acre site, which was leased in November 1978, is bounded by Sims Creek on one side. Because the site lies within the 100-year floodplain, the side bordering the creek bank required extra fill and retaining walls.

THE PLANNING AND DEVELOPMENT PROCESS

Holiday Inns, Inc., initiated the project after identifying its site in the targeted northeast market sector of Nashville. It then conducted a market analysis to define the demand potential of this market in general, as well as the potential and feasibility of the site in particular. Next, conceptual design of the hotel permitted the costs to be estimated. Lastly, the company management heard the results of a financial feasibility analysis (inclusive of operating pro formas), evaluated these data, and gave its authorization to proceed with the project.

The hotel caters to commercial and leisure travelers.

DESIGN

The size and architecture of this hotel differentiate it from Holiday Inns' traditional roadside motels. Twin masonry towers join to form a "V." At the point of the "V" is the 13,500-square-foot Holidome, which features a swimming pool with separate baby pool, a bar, a large-screen television, bumper pool facilities, table tennis, a putting green, a dry sauna, a whirlpool, and a gift shop.

Recognizing that the hotel would appeal to a mix of guests—to business travelers as well as to tourists—Holiday Inns considered the needs of both groups when planning the property. This facility includes 5,784 square feet of meeting space, which comprises: two meeting rooms of 450 square feet each; one meeting room of 684 square feet; and a 4,200-square-foot room (divisible into three equal, 1,400-square-foot sections) that has a banquet capacity of 400 persons. A dining room of 3,040 square feet (capacity 204) and a lounge of 3,224 square feet (capacity 208) complete the inventory of public facilities.

Most of the rooms—222 out of 394—have twin double beds, but 168 rooms provide king-size beds. These 390 rooms contain 216 square feet each. In contrast, four "parlors" offer 432 square feet of space each.

Although no extraordinary public approvals were required during the design or construction phases, the Board of Zoning Appeals did grant a variance to reduce the statutory amount of parking from 505 to 487 spaces.

The size and architecture of this Holiday Inn distinguish it from the traditional roadside facility.

FINANCING

The internally generated cash flow of Holiday Inns' operations entirely financed the project. Total project costs were $14,280,693, or $36,245 per guest room, 16 percent of which went on furniture, fixtures, and equipment.

MARKETING

The hotel caters to commercial and leisure travelers. The estimated mix of guests in 1983 was:

Commercial travelers	30%
Leisure travelers	27
Groups meeting at local convention center	15
Tourists	10
Others (including state and national associations)	18
	100%

The marketing program primarily aims to increase off-season commercial demand by using varied promotions. Also, however, the three members of the marketing staff make direct contact with corporate meeting planners to promote scheduling of meeting facilities, and solicit tour operators and state and national associations to sell rooms during the off-season period.

PROJECT DATA

Land Use Information

Site Area:	5.27 acres
Number of Buildings:	1
Number of Stories:	14
Number of Rooms:	394
Parking Spaces:	487
Parking Index:	1.24 spaces per guest room

Guest Room Mix

Room Type	Number of Rooms	Size (Square Feet)
Double/Double	222	216
King Regular	20	216
King Sofa	66	216
King Leisure	82	216
Parlor	4	432
	394	

Developer, Interior Design, & Management: Holiday Inns, Inc. Memphis, Tennessee

Architecture & Landscape Architecture: BWB Associates Memphis, Tennessee

Economic Information

Land Rent	$ 77,010
Site Improvement Cost	$ 916,717
Construction Cost	
Building Construction	$ 9,156,373
Fees (legal, architectural)	$ 521,954
Financing costs, insurance, & taxes during construction	$ 70,755
Furniture, Fixtures, & Equipment	$ 2,252,367
Operating Equipment (china, glass, silver, linen, etc., not in FFE)[1]	$ 108,728
Preopening Expenses	$ 331,029
Capitalized Interest	$ 845,760
Total Project Cost	$14,280,693

Cost per Room: $36,245

Operating Data

Year	Annual Average Occupancy (percent)	Annual Average Room Rent
1981[2]	74.4	$44.31
1982	74.8	$48.77
1983	77.1	$51.21

Notes
[1] Items with a short useful life.
[2] Nine months.

HOLIDAY INN

Suburban Franchise Hotel ✦ Westlake, Ohio

The Holiday Inn/Westlake is a commercially oriented suburban property located about 15 miles from both downtown Cleveland and the Cleveland–Hopkins International Airport. To enhance its appeal to commercial travelers, the hotel runs a courtesy airport limousine service. The Inn's Holidome and meeting facilities, however, appeal also to groups and to area residents—two demand segments that have already been successfully targeted by the hotel's marketing department. The Holidome, for instance, offers inducements for "hideaway" weekend retreats for local families.

Westlake is one of Cleveland's fastest growing and most affluent western suburbs. The hotel is therefore convenient to many upper-income area residents, as well as to a significant amount of commercial, office, and light industrial development. Current marketing programs include strategies for taking full advantage of this setting and for increasing the use of the hotel's facilities; one such strategy involves promoting a social and swim club to the Inn's residential, office, and commercial neighbors.

One of the major employers in the area, the Bonne Bell Corporation, lies just north of the Holiday Inn/Westlake, with only an eight-acre vacant parcel separating its headquarters from the hotel. The corporation is an important generator of room demand and of food and beverage business for the hotel; as a bonus, it makes its 1.5-mile jogging path with exercise stations available to guests of the Holiday Inn.

THE SITE

The Holiday Inn/Westlake occupies a nine-acre site on the western side of Crocker Road, less than one-half mile north of Interstate 90. Because the hotel is five stories high (the maximum height allowed by zoning restrictions), and because there are no intervening structures, the Inn is visible from the highway. Exit and entrance ramps serve Crocker Road from both westbound and eastbound lanes on Interstate 90.

The Holiday Inn/Westlake has 564 surface parking spaces.

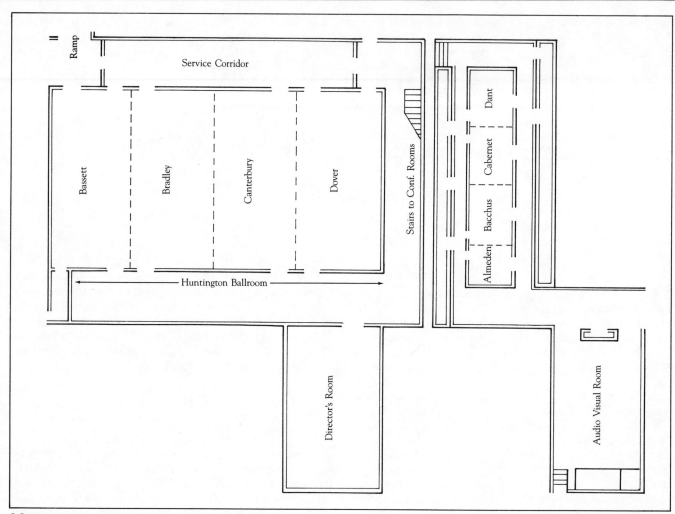

Meeting-room floor plan.

The site is essentially flat and was originally heavily wooded. During preparation for construction, in response to a requirement of the local planning department, the developers left many of the trees to buffer the hotel from the surrounding land uses. An additional requirement stipulated that 17 percent of the site be retained as "green area."

Land uses immediately surrounding the site include not only the Bonne Bell headquarters and plant, but also several other corporate installations to the north; a 70,000-square-foot office building, Interstate 90, a K-Mart, a supermarket, and a convenience shopping center to the south; service stations, a Red Roof Inn, and several office and corporate headquarters buildings to the east; as well as light industrial development to the west.

THE PLANNING AND DEVELOPMENT PROCESS

Fraser Mortgage Company, a family-owned firm headquartered in Westlake, had observed the local development activity and the contrasting lack of hotel accommodations. A family member conceived the idea that the development of a small motor hotel might be justified. After some research, and after discussions with potential users and hotel industry representatives, the concept evolved into the 265-room Holiday Inn/Westlake, a full-service hotel with a substantial amount of public space.

At one point, the plan had envisioned only 150 rooms, but, after they encountered difficulties in obtaining zoning in this community without regulations covering hotels, the developers decided to build a larger property and thereby avoid having to make a second zoning application. Ultimately, this was a good decision from a market standpoint as well; without this change of concept, the hotel would have been undersized, and neither the economic opportunity nor the value of the underlying land would have been optimized.

DESIGN

The frame-built facade of the Holiday Inn/Westlake conveys a country theme, with several Cape Cod elements. The result is a fresh look that differentiates the structure from that of a more standard Holiday Inn.

The indoor focal point is a four-story, covered atrium that houses most of the recreational amenities, as well as the Betsy Crocker Coffee Shop. A type of Holidome, this atrium is called The Oasis and extends to 11,000 square feet of floor space—lushly landscaped and brightened by a skylight.

Twenty of the hotel's 265 guest rooms are lanai suites overlooking The Oasis. These suites have king-size beds, wet bars, and tables large enough to accommodate private meetings. Guest rooms are located on all but the eastern side of The Oasis, off double-loaded corridors. The guest room block is of masonry construction.

Recognizing that the hotel would have to appeal to a mix of guests—commercial travelers, meeting/conference participants, and tourists—in order to be a viable project, the developers considered the needs and preferences of all three of these market segments in the facilities design and in the choice of decor. The several food and beverage outlets, for instance, provide varying experiences:

✦ Cahoon's. A formal dining room serving lunch and dinner, and decorated in a Victorian motif with leaded glass, copper, and oak. A nine-foot-high, hexagonal Wine Kiosk with leaded glass windows serves as a focal point for this 250-seat restaurant. The name of the dining room is that of the first residents of Westlake and is well known locally.

✦ Betsy Crocker. A coffee shop opening onto The Oasis and serving breakfast, lunch, and dinner daily. This name also encourages local patronage, as Betsy Crocker was the first schoolteacher in Westlake.

✦ The Upstairs Lounge. A quiet lounge resembling a private living room and intended primarily for subdued conversation. An open-air mezzanine overlooks The Oasis.

✦ Rapunzel's Lounge. An upbeat live-performance bar on weekends that offers more sedate entertainment on weeknights. The original concept for this room involved fast-paced entertainment exclusively. In response to guest reaction, however, the management decided to turn this lounge into a quieter room during the week.

The Inn's variety of recreational amenities attracts tourists, while also helping to differentiate the property in its marketing appeal to both commercial travelers and meeting attendees. The meeting and banquet space follows suit in targeting several market subsegments. This space comprises:

✦ A 6,000-square-foot ballroom, divisible into four sections.

✦ Four conference rooms, totaling 2,016 square feet, that may be used separately or as one room.

✦ An audiovisual theater that accommodates 60 persons in tiered, swivel-chaired rows. It offers a nine-by-nine-foot screen and is equipped to show both slides and movies.

✦ The Directors' Room, a facility designed for executive board meetings and small conferences that contains a built-in blackboard, a flipchart stand, 12 executive chairs, and an upscale boardroom table.

MARKETING

Four salespersons and one clerical support person constitute the marketing staff at the Holiday Inn/Westlake. The property's management has found the personal sales calls and contacts of the staff to be the single most effective initiative of the marketing program. Local radio and television spots were tried for the first few operating years but netted disappointing results. Local promotions such as charity programs have, however, proved valuable, as have the considerable benefits the hotel receives from its good working relationships with travel agents, and from its affiliation with Holiday Inn and with the Holidex reservation system.

EXPERIENCE GAINED

1) Project planning, development, and control

✦ Those involved in a project that will pioneer hotel development in a community should plan on spending a significant amount of time and money to educate local au-

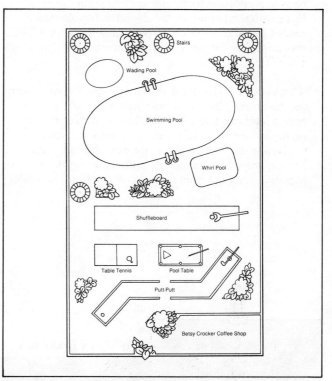

The four-story Holidome, called The Oasis, includes a 45-foot-long swimming pool, a sauna, a whirlpool bath, an exercise room, a game room, a putting green, a shuffleboard court, table tennis, and billiards.

thorities and to help create zoning regulations, building codes, and the like. If the community has not dealt with a project of this size before, the subject development will serve as a "guinea pig." The developer of such a project may also run into a small town mentality that assumes that a major commercial development will be lucrative enough to its backers that it can be forced to pay for other community improvements such as street paving and landscaping.

✦ While ensuring that project design and plans are complete, allow a contingency for revisions. The developers of this project spent $95,000 for additional work on plans that were not comprehensive.

✦ Recognize and make political use of the fact that a large suburban hotel project may act as a magnet to pull other commercial development into the area, raising the local tax base.

✦ Designate a single individual to monitor and control the project from conceptualization to opening. All contracts, expenditures, planning decisions, and other activities should process through this individual in order to obtain coordination of the development process.

2) Project costs

✦ Estimate preopening costs carefully, planning expenditures in proportion to the size and quality of the property. Preopening expenses at the Holiday Inn/Westlake exceeded initial estimates by 66 percent: although $300,000 was originally budgeted, actual expenses totaled about $500,000.

✦ Conformance with local authority requirements during the planning phase will not necessarily obviate unexpected later expenses. The developers on this project, for example, were required to put in an oversized elevator and to change the location of a fire exit after all plans had been approved by appropriate authorities, working drawings had been completed, and construction was under-

way. Again, the subject project may be paying for the education of local authorities as to appropriate fire, safety, traffic, and building codes for a project of this scope.

✦ Stipulate the amount of input and control that architects and designers will have on the management of the construction phase. Hiring a nonlocal equipment or interior designer may be much more costly than anticipated if, for instance, equipment should arrive at the construction site without proper supervision and instruction for the building crews.

3) Marketing and operations

✦ With a suburban hotel, direct sales may prove to be the most effective marketing method. At the Holiday Inn/Westlake, television, radio, and "giveaway" promotions were costly and largely unsuccessful. Direct sales efforts and local promotions, such as the contribution of meeting rooms to local charitable organizations, proved more productive.

✦ Generate a strategic business plan early in the development process. This plan should identify marketing objectives, management and organizational needs, staffing requirements, etc. All design, acquisition, staffing, and other such activities should tie into this strategic plan. With clear early decisions on the target market segments and on the type of facilities and services they will want, a hotel has a basis for evaluating potential purchases or expenditures.

✦ See that accounting and internal controls are carefully planned and "in place," both during construction and when operations begin. A company controller or an outside professional with broad experience in this type of project (from both the construction/development and operations angles) should prepare the plan of internal control and should conduct regular independent inspections. This person will help to prevent duplication of costs, untimely or unnecessary staffing, and other avoidable expenses.

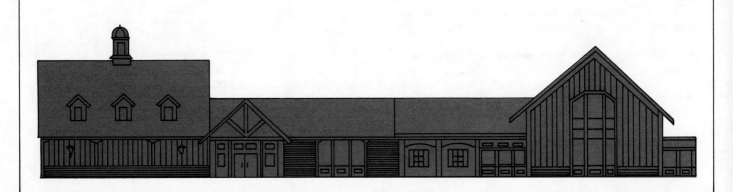

PROJECT DATA

Guest Room Mix	Number
Double/Double	113
King	132
Suites	20
	265

Food & Beverage Facilities	Number of Seats	Size (Square Feet)
"Cahoon's Dining Room"	250	3,365
"Betsy Crocker Coffee Shop"	75	1,500
"The Upstairs Lounge" and "Rapunzel's Lounge"	175	5,350
	500	

Meeting & Banquet Space	Banquet Seats	Theatre-Style Seats
Ballroom	600	1,000
Conference Rooms	150	375
Audiovisual Theater	—	60
Executive Boardroom	—	12
	750	1,447

Other Facilities & Services

- 564 parking spaces in surface lots.
- Holidome/health club, called "The Oasis," includes a 45-foot-long swimming pool, a sauna, a whirlpool bath, an exercise room with Universal equipment, a game room, a putting green, shuffleboard, table tennis, and billiards.
- Gift shop and car rental outlet.
- Wakeup service with complimentary coffee and newspaper.
- Secretarial and babysitting services.
- VIP limousine service to and from the airport.

Developer:	Fraser Mortgage Company Westlake, Ohio
Architect:	Bialosky & Manders Cleveland, Ohio
Interior Design:	Dimensional Interiors Beachwood, Ohio
Hotel Management:	Fraser Management Company Westlake, Ohio

Building Space Description	Gross Square Feet
Guest Rooms	99,065
Restaurants & Lounges	10,215
Lobby	2,080
Corridors	20,605
Kitchen	3,420
Mechanical & Housekeeping	8,245
Function Space	9,736
Retail/Lease	1,180
Recreational	12,225
Administrative Offices	4,800
Total	171,571

Economic Information

Site: 9 acres.

Economic Investment	Amount
Land acquisition	$ 440,000
Building & site costs	7,646,000
Fees (legal, architectural, interior design, etc.)	217,000
Financing costs, insurance, & taxes during construction	192,000
Operating equipment	150,000[1]
Preopening expenses	460,000
Working capital	895,000
Total investment[1]	$10,000,000[1]

Financing	
Equity—Fraser Mortgage	$ 1,200,000
Industrial revenue note, city of Westlake	7,800,000
Second mortgage— Broadview Savings & Loan	1,000,000
Total	$10,000,000

Note

[1] A separate capital expenditure by a leasing company provided $1.5 million for furniture, fixtures, and other equipment.

COMFORT INN

Economy Hotel ✦ Woodbridge, Virginia

Located one-half mile east of the Woodbridge/Occoquan interchange of Interstate 95, some 20 miles southwest of Washington, D.C., the 95-room Comfort Inn caters to business and pleasure travelers seeking comfort and convenience at a competitive price. The Inn is close to Mount Vernon, George Washington's estate, and equally near the numerous tourist attractions, events, museums, and theaters of Washington itself.

Room rates at this Comfort Inn are substantially below those charged for accommodations closer to the city. Thus, the Inn attracts rate-sensitive tourists who would prefer to make day trips to points of interest, as well as guests who have business in the vicinity or who are visiting friends or relatives nearby.

The Comfort Inn's site has an extent of 2.68 acres and lies on the eastern side of Horner Road. The land uses in the immediate area include a small strip shopping center to the north; a florist, a funeral home, and another shopping center to the south; an equipment rental establishment to the east; and an automobile dealership to the west. Generally, the Inn's neighbors comprise other service industries as well as residential concentrations.

The site is easily accessible from two interchanges on Interstate 95, although the property is not visible from this highway. To reach the property, southbound travelers take the Woodbridge/Route 1 exit, turn right on Gordon Boulevard/Route 123, and then turn left on Horner Road to the Inn. The suggested routing for northbound travelers involves taking the Woodbridge/Occoquan exit, bearing right toward Woodbridge on Route 123, and turning right on Horner.

In 1981, Quality Inns International announced that it was differentiating its product line to appeal to three distinct markets. One of the products of this differentiation, the Comfort Inns brand name provides an above-average room at a below-average price.

THE PLANNING AND DEVELOPMENT PROCESS

The developers of the Woodbridge Comfort Inn have been local residents for some time. They observed the business expansion in the market and, knowing the hotel supply situation there, decided that a budget/economy property would answer a need. They found the site, completed the site planning, obtained the necessary approvals, and negotiated all contracts within three months. The site was purchased on December 30, 1982; construction commenced in January 1983; and the Inn opened on May 27, 1983.

To provide financing, the Prince William County Industrial Development Authority passed an inducement resolution that authorized the developers to sell bonds. An underwriter then handled the sale of the bonds, which covered 100 percent of the project financing.

Prince William County approved the site and building plans; the site plan was also subject, however, to Virginia Department of Highways and Transportation approval on matters of vehicle access and amount of traffic generated.

DESIGN

A two-story brick structure with precast concrete interior walls, the Comfort Inn extends parallel to Horner Road. The lobby and office form a central unit, and two 48-room modules form wings on either side. Each 48-room module contains 16,588 square feet of guest rooms, while the middle section runs to 2,160 square feet and accommodates not only the lobby and an office, but also the manager's apartment, one small meeting room (828 square feet), an in-house laundry, a small amount of storage space, and a guest laundry room/game room.

Guest rooms range in size from 240 to 320 square feet and are reached from double-loaded corridors.

Lobby space at the Woodbridge Comfort Inn is modest and informal.

MARKETING

During this, the Inn's first year of operation, the general manager and assistant manager have been actively involved in its marketing program. Outside sales calls represent a permanent feature, as do continuing contacts with travel agents, bus tour operators, wholesalers, local association groups, and the Virginia Travel Council. Additionally, the Inn participates in Quality International's programs. The management company expects eventually to hire a sales and marketing staff member to work for both this property and another under its management. The company's philosophy maintains that even budget hotels need to be marketed well, and that overmarketing is preferable to undermarketing.

Projections of the market segmentation of guests here during the first operating year foresee this breakdown:

Commercial travelers	35%
In-transit tourists	30
Destination tourists	10
Military/government[1]	20
Bus tours	5
	100%

Further projections for these first 12 months of operation predict an occupancy level of about 70 percent and an overall average room rate of $36.00.

---

[1] From Fort Belvoir, Quantico, and the FBI.

EXPERIENCE GAINED

Based on the insights that the Madison Property Company gained in developing this Comfort Inn and several similar properties in the recent past, the company suggests:

◆ If at all possible, obtain a site directly visible from an interstate highway, at an interchange. Budget properties need visibility.

◆ Carefully consider the placement of the building on the site; the project may not present its best exposures to traffic patterns in the area. Passing traffic may view the back or the end of the building rather than the front of it, if the building clusters or centers around a restaurant or some other existing structure.

◆ Review the work of sign companies closely. On one occasion during the development of this property, a sign company positioned its product at the end of the building nearest the street but not nearest the hotel's automobile entrance. Potential guests left the interstate and drove toward the sign, eventually finding themselves either on the parking lot of a neighboring service station or in a ditch.

◆ Provide a weather-shielding overhang, marquee, or porte cochere at the lobby entrance for guest convenience. At the Woodbridge Comfort Inn, this consideration was omitted but will soon be added.

Guest rooms range in size from 240 to 320 square feet.

The typical Comfort Inn has 100 to 150 rooms. The Woodbridge facility is one of the smaller properties, with only 95 rooms. Guest rooms contain color televisions and direct-dial telephones.

PROJECT DATA

Guest Room Mix	Number	Size (Square Feet)
One Double Bed	46	240
Double/Double	37	288
King-Size Bed	8	320
Waterbed Suite	2	288
Jacuzzi Suite	2	320
	95	

Other Facilities & Services

- 156 parking spaces.
- Two outdoor hot tubs located in a raised wood deck in front of the Inn.
- Guest laundry room/game room with a limited number of washers, dryers, and game machines, plus candy, soft drink, and newspaper machines.
- Meeting room of 828 square feet that can also be rented for sleeping on capacity nights; has two bathrooms, a clothing rack, and a sofa that converts to a bed; several rollaway beds are also available.
- Complimentary coffee in the lobby.
- In-room movies.

Total square footage of building: 35,336 square feet.

Developer: Madison Property Company
Woodbridge, Virginia

Management: Madison Hotel Corporation
Woodbridge, Virginia

Economic Information

Site: 2.68 acres, purchased by the developer.

Economic Investment	Amount
Land acquisition cost	$ 308,000
Building and closing costs[1]	2,200,000
Legal fees	82,000
Financing costs, insurance, taxes, and interest during construction	450,000
Preopening expenses	60,000
Development overhead	50,000
Contingency and debt reserve	50,000
Total investment	$3,200,000
Total investment per guest room	$ 33,684

Financing: 100 percent financed through tax-exempt bonds: term, 20 years; fixed interest rate, 11.9 percent; first three years, only interest due.

Notes

[1]Includes site preparation; hard construction cost; architectural and design fees; furniture, fixtures, and equipment; and operating equipment (such as linen).

SUPER 8 LODGE

Economy Hotel ✦ Great Falls, Montana

Originally constructed in 1978 with 62 units, the Great Falls Super 8 Lodge adjoins a regional shopping mall and several food and beverage establishments. Two and one-half stories tall, the interior-corridor structure consists of rooms only, without additional amenities or facilities beyond a 24-hour desk. All rooms are furnished with a queen-size bed or beds, a color television, a direct-dial telephone, a full bathroom, and an individually controlled heating and air conditioning unit. Starting at $22.88 for single occupancy, room rates rise to $26.88 for double occupancy. As evidenced by a 55-room addition that opened in early 1984, the Super 8 has amply succeeded.

THE SITE

The Super 8 is situated just south of the central business district of Great Falls, on 13th Avenue South. Motorists cannot see it from any major highway, but it has easy access to Interstate 15 via Tenth Avenue. To the north and west are the Holiday Village Shopping Center and the adjacent food

and beverage outlets, respectively, while to the south and east are residential neighborhoods. A 109-room Holiday Inn and a 176-room Sheraton Inn stand about four blocks away on Tenth Avenue. The 1.6-acre site offers surface parking amounting to one space per guest room.

THE PLANNING AND DEVELOPMENT PROCESS

Midwest Lodging, Inc., was incorporated for the sole purpose of becoming a Super 8 Motel franchisee and developing this property in Great Falls. After a lengthy selection process, Midwest Lodging bought the present site on November 29, 1977, at a cost of $210,000 (about $3.00 per square foot). Construction began on the original 62-unit structure in February 1978 and took less than six months. The developer secured financing for the construction phase from the First Bank of Great Falls, and permanent financing from the First Bank with assistance from the Small Business Administration.

A typical Super 8 Lodge.

DESIGN

The architectural design derives from the English Tudor style, with beige stucco walls crossed by brown half-timbering—a common design for Super 8 Motels throughout the upper Midwest. To the exterior of the building, the developer has added a decorative balcony in the Tudor style for every two guest rooms. The balconies serve to cover the air conditioning exhaust grills, improving the motel's outward appearance.

All guest rooms are the same size, with only the arrangement of the furnishings differentiating them. (In later Super 8 developments, the offsetting of a wall has added space to the double rooms and reduced the size of single rooms by 24 square feet. As a result, the single rooms look less empty, with only the one bed, while the double rooms gain a more capacious look.) In the expanded units at Great Falls, as also in later Super 8 developments, the bathroom vanity is separated from the tub/shower and toilet with a door and wall, and from the bedroom with a false wall. With many travelers sharing rooms, this new design meets with wide success by accommodating two people in one room with greater privacy.

The economy hotel industry as a whole has suffered from a reputation for noisy guest rooms. At the Great Falls Super 8 Lodge, the developer installed extra sound board between guest rooms and insulated all inside walls with fiberglass. Midwest Lodging also used high-quality furnishings in each guest room. This decision raised the cost of initial construction but has saved money in the long run because the furniture has lasted well despite high occupancy levels.

In the newer units at Great Falls, the developer has installed both an elevator and a dumbwaiter (the latter for the use of cleaning and maintenance staff in moving supplies).

The original 62 units, however, do not benefit from either of these advantages. Although the building is only two and one-half stories tall, this design oversight means that those guests who travel with more than one piece of luggage may have a cumbersome task in carrying it up the stairs and down the hall.

MARKETING

The Great Falls Super 8 property relies heavily on the marketing department of the franchisor, Super 8 Motels (which receives 1 percent of gross room revenue to support national advertising for the chain). Super 8 Motels conducts its advertising through direct mail promotion to 17,000 U.S. travel agents, through advertisements placed in Republic and Northwest Orient flight magazines, and through sponsorship of 37 major sporting events seen in 24 million homes nationwide on ESPN, the cable television sports network. In addition, the chain carries out four quarterly promotions within its own system, each aimed at a different segment of the traveling public, e.g., Super 8 VIP Club members, senior citizens, or vacationers. On a local level, billboards promote the property, and the manager works closely with the Chamber of Commerce, Malstrom Air Force Base, and local businesses through semiannual direct mail and personal contacts.

The market mix is composed of commercial travelers (60 percent), tourists (25 percent), and convention business that overflows from nearby full-service properties (15 percent). Occupancy for the last three years has averaged over 90 percent—a situation that naturally called for the 1984 addition. The average room rate has risen from $15 in 1978 to $25 in 1983.

PROJECT DATA

Land Use Information
Site Area: 1.6 acres (69,696 square feet)
Total Rooms: 117
Parking Spaces: 117

Guest Room Mix

Room Type	Number	Size (Square Feet)
Queen Single	50	288
Queen Double	64	288 or 312
Handicap/Double	3	288
	117	

Developer and Management: Midwest Lodging, Inc. Aberdeen, South Dakota

Architect: Knight & Company Great Falls, Montana

Interior Design and Landscaping: Midwest Lodging, Inc. Aberdeen, South Dakota

Economic Information

	62 Units	55-Unit Addition
Economic Investment		
Land acquisition cost	$210,000	—
Site preparation cost	7,000	$ 5,000
Building construction cost	387,994	680,000
Furniture, fixtures, & equipment	119,407	147,500
Legal & architectural fees	8,938	5,000
Financing costs, insurance, & taxes during construction	8,548	20,000
Preopening expenses	18,272	-0-
Working capital	39,841	
Total investment	$800,000	$857,500
Total investment per guest room	$ 12,903	$ 15,591
Equity (percent of total investment)	25%	25%
Financed (percent of total investment)	75%	75%
	100%	100%

171

SIGNATURE INN

Economy Hotel ✦ Castleton, Indiana

The Signature Inn/Castleton is the third entry in a new chain. Its developer/operating agent—Master Developers, Inc.—was incorporated under the laws of Indiana on March 31, 1978, with the purpose of building, owning, operating, and franchising motels under the name "Signature Inns." On November 18, 1980, the company completed its capitalization of $4,500,000 through a public stock offering to Indiana residents.

Groundbreaking for the first Signature Inn was held on June 28, 1980, and it opened for business on March 12, 1981. In addition to the three properties already in existence, the chain has two additional facilities under construction and several others under development.

The concept of Signature Inns brings some new ideas to the lodging industry. Signature Inns specializes in providing services specifically for business and commercial travelers, who constitute a majority of U.S. motel guests, not only in the Midwest but nationwide.

Master Developers locates its motels, such as the Castleton property, at destination points of the business traveler.

Within these destination points, the ideal location is a "high traffic area" near food and beverage establishments. Signature Inns' motels do not provide on-premise food and beverage services; thus, construction and labor costs are minimized. This permits Signature Inns to give guests high-quality rooms at affordable prices.

THE SITE

The Signature Inn enjoys an excellent location in terms of visibility and accessibility from Interstate 465. Castleton, 10 miles northeast of downtown Indianapolis, is an upscale residential, retail, and commercial area. The site lies within the southwest quadrant of the interchange of Interstate 465 and Allisonville Road, adjacent to a Sunoco service station. Situated in the southeast quadrant is a Perkins Cake 'N' Steak restaurant, as well as a grocery store and retail outlets. The northwest quadrant contains a furniture store, a condo-

The Signature Inn in Castleton, Indiana, stands two stories tall and has a bronzed metal pitched roof, offset by piers of earthtone brickwork.

minium/apartment complex, and office buildings, while the northeast quadrant has the Castleton regional shopping mall and a variety of food and beverage outlets such as Chi Chi's, Mother Tucker's, Red Lobster, Wendy's, McDonald's, and Pizza Hut.

The site consists of 2.636 acres (114,824 square feet) and features virgin timber and natural storm drainage to a small lake. Zoning allowed for commercial use, with 126 hotel rooms plus one parking space apiece permissible.

THE PLANNING AND DEVELOPMENT PROCESS

Because of high interest rates and the difficulty of obtaining suitable financing for a large portion of the property's capital cost, a limited partnership program, Signature II, Ltd., was created to develop the Signature Inn/Castleton. The general partner was Signature Development Corporation, a wholly-owned subsidiary of Master Developers, Inc. The limited partners supplied the equity investment. The partnership hired and trained its own securities representatives to invest $1,975,000 of funds, or about $8,500 per partner, during a 15-month period ending March 15, 1983. The net proceeds of this public offering were $1,728,125. Construction financing came from Indiana National Bank through Indiana Mortgage Corporation, while First Indiana Federal Savings Bank furnished permanent financing in the amount of $1,650,000.

The general partner received a development fee of about $100,000 for developing the motel for the partnership. Other agreements made by Signature II, Ltd., include: (1) a franchise contract with Master Developers, Inc., which receives a 3 percent franchise fee based on gross room revenue; and (2) a management agreement also with Master Developers, Inc., which receives a fee of 4.5 percent of gross room revenue for performing accounting and management services.

The terms of the partnership provide for the allocation of the cash distributions, profits, losses, and tax credits on the following basis: 1 percent to the general partner and 99 percent to the limited partners until they receive an amount equal to their original investment. Thereafter, the benefits will be assigned at the rate of 15 percent to the general partner and 85 percent to the limited partners.

Signature II optioned the site for a six-month period in order to perform a market and site analysis and to clear zoning requirements. It then purchased the site on November 5, 1982, with construction commencing four days later. The construction phase lasted less than six months, and the property opened on May 26, 1983.

DESIGN

The architecture of the Signature Inn may be described as simple and modern, with an emphasis on function and on the quality of its furnishings.

The building stands two stories tall and has a bronzed metal pitched roof offset by piers of earthtone brickwork. The guest rooms contain 312 square feet each, 228 square feet of which is living area, including a large desk and work space and a reclining chair. The beds are queen-sized. Although no food and beverage facilities are provided, a small amount of quality meeting space is available off the two-story lobby. This block of space amounts to 2,279 square feet divided among five rooms. A 918-square-foot executive conference room with premium audiovisual equipment, an adjacent 150-square-foot conference room, and a convertible suite containing 587 square feet, complete the motel's inventory of meeting space.

Although the Signature Inn does not provide food and beverage service, it does offer a small amount of meeting space off its lobby.

Guest rooms contain 312 square feet, 228 square feet of which is living area. All beds are queen-sized.

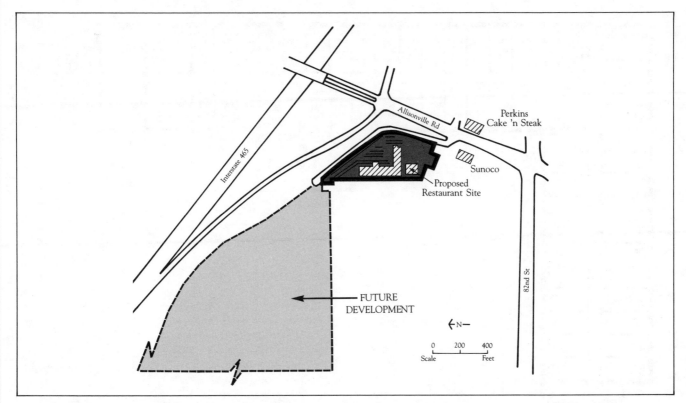

Master Developers locates its motels in "high traffic areas" near food and beverage establishments.

MARKETING

The Signature Inns concept involves economy-priced, limited-service accommodations without food and beverage facilities, catering to business travelers and providing special features to meet their needs. Room rates for single occupancy come to $33, and for double occupancy, $38. Although business travelers represent the primary market served, Signature Inns also targets pleasure travelers by offering free lodging for children under 12 and a senior citizen discount of 10 percent. The properties' market mix approximates 70 percent commercial and business travelers, 10 percent in-house groups, and 20 percent tourists and bus tours.

The Castleton Signature Inn offers these special features:

◆ A guest office where guests may use a typewriter and a calculator.

◆ Interview centers that provide appropriate settings for business interviews.

◆ Storage for guests' clothing and business items over the weekend.

◆ Telephone centers where business calls may be made in privacy and comfort.

◆ Free HBO movies, complimentary coffee, cable TV, and an outdoor pool.

No marketing department as such exists, but the manager and a secretary handle the local marketing responsibilities. Marketing tools include two roadside billboards, a monthly advertisement in the *Indianapolis Business Journal,* and word-of-mouth publicity from guests. Also, the motel has an "800" toll-free reservation number and a directory brochure. The local business, of course, became acquainted with the facility at the grand opening party that introduced it to the community.

EXPERIENCE GAINED

◆ Financing through limited partnership interests helps to minimize the inherent risk of the motel business. One of its advantages in this case was that the over 200 financially interested limited partners lived near the property and could help to promote it by directing potential guests there and by their own word-of-mouth advocacy.

◆ In future, properties should consider including more king-bedded rooms than they do now. These have substantial appeal both to tourist couples and to business travelers.

◆ With regard to motel fixtures, increasing the size of the vanity counter from three feet to four feet and making it separate from the bathroom have proved to be popular decisions at the Signature Inn/Castleton.

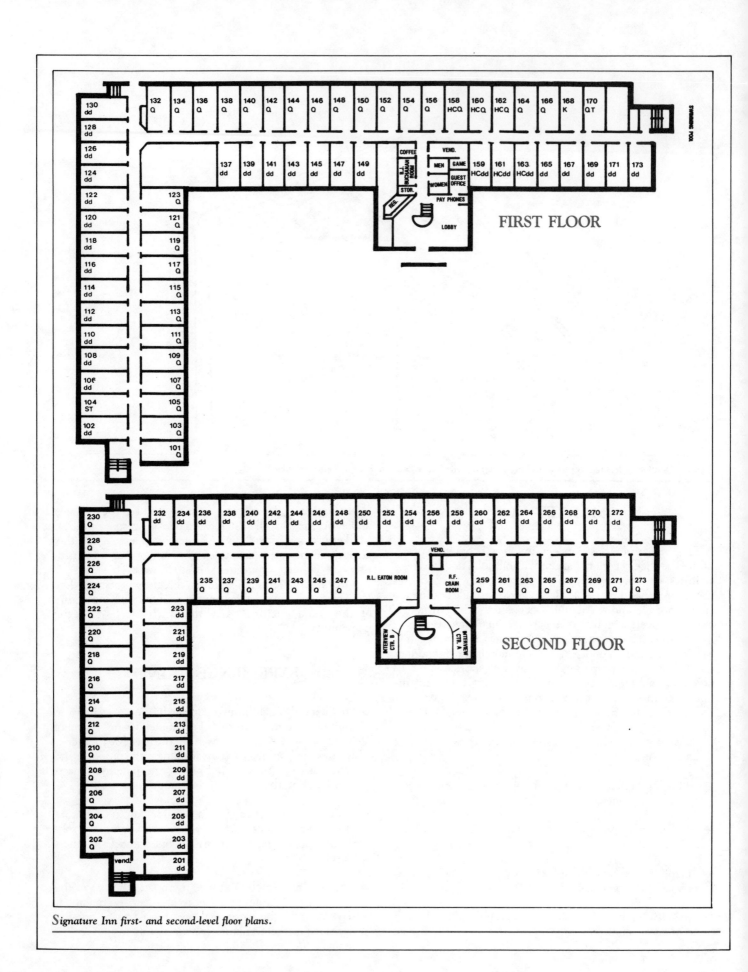

Signature Inn first- and second-level floor plans.

PROJECT DATA

Land Use Information
Site Area: 2.636 acres (114,824 square feet)
Total Rooms: 126
Parking Spaces: 126 surface spaces

Guest Room Mix

Room Type	Number	Size (Square Feet)
Studio	2	312
Double/Double	62	312
Queen Single	60	312
King Single	1	312
Suite	1	587
	126	

Meeting Space

Room Type	Number	Size (Square Feet)
Small Meeting Room	1	150
Professional Conference Room	1	918

Developer: Master Developers, Inc.
Indianapolis, Indiana

Architecture: LOM Corporation
Indianapolis, Indiana

Management: Master Developers, Inc.
Indianapolis, Indiana

Economic Information
Economic Investment

Land acquisition		$ 353,000
		($3.94 per sq. ft.)
Site improvement cost		99,000[1]
		$ 452,000
Cost per room	$ 3,587	
Building construction cost		2,126,000
Cost per room	16,873	
Furniture, fixtures, & equipment cost		455,000[2]
Cost per room	3,611	
Fees		73,000[2]
Cost per room	579	
Financing costs, insurance, & taxes during construction		20,000
Cost per room	159	
Preopening cost		17,000
Cost per room	135	
Working capital		135,000
Cost per room	1,071	
Development fees		100,000
Cost per room	794	
Total investment	$26,809	$3,378,000

Equity (percent of total investment)	51.0%[3]
Financed (percent of total investment)	49.0%
	100.0%

Notes
[1] Includes site utilities and landscaping.
[2] Excludes capital leases of $175,000 on telephone system for five years, televisions for seven years, and two signs for five years.
[3] Permanent financing was in the amount of $1,650,000 for a 15-year term with a 25-year amortization schedule. The rate is 13½%, fixed for the first five years, with adjustments at the fifth and tenth years tied to the Treasury constant. There is a substantial prepayment penalty; however, six months before the fifth and tenth anniversary dates, there is a window for prepayment without penalty.

GRANADA ROYALE HOMETEL

All-Suite Suburban ✦ Bloomington, Minnesota

The Granada Royale Hometel in Bloomington, Minnesota, is but one representative of an interesting departure from the mainstream of hotel development trends. In recent years, the lodging industry has in fact experimented with several new concepts to better meet the needs of specific market subsegments. One such experiment began in 1969 with Granada Royale Hometels and achieved its most upscale form in 1972 with Guest Quarters. The all-suite hotel as developed by these two chains stresses the guest room's combining both a parlor and a bedroom, as well as, in some cases, a kitchen. This kind of hotel eliminates or downplays restaurants and other traditional public space. The apparent market success of these two chains has encouraged others such as Brock Hotel Corporation and Brookhollow Inns to develop similar properties, and even large national chains have diversified to include all-suite facilities. (In December 1983, Holiday Inns acquired the Granada Royale Hometels system and added it to its Embassy Suites division.)

THE CONCEPT

These hotels feature guest room space that is larger than normal, with a living/parlor area separated from the sleeping area, and with cooking and refrigeration equipment. The homelike public space usually offers only limited amenity packages.

Because all-suite hotels are so new in concept, their site and market objectives frequently differ from those of standard hotels. While all-suite chains generally choose sites that stand to benefit directly from local commercial and retail activity, exactly how near a site is to commercial demand generators depends on the market position of the particular chain. Additionally, because most of the captured commercial demand is confined to one market area, highway visibility makes less difference here than it does to conventional lodging properties.

Although most all-suite hotels have minimal public meeting and banquet space, they are still gaining increased acceptance in the executive corporate meetings market. Functions such as board meetings are increasingly taking place at all-suite properties because corporate meeting planners are attracted to:

✦ The lower overall volume of in-house group business than occurs in a conventional hotel;

✦ The higher level of personal service; and

✦ The guest accommodations—more spacious than standard hotel rooms, with separate living areas conducive to work as well as to relaxation.

International travelers, who typically stay longer, also enjoy the relatively spacious accommodations. Additionally, these travelers are less price sensitive than many domestic travelers, as their native countries have, in most cases, higher average room rates than those in effect in this country.

All-suite hotels can boast higher annual occupancy levels than their conventional competitors as a result of their stronger penetration both of the weekday transient commercial demand and of the long-term, seven-day-a-week demand that may represent as much as 15 to 20 percent of business. These hotels also improve upon their competitors by achieving substantially higher average room rates.

Significantly, the all-suite concept is not a homogeneous one. While much diversity exists between properties, all-suite hotels fall roughly into three categories: urban, suburban, and residential.

High-end urban properties presently include Guest Quarters and Brock Park Suite Hotels. These are characteristically of mid- to high-rise construction and situated in urban locations near full-service hotels.

Granada Royale Hometels typify the suburban all-suite category. These (usually mid-rise) properties stand in suburban commercial areas.

Residential all-suite properties encompass Brock Residence Inns, Brookhollow Inns, and Lexington Motor Inns. This category is the most land intensive of the three, and its hotels offer the largest number of in-room amenities and the fewest in-hotel support services.

GRANADA ROYALE HOMETELS

BACKGROUND AND EVOLUTION

The first Granada Royale Hometel opened in Phoenix in 1969. Plans for a 75-unit apartment complex had been amended to add lobby space, a telephone system, and a laundry. Later Hometels have looked somewhat less like apartments, but have still provided a residential atmosphere. The guest-unit kitchens, for instance, have gone from complete apartment-style facilities to smaller, galley kitchen/wet bar combinations.

In 1972, the six-story, 191-suite Granada Royale Hometel in Omaha initiated another change with its enclosed atrium. This design choice has been generally repeated in cold climates. All future Hometels will employ an enclosed, skylighted atrium rather than the open one that previous properties had used as a kind of trademark.

Marketing efforts for Hometels started with the offering of a full complimentary American-style breakfast cooked to order, plus unlimited evening cocktails during a two-hour open bar. Hometels' goal was to strengthen local market presence through word-of-mouth advertising. Recently, Granada Royale Hometels has begun a national advertising campaign and more extensive marketing efforts through a new national sales organization and public relations program.

The first Hometels offered no food and beverage service, aside from the complimentary breakfast and afternoon cocktails. They also afforded very limited meeting facilities. Later Granada Royale designs, however, have incorporated full-service restaurants, which were leased to experienced outside operators.

The Granada Royale Hometel in Bloomington, Minnesota.

DESIGN

Granada Royale Hometels traditionally use a Spanish architectural theme, with four to eight floors of 200 to 300 suites surrounding a landscaped atrium/courtyard. (When the open atrium design was used in all of Hometels' earlier warm-weather locations, it increased building costs by up to 5 percent. On the other hand, in earlier cold-climate locations and in all of the newer structures, where the company has preserved the lush garden atmosphere of the courtyard by enclosing it with a skylighted ceiling, these building costs have amounted to as much as 10 percent higher than the old ones.) Hometel suites average nearly 560 square feet of living room and bedroom space. Normally, 5 percent of the suites are executive suites, which are standard except for an attached boardroom for meetings of eight to 12 persons.

THE GUEST SPACE

Granada Royale Hometels provide each guest with a two-room suite that includes a separate bedroom, a separate living room with a queen-size hide-a-bed, a wet bar, and a galley kitchen with range, refrigerator, pots, pans, dishes, and tableware. The dining area has a large table that can double as a desk or a conference table. Both the bedroom and the living room have a telephone and a television set, and the bedroom's television runs by remote control.

Guest room appointments resemble those found in a similar-priced traditional guest room but not those found in a suite accommodation in a typical hotel, although every Hometel suite does contain high-quality fixtures and furnishings. Each bedroom, for example, has two large armoires custom designed for the company at a cost of $800 apiece, and each suite benefits from the chain's expenditure of about 50 percent more for its carpeting than is spent on the average by the industry as a whole. In addition, the countertops in many Hometels are either marble ones imported from Italy or ceramic tile ones from Mexico.

AMENITIES AND SERVICES

Most Granada Royale Hometels offer a pool, a whirlpool bath, and a gift shop, while some also offer a steam room and a sauna. Clubhouses or patio/reception areas in the hotel's central courtyards serve as settings for the complimentary breakfasts and cocktails. All Granada Royale Hometels offer some meeting rooms.

Personalized service is central to the Hometel image, although the service offered is necessarily less extensive than that offered by full-service convention hotels or by urban suite operations such as Guest Quarters. Typical Hometel services and amenities include:

✦ A full-service restaurant, offering lunch and dinner, at most locations.

- ◆ Meeting space—up to 12,000 square feet—at all properties.
- ◆ Banquet and catering capabilities provided or available at most locations.
- ◆ Car rental referral service at all locations.
- ◆ Room service at all locations with restaurants.
- ◆ Coin-operated washers and dryers on all premises, usually on every other floor.
- ◆ Tennis, golf, and horseback riding available off the premises in some cities.
- ◆ Outdoor gas grills in all open atrium/courtyards.

SITES

Granada Royale Hometels has generally developed sites in middle- to upper-middle-class suburban areas, near regional shopping centers, with the ideal location one between the best residential section and the best business district. The management believes that potential sites need not be in dense commercial areas but must be convenient to such areas, because most properties cater primarily to corporate travelers. Thus, Hometels may be closer to residential neighborhoods than is usual for suburban hotels, and this situation enhances their capture of such demand segments as families on getaway weekends and corporate personnel who are relocating.

Construction costs of Hometels range between $13 and $30 million, depending on land costs and on the number of suites and floors.

MARKETING

The chain receives its strongest market support from mid-level professionals employed by medium-sized companies. These professionals are between 25 and 54 years old and earn more than $40,000 per year. Many guests hold sales or marketing positions. They generally patronize Granada Royale Hometels because they are "trading up" to obtain a better price/value relationship through Hometels' larger guest space and through its complimentary food and beverages. Granada Royale Hometels also capture family weekend demand; however, many properties find it necessary to offer package programs with discounted rates to attract these guests. Nationwide, Granada Royale's market is composed as follows:

Single commercial travelers and small corporate meetings	73%
Tourists and others	27
	100%

The broad market appeal of the Hometel concept has enabled chain performance to rise consistently above that of the industry as a whole. Over the last five years, Granada Royale has not only increased its total market penetration but has also significantly raised its average room rate. Comparative performance both in secondary markets such as El Paso and in primary markets such as Kansas City has been strong. In fact, most Granada Royale Hometels compete effectively with mid-market hotels and motor inns such as Marriott Hotels, Sheraton Hotels, Hilton Inns, and, to a lesser extent, with first-class hotels and quality independent properties.

THE BLOOMINGTON PROPERTY

At the Granada Royale Hometel in Bloomington, Minnesota, all 219 suites overlook the enclosed, skylighted atrium/courtyard with its Spanish-style fountains. The lushly landscaped facility features a pool, sauna, steam room, and whirlpool, while a full-service, 140-seat restaurant serves lunch and dinner and caters banquets and receptions. A gift shop may be found in the lobby, and the Hometel provides free parking, a coin-operated laundry, and free transportation to the Minneapolis-St. Paul International Airport. Four meeting rooms offer 6,000 square feet of space. The hotel, which stands on leased land, opened in 1981.

PROJECT DATA

Land Use Information
Site Area: 4.8 acres (207,345 square feet)
Parking Spaces: 425

Land Use Plan

	Square Feet
Building	342,396 (total of eight floors)
Drives and Parking	108,678
Recreation, Landscaping	55,800

Guest Room Mix

Type	Number	Size (Square Feet)
King	85	522
Double/Double	120	556
Executive	14	1,030
	219	

Economic Information
Construction Cost: $8,072,480

RAMADA RENAISSANCE

Multitiered Marketing Strategies ◆ Atlanta, Georgia

Until recently, almost every hotel chain confined itself to one well-defined market segment. Those chains that appealed to the budget, middle, executive, or luxury markets were clearly distinguishable. While an occasional chain property might position itself to cater to a nontraditional market, the focus of the parent company remained unchanged.

A recent phenomenon that is gathering momentum is the diversification of major lodging chains into markets above or below their usual focuses. Quality Inns was the first company to attempt a multitiered marketing strategy. It introduced Comfort Inns (economy) and Quality Royale (executive) to complement its Quality Inn (middle-market) line. This effort was quickly followed by Ramada's announcement, first of Ramada Renaissance, then of Ramada Hotels.

RAMADA'S CONCEPT

Ramada has structured its stratification somewhat differently from that of Quality Inns. While Quality's products address the budget, mid-priced, and executive markets, all three of the Ramada property lines fall within the mid-priced to executive range. Ramada Inns are not budget properties, nor do Ramada Renaissance operations attract the true lux-

The 510-room Ramada Renaissance Hotel in Atlanta was built for approximately $63,000 per room.

The Ramada Renaissance Hotel in downtown San Francisco is part of Ramada's effort to target the "mid-priced luxury" market.

ury customer. Some luxury-market customers do in fact stay at these properties, but the latter are really only designed to capture the middle- to upper-middle market. Renaissance properties may maintain the same quality standards and offer the same level of service as do many traditional luxury hotels. But they offer these similar services and provide comparable amenities for what Ramada believes to be a better price/value ratio.

Ramada products differ from each other not only in price range (within the middle market), but also in the market area in which they are located. As a result, they also differ in the nature of the customers who visit their market areas. For example, customers traveling to a very small city neither expect nor need some amenities and levels of service. Thus, the attentions of a doorman are probably unjustified at a roadside property where customers park a few steps from their rooms. Similarly, 24-hour concierge service is unnecessary in a market whose entertainment and dining options are limited. In a major city, however, these services are not only desirable but expected, as are extended hours and options for food and beverage service.

Upscale operators such as Sheraton, Hilton, Hyatt, and Westin are precluded from many smaller and medium-sized cities by the nature of their operations. They are, therefore, losing potential custom in these small or medium-sized markets. Budget operators, on the other hand, are precluded from entering the medium-sized and certainly the major downtown markets by the nature of *their* operations. Ramada's strategy has been to provide a product in every market from the lower end of the mid-priced range to the upper end of it. For example, Washington, D.C., Atlanta, and Denver each have a Ramada Inn, a Ramada Hotel, and a Ramada Renaissance. Whatever customers' reasons for travel, they will find appropriate Ramada accommodations in these cities.

Ramada will retain a renovated Ramada Inn product line to appeal to the large value-oriented market to which it has always catered. More than $90 million has been spent on redesigning and refurbishing most Inns owned by the parent company, and another $300 million has been spent by franchisees. Less profitable hotels have been sold, and by the end of March 1983, 156 franchise properties that could not or would not go along with the product improvement program had been removed from the system. Ramada Inns are typically found in cities and towns near major thoroughfares. They offer amenities such as informal and specialty restaurants, meeting space, convenient parking, pools, and lounges (the latter often featuring entertainment).

Ramada Hotels function as a middle tier between Ramada Inns and Ramada Renaissance hotels. The mid- to high-rise Ramada Hotels stand at airports, in the suburbs of major cities, and in some downtowns. They offer a larger variety of dining and entertainment options, more meeting space, more recreational facilities, and a higher level of service than do Ramada Inns, but they lack some of the special amenity packages required of all Ramada Renaissance hotels, such as concierge floors.

On the uppermost tier, Ramada Renaissance hotels have positioned Ramada to compete with executive-class chains.

Major distinctions between Renaissance products and Ramada Hotels again fall along the lines of higher levels of service and more amenities. Located near major airports or in the downtown business districts of larger cities, both domestic and foreign, Ramada Renaissance hotels offer accommodations, services, and amenities usually found only in luxury hotels, but at a lower price.

THE ATLANTA PROPERTY

The 510-room Ramada Renaissance Hotel in Atlanta houses one ballroom, 13 meeting rooms, and six boardrooms; it offers an indoor pool, a whirlpool, an exercise room, a gift shop, a car rental counter, airport shuttle service, a club floor, 24-hour concierge service, and a game room. The hotel has four distinct food and beverage areas.

The hotel opened a week earlier than was projected and came in at $800,000 under its construction budget. The final cost for the property amounted to about $63,000 per room, which includes almost $10,000 per room for land cost, loan interest at approximately 18 percent, and expenses for extraordinary site work.

The marketing strategy for the hotel has aimed to establish a strong commercial-business base and has so far succeeded. After only a few months of operation, the hotel achieved an occupancy rate of 83.1 percent. Both this rate and the average daily room rate have substantially exceeded projections, while the lobby bar and the formal dining room have both surpassed the developer's most optimistic expectations.

*T*he Ramada Renaissance Hotel in Washington, D.C., has 341 rooms, 16 suites, and two restaurants. Single rooms command $85 to $95 per night, and doubles, $105 to $115.

PROJECT DATA

Land Use Information
Site Area: 9.5 acres

Guest Room Mix

Type	Size (Square Feet)	Number
Double	375 (approx.)	233
King	375 (approx.)	160
Suite	(Various)	32
Presidential	(Four rooms)	2
Honeymoon	(Five rooms)	1
Miscellaneous	(Various)	82
		510

Restaurants

Name	Type	Seats
"La Martine"	Entertainment Lounge	114
"Le Cygne"	Fine Dining	150
"Summerfield's"	Informal Dining	100
"Lobby"	Lounge	60

Public Space

Type	Size (Square Feet)	Number
Grand Ballroom	5,000	1
Meeting Room	600 each	13
Boardroom	264 each	6

Economic Information
Site Acquisition Cost: $3,800,000
Site Improvement Cost: $642,403 (rock, grading, drainage, etc.)

Construction Cost

Hard costs	$16,082,000 (excluding parking)
Soft costs	5,215,597
Furniture, fixtures, and equipment	6,284,000
Total	$27,581,597

Parking

Structured	$762,000
Unstructured	116,000
Total	$878,000

Developer: Ramada Inns, Inc.
Phoenix, Arizona

Architect: Rabun, Hatch & Dendy
Atlanta, Georgia

Interior Design: Trisha Wilson Associates
Dallas, Texas

APPENDICES

APPENDIX A

SELECTED LIST OF HOTEL CHAINS

Americana Hotels
532 S. Michigan Avenue
Chicago, Illinois 60605

Best Western
Box 10203
Phoenix, Arizona 85064

Brock Hotel Corporation
4441 W. Airport Freeway
Irving, Texas 75062

Days Inn
2751 Buford Highway, N.E.
Atlanta, Georgia 30324

Doral Hotels
600 Madison Avenue
New York, New York 10022

Downtowner Inns
5350 Poplar Avenue
Memphis, Tennessee 38119

Dunfey Hotels
500 Lafayette Road
Hampton, New Hampshire 03842

Econo-Travel Motor Hotels
20 Koger Executive Center
Norfolk, Virginia 23502

Four Seasons Hotels
1100 Eglington Avenue East
Toronto, Ontario M3C18H

Friendship Inns of America
739 S-400 West
Salt Lake City, Utah 84101

Gulf & Western Hotels
One Gulf & Western Plaza
New York, New York 10023

Helmsley Hotels
455 Madison Avenue
New York, New York 10022

Hilton Hotels Corp.
9880 Wilshire Blvd.
Beverly Hills, California 90024

Holiday Inn, Inc.
3742 Lamar Avenue
Memphis, Tennessee 38118

Howard Johnson's
220 Forbes Road
Braintree, Massachusetts 02184

Hyatt Hotels
9700 W. Bryn Mawr
Rosemont, Illinois 60018

Imperial 400 Motor Inns
1830 N. Nash Street
Arlington, Virginia 22209

Inter-Continental Hotels
200 Park Avenue
New York, New York 10166

Knights Inn
6561 E. Livingston
Reynoldsburg, Ohio 43068

L-K Motels
1125 Ellenkay Drive
Marion, Ohio 43302

La Quinta Motor Inns
Century Building
San Antonio, Texas 78216

Loews Hotels
666 Fifth Avenue
New York, New York 10103

Marriott Corporation
One Marriott Drive
Washington, D.C. 20058

Meridien Hotels
1350 Avenue of the Americas
New York, New York 10019

Motel 6 Inc.
51 Hitchcock Way
Santa Barbara, California 93105

Omni International Hotels
One Omni International Plaza
Atlanta, Georgia 30335

Quality Inns International
10750 Columbia Pike
Silver Spring, Maryland 20901

Radisson Hotels
12805 State Highway 55
Minneapolis, Minnesota 55441

Ramada Inns
3838 E. Van Buren Street
Phoenix, Arizona 85008

Red Carpet Inns International
454 Moss Trail
Goodlettsville, Tennessee 37072

Red Roof Inns, Inc.
4355 Davidson Road
Amlin, Ohio 43002

Regent International Hotels
600 Second Street, N.W.
Albuquerque, New Mexico 87102

Rodeway Inns International
2525 Stemmons Freeway
Dallas, Texas 75207

Sheraton Hotels
60 State Street
Boston, Massachusetts 02109

Sonesta International Hotels Corp.
John Hancock Tower
Boston, Massachusetts 02116

Stouffer Hotels
29800 Bainbridge Road
Solon, Ohio 44139

Summit Hotels International
2525 Stemmons Freeway
Dallas, Texas 75207

Super 8 Motels
224 Sixth Avenue, S.E.
Aberdeen, South Dakota 57401

Thunderbird/Red Lion Motor Inns
4001 Main Street
Vancouver, Washington 98666

TraveLodge International
250 TraveLodge Drive
El Cajon, California 92090

Trusthouse Forte Ltd.
810 Seventh Avenue
New York, New York 10019

Westin Hotels
Western Building
Seattle, Washington 98121

APPENDIX B

Preliminary Development Commitment Agreement
for the
Development of the Downtown Hotel/
Convention Center/Retail Complex in Pueblo, Colorado,
between
the City of Pueblo, Colorado, and

———————————————

This Preliminary Development Commitment Agreement, made this _____ day of _____, 19 ____, by and between the City of Pueblo, Colorado (hereinafter referred to as "City"), and _____ (hereinafter referred to as "Developer").

WITNESSETH THAT

WHEREAS, the City, a municipal corporation of the State of Colorado, wishes to implement a program for the purpose of rebuilding and revitalizing the core area pursuant to state and local laws; and

WHEREAS, the City has retained development consultation services from the firm of _____

_____
and has authorized them to act in cooperation with the Developer to determine the size, reuse characteristics, and the potential relationships of publicly provided facilities to complement the construction of privately owned facilities as part of an integrated project to be redeveloped in Pueblo, Colorado, and to assist the City's needs to define financial implications for public involvement in the aforementioned project elements; and

WHEREAS, _____, in concert with the Developer, has indicated that the designated site area, defined as the blocks bordered by 1st Street, Santa Fe Avenue, Union Avenue, Richmond Avenue and Mechanic Street, or any contiguous parcel(s) that might be subsequently designated, is appropriate for the development of a combination of public and private buildings; namely, a "mixed-use" redevelopment project consisting in part of the following uses and approximate sizes: a hotel of 300 rooms; retail facilities of 60,000 square feet gross leaseable area; exhibition and meeting space of between 30,000 and 40,000 square feet gross floor area; and a variety of public site improvements (parking garage, plazas or malls, etc.); and

WHEREAS, the parties hereto deem it to their mutual benefit to cooperate and coordinate the development to maximize its attraction and beauty as an asset mutually beneficial to each party hereto; and

WHEREAS, each party hereto deems it to be to its mutual benefit to outline and establish this Preliminary Development Commitment Agreement as a guideline for all subsequent cooperation and interaction between said parties; and

WHEREAS, each party hereto recognizes and deems it to its mutual benefit, subject to further determinations of feasibility, to commit the maximum coordination for public and private financing of the project in order to maximize the commitment to high standards of quality, use and utility; and

WHEREAS, to accomplish the purpose herein described, the City has determined that the public interest can best be served by the execution of this Preliminary Development Commitment Agreement with the Developer in which the Developer: warrants the contribution of in-kind consultation and packaging services in conjunction with the filing of federal grant applications related to the project; warrants to program and construct the privately owned components of the Preferred Development Program in concert with the publicly owned components of said Program, which shall be designed and constructed under applicable state and local law; and

WHEREAS, in recognition that both the City and the Developer shall incur project-related costs prior to the site being secured by the public sector (October 30, 1980), the City and the Developer agree that in the event either party defaults on the terms of this Agreement prior to November 1, 1980, the party not in default shall be fully reimbursed for all reasonable and documented project-related costs up to a maximum of Twenty Thousand Dollars ($20,000). The party not in default

may, solely at its discretion waive the payment of such funds, concur in an extension date to facilitate public ownership of the project site, and continue to operate under the terms of this Agreement; and

WHEREAS, the City shall continue its association with _____

_____, during the provision of architectural and engineering services in the construction of said components; and

WHEREAS, this Preliminary Development Commitment Agreement is to be followed by more definitive agreements specifically defining the roles and responsibilities of all involved parties in the development of this Project.

NOW, THEREFORE, for and in consideration of the mutual promises herein contained, the receipt and sufficiency of which is hereby acknowledged, the parties heretofore mutually agree as follows:

Section 1. Public Sector Commitments

A. The City hereby acknowledges that the public capital funds necessary to construct the Convention/Conference Center and the project infrastructure (parking, utilities, roads, etc.) are not now locally available, therefore necessitating the City's application for state and/or federal funding assistance to carry out its construction obligations. As a priority commitment the City is now prepared to apply for funds available under the Urban Development Action Grant Program and programs of the United States Economic Development Administration. The remaining public funds shall be provided from federal Community Development monies and appropriate local sources on a timely basis. Depending upon the timely execution of preliminary development commitments, the City shall obligate itself and its consultants to make appropriate applications for the aforementioned federal grants no later than April 30, 1980.

B. The City shall commit its resources and efforts in a timely manner to the completion and adoption of an Urban Redevelopment Plan as required under applicable Colorado law. This plan is to be completed and adopted no later than April 30, 1980. The Redevelopment Plan shall reflect the findings of the redevelopment programming efforts undertaken to date and shall include at least the following additional items: the development of a land acquisition and financing strategy oriented toward the acquisition of any land necessary to effectuate the formal Redevelopment Plan and Program; a detailed description of land acquisition procedures; a detailed description of relocation requirements; and a description of the general procedures to be used for property demolition and land disposition.

C. The City shall devise a budget by identified sources for immediate site acquisition as contained in the execution schedule to be outlined in the Redevelopment Plan. . . . For purposes of this Agreement, land acquisition parcels shall be defined as follows: all land necessary to create a site sufficient to accommodate the hotel facility, the retail facility, the convention/conference center, the parking structure and related landscaped open space and access areas. Collectively, these areas total approximately 448,450 square feet or 10.3 acres and shall include land allocated to the following uses: hotel facility—43,000 square feet or 0.99 acres; convention/conference center—38,400 square feet or 0.88 acres; parking structure—103,950 square feet or 2.39 acres; access to the parking structure—15,600 square feet or 0.36 acres; related landscaped areas—212,925 square feet or 4.89 acres. It is understood by the parties to this Agreement that the City shall adopt a tentative budget for land acquisition (including obtaining the funds described therein) subject to the exact amount stipulated by land acquisition appraisals no later than April 30, 1980.

D. The City or its designated agency shall undertake land acquisition appraisals for those identified parcels during the time period commencing no later than April 30, 1980, and ending no later than June 30, 1980. The City or its designated agency shall initiate the acquisition of these previously identified parcels during the time period commencing no later than June 30, 1980, and ending no later than October 30, 1980. The City or its designated agency shall undertake land acquisition procedures which shall include negotiations concerning the methods and value of land acquisition and the procedures to be followed in the event that con-

demnation is required. If it is necessary to alter the originally defined land acquisition schedule, the City or its designated agency must offer, and the Developer must accept, no later than July 30, 1980, the revised land acquisition schedule. If the Developer deems the revised schedule detrimental to the feasible development of the project, he may, at his option, declare the conditions imposed under this Preliminary Development Commitment Agreement null and void.

E. The City or its designated agency shall undertake procedures to relocate existing tenants and demolish existing structures in the previously identified acquisition parcels. The relocation and demolition process on these identified parcels shall be undertaken during the time period commencing no later than July 30, 1980, and ending no later than September 30, 1981.

F. The City shall ensure that the enactment of appropriate zoning, street access and the issuance of all necessary permits, licenses, and approvals of any kind which shall be required with respect to the Developer's construction shall be available on proper application, payment of requisite fees, and other compliance with applicable laws, rules and regulations.

G. The City shall make available to the Developer a site, together with the provision of City sewer service adequate to service the proposed development, within the previously described acquisition area, for development of a hotel facility and a retail facility (see Section 1, Item C) including directly related landscaped open space and access areas. The sewer hookups to the project shall be provided at no charge to the Developer. The City shall also cause the provision of water, natural gas and electrical services to the site adequate to service the proposed development. The Developer agrees to pay for utility hookup charges required by these quasi-public utility companies. These sites shall be made available to the Developer by either of the following two means at the Developer's option:

1. Fee

The City or its designated agency shall dispose of the hotel facility site and the retail facility site to the Developer at a negotiated fee, based upon reuse appraisals conducted under permissible law to determine fair market value for sale to the Developer. If the Developer wishes to purchase the site, the City agrees to provide a land write-down on the cost of land acquisition to the private sector. The City hereby commits to conduct these appraisals during a period commencing no

later than April 30, 1980, and ending no later than June 30, 1980.

2. Lease

The City or its designated agency hereby pledges itself to consider, in lieu of Item 1 (G.1) above, leasing the previously identified hotel facility site and retail facility site to the Developer according to such terms and conditions as can be mutually agreed upon by the parties.

These dispositions, within the previously identified acquisition area, disposed of either through title fee simple or a lease, shall be determined no later than April 30, 1980, through the execution of a Land Disposition Agreement or a Parcel Lease Agreement.

H. The City agrees that the capital cost of the Convention/Conference Center shall be publicly financed. The Convention/Conference Center shall be designed and constructed concurrently with the hotel facility under the terms of a subordinated lease agreement with the City to be subsequently negotiated. The following design/financial specifications shall serve as a pro forma statement of the quality level associated with the development of the Convention/Conference Center, with said specifications subject to modification by the City, with the concurrence of the Developer, or his assigned designated hotel operator, from a time period commencing upon execution of this Agreement and subsequent execution of more definitive agreements no later than April 30, 1980:

MAXIMUM PROGRAM OF SPACES CONVENTION/ CONFERENCE CENTER

Exhibit Area/Banquet Hall	16,000 NSF
Meeting Rooms	8,000
✦ 6 rooms @ 500 SF	
✦ 4 rooms @ 1,000 SF	
Storage	2,000
Receiving	1,500
Lobby Space	3,000
(and Prefunction Areas)	
Office	1,800
Coat Room	250
Toilet Rooms	1,200
Undesignated Space	250
Net Area (85%)	34,000 NSF
Gross Area (100%)	40,000 GSF

The City shall publicly finance the capital costs of the program of spaces itemized above in a range of 30,000 to 40,000 gross square feet at an average per-square-foot cost of Ninety-Five Dollars ($95.00). The maximum total development cost of the Convention/Conference Center shall be approximately Four Million Two Hundred Thousand Dollars ($4,200,000) which shall include the following approximate allocation of capital expenditures:

- ◆ Construction cost estimate (including site improvements, landscaping and contingencies) — $2,549,400
- ◆ Professional services (including architect, engineer and contingencies) — 252,000
- ◆ Construction management fees (including contingencies) — 210,000
- ◆ Furniture, fixtures and equipment — 888,700
- ◆ Estimated land costs — 299,900

TOTAL — $4,200,000

The City further agrees to provide the initial furniture, fixtures and equipment for the Convention/Conference Center, to replace structural and mechanical defects which occur during the lease and to be responsible for payment of hazard insurance on the structure and its contents. In return, the City requires the Developer, or his designated hotel operator, to enter into an exclusive marketing and management agreement, the terms of which are delineated in Section 2, Item G of this Agreement. Since the convention center is publicly owned the City shall not require the Developer to pay property taxes or debt service charges on the convention/conference space.

1. The City agrees to offer second mortgage financing to the Developer for private costs associated with development of the private components of the project. This second mortgage instrument, which would be financed through funds received under the Urban Development Action Grant Program of the United States Department of Housing and Urban Development, shall be subordinated to the cash flow required to satisfy any first mortgage instrument and all operating expenses of the private facilities. An amount of the cash then available, which shall be subsequently negotiated between the Developer and the City, shall then be directed to pay for the debt service on the second mortgage, prior to any return on equity. If circumstances in any given year during the duration of the second mortgage prove insufficient in terms of cash flow to meet the full debt payment on the second mortgage instrument, the Developer then

shall pay the available portion of the proceeds to the City, and shall defer the balance to the 21st year of the hotel operations. The accumulation of these deferred charges would be on a non-interest basis and shall become due in the 21st year, in an amount to be subsequently negotiated between the Developer and the City.

J. The City agrees to assist the Developer in securing municipal development bond financing for the private costs associated with the development of the private components of the project (see Section 2, Item F for the terms of participation).

K. The City shall develop, or cause to be developed, a minimum of 500 parking spaces as an integral part of the project, adjacent or contiguous to the proposed project area, and available to the Developer. However, nothing herein contained shall prevent charges for use of such facilities. Any charges for use of such facilities shall be based upon reasonably necessary rates to cover operating fees, management fees, operational expenses and debt services, and such other necessary and incidental expenses, including payment in lieu of taxes as may become necessary or desirable for the City of Pueblo. The City shall guarantee an adequate number of parking spaces and shall make provisions for potential future changes in supply. These parking spaces are to be available no later than September 30, 1983.

Section 2. Private Sector Commitments

A. The Developer agrees to either purchase the required portions of the site in fee simple from the City at a written-down cost or lease the required portions of the site under lease terms and conditions that are commensurate with fair market value. This land disposition shall be manifested through a Land Disposition Agreement to be conditionally executed no later than April 30, 1980.

B. The Developer agrees that the design of the private sector components of the project is of paramount importance to the City and for that reason will allow the appropriate public agencies designated by the City to exercise the approval rights (including the selection of the architect) over the design plans of the private sector components of the complex. In selecting project architects, the Developer shall submit not less than three (3) acceptable architectural firms. The City shall then select from those submitted by the Developer and designate one to serve as the project architect. It is understood by the parties hereto that the preferred architect selected by the City shall then negotiate a

contract for services for the planned hotel and retail facilities with the Developer.

C. The Developer agrees that the joint public/private objective manifested through the coordinated design process can best be realized by the designation of the same construction management entity for the public and private components of the project. In selecting a construction manager, the Developer shall submit not less than three (3) acceptable firms. The City shall then select one from those submitted and designate one to serve as the construction manager for the public components, with the expressed understanding that the selected construction manager shall negotiate a contract for services with the developer of the private components.

D. The Developer shall secure the appropriate financing mechanism for the private components during the time period commencing no later than April 30, 1980, and terminating no later than January 31, 1981, within the requirements of the Redevelopment Plan and the potential contractual commitments arising between the City as grant recipient and the appropriate public funding agency involved.

E. The Developer agrees to construct a hotel facility at the location designated in the Land Disposition Agreement and consistent with the publicly adopted Redevelopment Plan. The Developer also agrees to cause the development of a retail facility on the site, either through agreement to construct the facility or exercising assignability to a successor organization mutually acceptable with the City. The following design/financial specifications shall serve only as a pro forma statement of the quality level associated with development of the hotel facility, with said specifications subject to modification by the Developer, with concurrence by the City, from the time period commencing upon execution of this Agreement and subsequent execution of more definitive agreements no later than April 30, 1980:

1. Hotel Facility

The minimum required standards, architectural requirements and physical development guidelines for the hotel component of this project . . . represent the acceptable minimum required by _____, and are in no way meant to limit the quality level of a proposed project from being designed in a manner superior to those standards.

The total development costs of the hotel facility shall be approximately Fifteen Million Nine Hundred Thousand Dollars ($15,900,000) which shall include the following approximate allocation of capital expenditures:

- ◆ Construction cost estimate (including site improvements, landscaping and contingencies) — $10,843,800
- ◆ Professional services (including architects, engineer, legal, project administration and contingencies) — 636,000
- ◆ Furniture, fixtures, and equipment (FF&E) — 2,241,900
- ◆ Start-up costs (including pre-opening expenses, operating losses [years one and two], other costs and contingencies) — 492,900
- ◆ Working capital (including construction and permanent loan fees and construction loan interest) — 1,224,300
- ◆ Estimated land costs — 461,100
  TOTAL — $15,900,000

2. Retail Facility

The following design/financial specifications shall serve as a pro forma statement on the quality level associated with the development of the retail facility, with said specifications subject to modification by the Developer, or a subsequently assigned successor organization, with concurrence by the City, upon execution of this Agreement and subsequent execution of more definitive agreements no later than April 30, 1980. The Developer shall cause the development of 60,000 gross square feet of retail space to be leased to a minimum of eighteen (18) tenants and/or shopowners offering a wide variety of specialty and convenience merchandise. This retail space shall be designed in such a way as to complement existing retail space along Main Street in the downtown area and to provide continuity in pedestrian travel between the parking structure and the central business district. The total development costs of the retail facility shall be approximately Three Million Six Hundred Thousand Dollars ($3,600,000) which shall include the following approximate allocation of capital expenditures:

- ◆ Construction cost estimates (including site improvements, landscaping and contingencies) — $2,401,200
- ◆ Professional services (including architects, engineer, legal, project administration and contingencies) — 255,600
- ◆ Start-up costs (including pre-opening expenses, tenant inducements, operating losses [years one and two], leasing fees and contingencies) — 306,000
- ◆ Working capital (including construction and permanent loan fees and construction loan interest) — 367,200
- ◆ Estimated land costs — 270,000
  TOTAL — $3,600,000

Construction of the private components shall be initiated no later than September 30, 1981, and completed no later than September 30, 1983.

F. The Developer agrees to pay a fee to the City, up to Twenty Thousand Dollars ($20,000), to cover the costs associated with the issuance of municipal development bonds if they are used to finance the private portions of the project. This fee shall cover costs incurred by the City associated with retaining appropriate private sector assistance to aid the City in ascertaining the feasibility of such a bond issuance. It is anticipated that the City shall retain the services of a bond counsel, a market analyst, a financial analyst and other appropriate professionals in this regard. The Developer agrees to pay this fee in full prior to the City securing the professional assistance required.

G. The Developer, or his designated hotel operator, agrees to enter into an exclusive marketing and management agreement with the City whereby the hotel operator shall receive all catering and operating revenues and assume all catering and operating costs associated with use of the Convention/Conference Center. The Developer, or his designated hotel operator, also further agrees to make all needed capital expenditures for replacement of furniture, fixtures and equipment in the Convention/Conference Center.

Section 3. Cooperative Commitments

The parties to this Preliminary Development Commitment Agreement agree to enter into more definitive agreements which shall supersede this Agreement. These agreements shall include but shall not be limited to a General Development Agreement, a Land Disposition Agreement or a Parcel Lease Agreement, a Subordinated Lease Agreement, a Parking Lease Agreement. These agreements shall be negotiated and conditionally executed no later than April 30, 1984, with subsequent execution upon the federal grant commitments being received by the City.

Section 4. Miscellaneous

This Preliminary Development Commitment Agreement entered into on the date here first written above, shall bind the parties hereto for a period not to exceed nine (9) months. It is initially agreed by the parties hereto that this Preliminary Development Commitment Agreement may be given such extension or extensions to reasonably effectuate the purpose hereof where a delay is caused for unforeseen reasons or other complications beyond the control of either party hereto. Neither party shall unreasonably withhold such extension.

IN WITNESS WHEREOF, the parties hereto have hereunto caused their hand and seal to be affixed the day and year above first written.

The City of Pueblo, Colorado

By: _____   By: _____
Title: _____   Title: _____
Date: _____   Date: _____

APPENDIX C

UNNEGOTIATED MANAGEMENT AGREEMENT

AGREEMENT, made as of the ___ day of _____, 19___, between the Owner, hereinafter named, and

_____
(hereinafter called "Operator"):

WITNESSETH:

WHEREAS, Owner proposes to construct, furnish, and equip a first-class _____ containing approximately _____ square feet, and to be known as _____

_____ (hereinafter referred to and defined as the "Site"); and

WHEREAS, Owner desires to obtain the benefits of Operator's expertise in the management and operation of the Site by turning over to Operator all control and discretion in the operation, direction, management, and supervision, and Operator desires to assume such control and discretion upon the terms and conditions set forth in this Agreement.

NOW, THEREFORE, in consideration of the mutual promises and covenants herein contained, Owner and Operator agree as follows:

ARTICLE I

DEFINITIONS

(a) *Basic Fee:* The sum of _____ of Gross Revenues paid monthly, for a Fiscal Year, or prorata portion thereof if applicable.

(b) *Budget:* An estimate of revenues and expenditures (including capital expenditures and replacements).

(c) *Building:* The _____

_____ building and improvements to be located on the Site, which will be fully air conditioned, will have _____ guest rooms (each with bath), conference facilities, audio visual control room, restaurant(s), bar(s) and banquet facilities, and other public rooms, commercial space, recreational facilities, including swimming pool, landscaped grounds, and other facilities necessary for the operation of a first-class _____, together with all fixtures and equipment

necessary for the efficient operation of the buildings and other improvements, including without limitation heating, air conditioning, lighting, sanitary, laundry, refrigeration, kitchen, elevator, and other similar fixtures and equipment.

(d) *Executive Committee Members:* The members of this committee shall be the general manager, the director of food and beverage, the director of marketing, the director of rooms, and the controller.

(e) *General Manager's Maximum Salary:* An annual base salary not to exceed _____ for the first _____ Operating Years, thereafter as reflected in the Budget.

(f) *Fiscal Year:* The year ending

_____, which is the fiscal year established by Owner for the Property.

(g) *Furnishings and Equipment:*

(i) The Operating Equipment;

(ii) All furniture, furnishings, and specialized _____ equipment (which term shall mean and include all equipment required for the operation of kitchens, laundries, dry cleaning facilities, bars, special lighting, and other equipment, except such as are permanent fixtures forming a part of the Building);

(iii) Office furniture and equipment (including, without limitation, audio visual equipment);

(iv) Such other furnishings and equipment as are requisite for the efficient operation of a first-class _____ (including, without limitation, utensils and other similar items).

(h) *Incentive Fee:* _____ per cent (___%) of the Gross Operating Profit for a Fiscal Year, or prorata portion thereof if applicable.

(i) *Operating Equipment:* All chinaware, glasses, linens, utensils, silverware, and uniforms necessary for the operation of the Property.

(j) *Operating Supplies:* Supplies, cleaning materials, food and beverages, fuel, stationery, household stores, matches, soap, and other consumable items.

(k) *Operating Year:* A year of operation under this Agreement.

(l) *Owner:* _____

_____

(m) *Property:* The Building, the Site, the Furnishings, and Equipment, together with all entrances, exits, rights of ingress and egress, riparian rights, easements, and appurtenances thereunto belonging or appertaining.

(n) *Replacement Reserve:* Initially, the amount of $_____ per rentable unit; at the beginning of each Fiscal Year thereafter, the amount reflected by that year's Budget.

(o) *Site:* A tract of real property described in Exhibit A attached hereto on which the Building is located.

(p) *Term:* The original term shall be five (5) years commencing _____, 19___, and ending _____, 19___, and the Operator shall have the right as set forth in Article III, to renew the term for three (3) successive periods of two (2) years each.

(q) *Working Capital:* The amount of $_____ per rentable unit, until further notice by Operator.

ARTICLE II

OWNER'S TITLE

The Owner represents and warrants as follows:

(1) The Owner is the owner or ground lessee of the property and has full power and authority to enter into this Agreement.

(2) The Property is zoned for use as a

_____, and all necessary governmental and other permits and approvals for such use and for the food and beverage (including the sale and service of liquor) operations on the Property have been obtained and are in full force and effect.

(3) Throughout the term of this Agreement, the Owner will maintain full ownership of or right to use the Property and will pay, keep, observe, and perform all payments, terms, covenants, conditions, and obligations under any lease or other concession, any deed of trust, mortgage, or other security agreement, and any real estate taxes or assessment covering or affecting the Property or any part thereof.

ARTICLE III

TERM OF AGREEMENT

1. This Agreement shall continue for the term described in Article I(p) hereof. The Operator shall have the right and option to renew such term for successive periods as set out in Article I(p) hereof, upon the following terms and conditions:

(a) Each renewal term shall be upon the same terms, covenants, and conditions as in this Agreement;

(b) The term of this Agreement shall have been renewed for the prior renewal term;

(c) Operator shall exercise its right to renew the term by written notice to the Owner at least three (3) months prior to the expiration of the then existing term.

The phrase "term of this Agreement" as used herein shall mean the original term and any renewal or renewals thereof then in effect in accordance with the provisions of this Article III.

ARTICLE IV

DUTIES OF OPERATOR

During the term of this Agreement, Operator agrees, for and in consideration of the compensation hereinafter provided, and the Owner hereby grants to Operator the sole and exclusive right, to supervise and direct the management and operation of the Property as the agent of the Owner. Without limiting the generality of the foregoing, Owner grants to Operator the sole and exclusive right, and Operator agrees:

1. To operate the Property in the same manner as is customary and usual in the operation of comparable facilities, to provide such services as are customarily provided by operators of _____ of comparable class and standing consistent with the Property's facilities, and to consult with the Owner and keep the Owner advised as to all major policy matters affecting the Property; provided, however, that Operator will make no major policy changes, not reflected in the Budget, without prior approval of Owner. In this connection, Operator shall have all reasonable discretion in the operation, direction, management, and supervision of the Property, including without limitation, labor policies, credit policies (including entering into agreements with credit card organizations), cashiering, terms of admittance, charges for rooms, guest services, leasing, licensing and granting of concessions for commercial space in or on the Property, entertain-

ment and amusement, food and beverages, purchasing of Operating Equipment, maintenance of the Property, repairs to and replacements of Furnishings and Equipment, the institution of such legal proceedings as are necessary in connection with tenants or otherwise in the operation of the Property, all matters relating to employee safety, health and welfare, insurance, benefits and the like, and all phases of advertising, promotion, publicity, marketing, and sales strategy relating to the Property.

2. To submit for Owner's approval within ninety (90) days of execution hereof a Budget in reasonable detail for remainder of the present Fiscal Year, including a schedule of room rentals and a schedule of expected special repairs and maintenance projects and capital replacement budget. At least thirty (30) days before the beginning of each successive Fiscal Year, Operator shall submit for Owner's approval such a Budget for the ensuing Fiscal Year. Such Budget shall in general form the basis on which expenditures for the Property shall be made, it being understood and agreed that Operator may deviate from such Budget if in Operator's reasonable judgment a deviation is necessary or desirable for the efficient operation of the Property as a first-class _____ _____. Operator makes no guarantee, warranty, or representation whatsoever in connection with the Budgets, such being intended as reasonable estimates only.

3. To hire, promote, discharge, and supervise the work of the management staff (i.e., general manager, assistant managers, and department heads) of the Property and to supervise through said management staff the hiring, promoting, discharge, and work of all other operating and service employees performing services in or about the Property, all in the name of the Owner. Except as provided in the third paragraph of this paragraph 3, all of such employees shall be on Owner's payroll and Operator shall not be liable to such employees for their wages or compensation. Operator will, in the hiring of the management staff and other operating and service employees of the Property, use or cause said management staff to use reasonable care to select qualified, competent, and trustworthy employees. Operator will negotiate, pursuant to rules and regulations as promulgated by the National Labor Relation Board and on the Owner's behalf, with any labor union lawfully entitled to represent such employees, but any collective bargaining agreements or labor contracts resulting therefrom shall be first approved by Owner who shall be

the only authorized person to execute the same. Operator will not enter into any agreement with an employee for an annual basic salary in excess of the General Manager's Maximum Salary without the consent in writing of the Owner. It is understood that Operator may arrange a bonus plan with Owner to be paid to the general manager and the other members of the Executive Committee as an incentive to maximize the Gross Operating Profit.

Since the general manager of the Property may need to reside at the Property and be available full time in order to perform properly the duties of his employment, it is further understood and agreed that the general manager of the Property (including his wife and dependent children), in addition to his salary and fringe benefits, may receive the normal maintenance customarily provided a general manager of a first-class _____ _____, including free room and board, automobile, laundry and valet, and reimbursement for any and all expenses, including business entertainment and traveling expenses, which such general manager may reasonably incur in the performance of his duties.

The general manager and other Executive Committee Members assigned to the Property shall be employees of Operator, and Owner shall reimburse Operator monthly, in advance, for the total aggregate compensation, including salary and fringe benefits. With the approval of Owner, Operator may assign other employees of Operator or any of its subsidiaries or affiliates as members of the management staff of the Property, and unless Operator shall elect (as hereinafter provided) to have such employees treated as employees of the Owner, the Owner shall reimburse Operator for the total aggregate compensation, including salary and fringe benefits, paid or payable with respect to such employees. Operator shall have the right to elect to have some or all of such employees treated as employees of the Owner and, in such event, the Owner shall pay directly the total aggregate compensation, including salary and fringe benefits, payable with respect to such employees, provided, however, that should Operator elect to continue to pay all or any part of the fringe benefits payable with respect to such employees, the Owner shall reimburse Operator in an amount equal to such fringe benefits paid by Operator. The term "fringe benefits" as used herein shall mean and include the employer's contribution of F.I.C.A., unemployment compensation and other employment taxes, and pension plan contributions, workmen's compensation, group life and accident and health insurance, dental insurance, premiums and profit sharing, disability, and other similar benefits paid or payable by the employer with respect to employees in other _____ _____ operated by Operator.

Operator may, with Owner's approval, from time to time find it desirable to assign one or more of its supervisory employees to the Property on a temporary basis. Owner agrees to reimburse Operator for all actual expenses to and from the Property and for all room and board while at the Property for such employees while on Property business.

4. To consummate in the name of and for the benefit of the Owner, arrangements with concessionaires, licensees, tenants, or other intended users of the facilities of the Property.

5. To enter into contracts in the name and at the expense of the Owner for the furnishing to the Property of electricity, gas, water, steam, telephone, cleaning (including window cleaning where necessary), vermin exterminators, elevator and boiler maintenance, air-conditioning maintenance, master television antennae installation and service, laundry service, dry cleaning service, and other utilities, services, and concessions which are provided in connection with the maintenance and operation of a first-class _____ in accordance with standards comparable to those prevailing in other such _____ _____.

6. To purchase all Operating Supplies (as hereinabove defined) and other materials and supplies in the name of, for the account of, and at the expense of the Owner. Owner acknowledges that Operator may perform services as a representative of the manufacturer of any of such items in order to secure the benefits of lower costs in connection with purchasing arrangements for Owner.

7. To make or install, or cause to be made or installed, through a schedule of preventative maintenance and supervisory program, at Owner's expense and in the name of the Owner, all necessary or desirable repairs, decorations, renewals, revisions, alterations, rebuildings, replacements, additions, and improvements in and to the Site, and Building, and the Furnishings and Equipment; provided, however, that such are included in the Budget or do not exceed _____

($ _____) per item. Operator also agrees that all needed repairs are re-

corded and serviced on a priority basis through the use of a work order system.

8. To apply for and obtain and maintain in the name and at the expense of the Owner, all licenses and permits required of the Owner or Operator in connection with the management and operation of the Property. The Owner agrees to execute and deliver any and all applications and other documents and to otherwise cooperate to the fullest extent with Operator in applying for, obtaining, and maintaining such licenses and permits.

9. To cause at Owner's expense all such acts and things to be done in and about the Property as shall be necessary, and the Owner covenants throughout the term of this Agreement at its expense, to comply with all statutes, ordinances, laws, rules, regulations, orders, and requirements of any federal, state, or municipal government and appropriate departments, commissions, boards, and officers having jurisdiction in the premises respecting the use of the Property or the construction, maintenance, or operation thereof, as well as with all orders and requirements of the local Board of Fire Underwriters or any other body which may hereafter exercise similar functions; provided, however, that if the Owner shall adequately secure and protect Operator from loss, cost, damage, and expense by bond or other means satisfactory to Operator, the Owner, at its sole expense and without cost to Operator, shall have the right to contest by proper legal proceedings the validity of any such statute, ordinance, law, rule, regulation, order, or requirement provided such contest shall not result in the suspension of operations of the Property. Subject to the foregoing, the Owner may postpone compliance with any such law, ordinance, order, rule, regulation, or requirement to the extent and in the manner provided by law until final determination of any such proceedings. The Owner shall prosecute all such proceedings with all due diligence and dispatch. Notwithstanding the foregoing, if failure to comply promptly with any statute, ordinance, law, rule, regulation, order, or requirement would result in the suspension of operations of the Property or would expose Owner or Operator to the imminent danger of criminal liability other than the payment of fines, then in such event Operator may (but shall not be obligated to) cause the same to be complied with at Owner's expense.

10. As agent for Owner, to deposit in a banking institution or institutions in accounts in Operator's name all monies furnished by Owner as working capital and all monies received by Operator for or on behalf of Owner and to disburse and pay

the same on behalf of and in the name of the Owner in such amounts and at such times as the same are required in connection with the ownership, maintenance, and operation of the Property on account of:

(a) All taxes, assessments, and charges of every kind imposed by any governmental authority having jurisdiction, including interest and penalties thereon, unless payment thereof is in good faith being contested by Owner, at its sole expense and without cost to Operator, and enforcement thereof is stayed and Owner shall have given Operator written notice of such contest and stay and authorize the non-payment thereof not less than ten (10) days prior to the date on which such tax, assessment, or charge is due and payable.

(b) All costs and expenses of maintaining, operating, and supervising the operation of the Property, including, without limitation, the following:

(i) The cost of all purchases of Operating Supplies.

(ii) The salaries, fringe benefits, and expenses of Property employees, including the executive staff and general manager.

(iii) The cost of the Property's fair share of any group advertising, marketing, reservation billing, or audit system services for _____ operated by Operator, it subsidiaries, or affiliates, or by the franchisor, and which are deemed desirable or are required by Operator or the franchisor.

(iv) Out-of-pocket expenses incurred for the account of or in connection with the Property, including reasonable traveling expenses of executives and employees of Operator and its subsidiaries and affiliates.

(v) All costs and expenses of any separate advertising, business promotion, or personnel training program of the Property alone, separate and distinct from any other _____ operated by Operator or its subsidiaries or affiliates.

(vi) All expenditures, which are of an ordinary nature, or which have been covered in the annual Budget for the then current year, for repairs and maintenance, Operating Equipment, Furnishings and Equipment (other than Operating Equipment), and for capital improvements.

(vii) Premiums for insurance maintained pursuant to this Agreement.

(viii) Legal fees.

(ix) The Basic Fee and/or Incentive Fee and all reimbursements or other payments due to Operator under the provisions of this Agreement.

(x) Cost and expense of utilities, services, and concessions at the Property and any and all other expenditures provided for in this Agreement.

(xi) The expense of the Property's membership in any trade associations which Operator deems desirable.

(xii) Any other charge, item or expense or other item which Owner in writing directs to be paid.

(xiii) The Replacement Reserve provided for in this Agreement.

Subject to maintaining reasonable reserves for replacements and working capital requirements, Operator, upon Owner's written request, shall transfer such funds as Owner shall request from bank accounts maintained pursuant to this paragraph 10 to a bank account opened and maintained solely by Owner.

11. At Owner's request to take out and maintain on behalf of Owner and at Owner's expense, at all times during the term of the Agreement, insurance as provided in the Insurance Rider attached hereto and made a part of this Agreement for all purposes.

12. To deliver or cause to be delivered to the Owner statements as follows:

(a) On or before the end of each calendar month, Operator shall deliver or cause to be delivered to the Owner a profit and loss statement showing the results of operation of the Property for the preceding calendar month and the Fiscal Year to date, and having annexed thereto a computation of the management fee for such preceding month and the Fiscal Year to date. Such statement and computation shall be prepared by the controller for the Property and taken and made from the books of account of the Property.

(b) Within ninety (90) days after the end of each Fiscal Year, Operator will also deliver or cause to be delivered to the Owner a balance sheet and related statement of profit and loss (including all supporting departmental schedules of revenues and expenses), audited by independent public accountants recognized in the

field, approved by both Owner and Operator and retained by Owner, showing the assets employed in the operation of the Property and the liabilities incurred in connection therewith, as at Fiscal Year end, and the results of the operation of the Property during the preceding Fiscal Year, and having annexed thereto a computation of the management fee for such year. At Operator's option such independent accountants approved by both Owner and Operator may be retained at Owner's expense to prepare monthly statements,

including those agreed to in the last paragraph (a) and semiannual statements.

All costs and expenses incurred in connection with the preparation of any statements, budgets, schedules, computations, and other reports required under this paragraph 12 or under any other provisions of this Agreement shall be borne by the Owner.

13. To institute, in its own name or in the name of Owner, but in any event at the expense of Owner, any and all legal actions or proceedings to collect charges, rent or other income from the Property or to oust or dispossess guests, tenants, or other persons in possession therefrom, or to cancel or terminate any lease, license, or concession agreement for the breach thereof or default thereunder by the tenant, licensee, or concessionaire; provided, however, that Operator shall not institute any legal actions or proceedings to oust or dispossess tenants or other persons in possession thereunder, or cancel or terminate, any lease, license, or concession agreement having a then unexpired term of one year or more, without prior consent of Owner.

14. Unless otherwise directed by Owner, Operator may (but shall not be obligated to) take at Owner's expense any appropriate steps to protest and/or litigate to final decision in any appropriate court or forum any violation, order, rule, or regulation affecting the Property. Any counsel to be engaged under this or the next preceding paragraph shall be mutually approved by Owner and Operator.

15. In the performance of its duties as Operator, Operator shall act solely as the agent of the Owner. All debts and liabilities to third persons incurred by Operator in the course of its operation and management of the Property shall be the debts and liabilities of the Owner only, and Operator shall not be liable for any such debts or liabilities.

ARTICLE V

MANAGEMENT FEE

As compensation for the services to be rendered by Operator during the term of this Agreement, the Owner shall pay to Operator, at its principal office (or at such other place, if any, as Operator may from time to time designate in a written notice to Owner) and at the times hereinafter specified, the Basic Fee and the Incentive Fee, derived from the Property in each Fiscal Year, or portion thereof if applicable. Such management fees shall be paid in monthly installments as follows: on the fifth day of each month Owner shall be sent a statement and shall pay the Basic

Fee derived from the Property from the preceding month; on the fifth day of the first month of each fiscal quarter owner shall be sent a statement and shall pay the Incentive Fee derived from the Property the preceding quarter.

If the aggregate installments of the management fee paid in any Fiscal Year shall be more or less than the total annual management fee due for the entire Fiscal Year, Operator, or Owner, as the case may be, shall pay to the other the amount of such overpayment or underpayment within ninety (90) days after the end of each such Fiscal Year.

For the purpose of determining the Incentive Fee, the Gross Operating Profit shall be determined in accordance with the "Uniform System of Accounts for Hotels (Seventh Revised Edition, 1979)" as adopted by the American Hotel/Motel Association and as from time to time supplemented or amended (hereinafter referred to as "Uniform System of Accounts for Hotels"). Gross Revenues shall include all revenues and income of any kind derived directly or indirectly from the Property (including store and building rentals from the Property building, and rentals or other payments from sublessees and concessionaires, but not the gross receipts of such sublessees or concessionaires), whether on a cash basis or on credit, paid or unpaid, collected or uncollected, determined in accordance with sound accounting practices and in accordance with the Uniform System of Accounts for Hotels, excluding, however, (a) federal, state, and municipal excise, sales, and use taxes collected directly from patrons or guests or as a part of the sales price of any goods, services or displays, such as gross receipts, admission, cabaret, or similar or equivalent taxes and (b) gains arising from the sale or other disposition of capital assets. Proceeds from use and occupancy insurance shall be included in determining the Gross Operating Profit and Gross Revenues derived from the Property and in computing the management fee.

ARTICLE VI

GENERAL COVENANTS OF OWNER AND OPERATOR

1. Books and records. The Operator shall keep, and on behalf of the Owner shall supervise and direct the keeping of, full and adequate books of account and such other records reflecting the results of operation of the Property. Such books and records shall be kept in all material respects in accordance with the Uniform System of Accounts for Hotels. Operator agrees to establish an aggressive internal audit program designed to stay abreast of all operational responsibilities and to provide constructive development of such responsibilities.

2. *Opening Inventories and Working Capital.* Owner agrees to provide at its expense, and Operator shall order on behalf of the Owner, sufficient initial inventories of Operating Supplies for the operation of the Property. The Owner further agrees that, at the commencement of this Agreement and thereafter, upon the request of Operator, to provide and maintain all Working Capital required for the uninterrupted and efficient operation and maintenance of the Property. Operator shall in no event be required to advance any of its own funds for the operation of the Property, nor to incur any liability in connection herewith unless Owner shall have furnished Operator with funds necessary for the discharge thereof.

3. *Operating Expenses.* The Owner shall be solely liable for the costs and expenses of maintaining and operating the Property, and subject to the provisions of Article IV, the Owner shall pay all costs and expenses of maintaining, operating, and supervising the operation of the Property, including, without limitation, the salaries of all of its personnel.

4. *Owner's Right of Inspection and Review.* Operator shall accord to the Owner, its accountants, attorneys and agents, the right to enter upon any part of the Property at all reasonable times during the term of this Agreement for the purpose of examining or inspecting the same or examining or making extracts of books and records of the Property or for any other purpose which the Owner, in its discretion, shall deem necessary or advisable, but the same shall be done with as little disruption to the business of the Property as possible. Books and records of the Property shall be kept at the Property or such other place as the parties may hereafter agree. In all cases proper identification must be given to management in charge of the Property before inspection or review is granted.

5. *Replacement Reserve.* At the commencement of this Agreement and at the beginning of each Fiscal Year thereafter, a Replacement Reserve shall be created by Owner in accordance with that year's Budget, for the purpose of making capitalized replacements, substitutions, and additions to the Furnishing and Equipment of the Property. Such fund will be deposited in an account in Operator's name. Any expenditure for replacement of, substitution of, or additions to Furnishings and Equipment during each Fiscal Year may be made by Operator without

Owner's consent up to the then remaining balance in such reserve fund. Any expenditure in excess of the reserve fund shall be subject to the Owner's approval, which approval shall not be unreasonably withheld. Upon termination of this Agreement any remaining balance of the reserve fund shall be paid to Owner.

6. *Right of Set-Off.* Operator shall have the right of set-off against any payments to be made to Owner by Operator hereunder and against all funds from time to time in the bank accounts provided for herein.

7. *Indemnification of Operator.* Operator, its agents and employees, shall not be liable to Owner or to any other person for any act or omission, negligent, tortious or otherwise, of any agent or employee of Owner or Operator in the performance of this Agreement, except only the fraud or gross negligence of Operator, and Owner hereby agrees to indemnify and hold harmless Operator, its agents and employees, from and against any liability, loss, damage, cost, or expense (including attorney's fees) by reason of any such act or omission.

8. *Employment of Executive Committee Members.* Owner agrees that if any of the Executive Committee Members of the Property leaves the employ of Operator for any reason, including termination by the Operator, Owner shall not hire or cause to be hired such Executive Committee Members in any capacity for at least one year following such termination of employment with Operator.

ARTICLE VII

TRADE NAME

The trademarks and service marks of both Owner and Operator may be used in connection with the operation of the Property. It is expressly agreed that neither party will, by virtue of the operations under this Agreement, acquire any right to any trademark or service mark of the other party. Each party agrees to cooperate with the other party by all reasonable means in the protection of its trademarks and service marks.

Anything contained in this Article VII to the contrary notwithstanding, upon the expiration or earlier termination of this Agreement, the Owner shall have the right to use in connection with the operation of the Property any and all items of Operating Equipment and Operating Supplies then on hand bearing the trademarks or service marks of Operator but shall not reorder any such item; and thereafter the Owner shall not use any trademark or service mark of Operator for any purpose. It

is expressly provided, however, that Operator may replace any such items at its expense, and from and after such replacement Owner shall have no right to use such items bearing Operator's trademarks or service marks.

ARTICLE VIII

NOTICES

Any notice by either party to the other shall be in writing and shall be given, and be deemed to have been duly given, if either delivered personally or mailed in a registered or certified postpaid envelope addressed to the address set forth on the signature page hereto, or, if the address for notice of either party shall be duly changed as hereinafter provided, delivered or mailed as aforesaid to such party at such changed address. Either party may at any time change the address for notices to such party by the delivery or mailing, as aforesaid, of a notice stating the change and setting forth the changed address.

ARTICLE IX

SUCCESSORS AND ASSIGNS

1. *Assignment by Operator.* Operator, without the consent of the Owner shall have the right to assign this Agreement to any successor or assignee of Operator which may result from any merger, consolidation, or reorganization or to any corporation or firm, 50 percent or more of whose voting stock or control is owned directly or indirectly by Operator, or to another corporation which shall acquire all or substantially all of the business and assets of Operator. Upon execution of any assignment as aforesaid, notice thereof in the form of a duplicate original of such assignment shall be delivered to the Owner forthwith.

Except as hereinabove provided, Operator shall not assign this Agreement without the prior written consent of Owner. Any consent granted by the Owner to any such assignment shall not be deemed a waiver of the covenant herein contained against assignment in any subsequent case.

2. *Sale, Lease, or Assignment by Owner.*

(a) Owner shall not sell or lease the Property or any part thereof or assign this Assignment, or any interest therein, without the prior written consent of Operator. If Owner shall have received a bona fide written offer to purchase or lease the Property, the Site, or the Building, and Owner, pursuant to the terms of such offer, desires to sell or lease the Property, Site, or Building, to the prospective purchaser or lessee, Owner shall give written notice thereof to Operator, stating the name of the prospective purchaser or tenant, as the case may be, including the names and addresses of the owners of the capital stock, partnership interests, or other proprietary interests in said prospective purchaser or tenant, the price or rental, and all the terms and conditions of such proposed sale or lease, together with all other information with respect thereto which is requested by Operator and reasonably available to Owner. Within sixty (60) days after the date of receipt by Operator of such written notice from Owner, Operator shall elect, by written notice to Owner, one of the following alternatives:

(i) To purchase or lease the Property, Site, or Building (to whichever of the same offer shall apply and Owner so desires to sell or lease) at the same price or rental and upon the same terms and conditions as those set forth in the written notice from the Owner to Operator. In the event that Operator shall have elected to so purchase or lease the Property, Site, or Building in accordance with the provisions of the preceding sentence, Owner and Operator shall promptly thereafter enter into an agreement for the sale or lease at the price or rental and on the terms aforesaid and shall consummate such transaction in accordance with the terms thereof.

(ii) To consent to such sale or lease and to the assignment of this Agreement to such purchaser or lessee, if such sale or lease is in fact consummated. Concurrently with the consummation of such sale or lease, the purchaser or lessee, as the case may be, shall in writing, under an assumption agreement in form and substance reasonably satisfactory to Operator's counsel, assume and agree to perform this Agreement, an executed copy of which assumption agreement shall be promptly delivered by Owner to Operator. It is expressly understood and agreed, however, that notwithstanding Operator's consent to such sale or lease and assignment of this Agreement and the execution and delivery of said assumption agreement, Owner shall not be released from any of its obligations hereunder. To the fullest practical extent, Owner shall give to Operator sufficient written notice of the date on which such sale or lease is to be consummated in order to give Operator an opportunity to be present at such time.

(iii) To terminate this Agreement (if and only if Operator shall not have exercised its rights under clause (i) or (ii) above), which notice of termination shall fix a date of termination not less than six-

ty (60) days nor more than ninety (90) days after the date of receipt by Operator of Owner's original 60-day notice. If Operator shall elect to terminate this Agreement as provided in this clause (iii), Owner shall, and as a condition to such sale or lease, in the sales agreement or lease, as the case may be, require the prospective purchaser or lessee to indemnify and save Operator harmless against any and all losses, costs, damages, liabilities, claims, and expenses, including reasonable attorney's fees, arising or resulting from the failure of the Owner or such prospective purchaser or lessee to provide any of the services contracted for in connection with the business booked for the Property to and including the date of such termination, including any and all business so booked as to which facilities and/or services are to be furnished subsequent to the date of termination, provided that any settlement by Operator of any such claims shall be subject to the prior written approval of Owner which shall not be unreasonably withheld. If, within ninety (90) days after the date of receipt by Operator of the Owner's original 60-day notice, the Owner shall not consummate said sale or lease of the Property, the Site, or the Building to the prospective purchaser or lessee named in the original notice to Operator at the price or rental and on terms no less favorable to the Owner than those at which such property was offered for sale or lease to Operator, then the termination notice theretofore served by Operator upon the Owner shall be null and void, and this Agreement shall continue in full force and effect, and the Property, the Site, and the Building shall again be subject to the restrictions of this subparagraph 2(a) of Article IX. Operator agrees that upon the terms and conditions set forth in this subparagraph 2(a), it shall elect one of the alternatives set forth in clauses (i), (ii) and (iii) above. If Operator shall fail, neglect, or refuse to so exercise any of said alternatives within the said 60-day period, the same shall be conclusively deemed to constitute an election and consent under paragraph 2(a)(ii) above and the provisions thereof shall prevail as if Operator had in writing consented thereto. Any consent granted by Operator to any such sale or lease and assignment shall not be deemed a waiver of the covenant herein contained against sale, lease or assignment in any subsequent case.

(b) Nothing herein contained shall prevent Owner from assigning this Assignment to any bank, insurance company, or other financial institution as collateral security to any first mortgage on the Property.

(c) Except as provided in subparagraph 2(d) of this Article IX, the voluntary or involuntary sale, assignment, transfer, or other disposition, or transfer by operation of law (other than by will or the laws of intestate succession) of a controlling interest in the Owner (i.e., the possession, directly or indirectly, of the power to direct or cause the direction of the management and policies of Owner, whether through the ownership of voting securities or by contract or otherwise) shall be deemed a sale or lease of the Property within the foregoing provisions of subparagraph 2(a) of this Article IX, and shall be subject to the same rights of Operator as set forth in said subparagraph 2(a) with respect to the sale or lease of the Property. Owner, from time to time, upon the written request of Operator, shall furnish Operator with a list of the names and addresses of the owners of the capital stock, partnership interests or other proprietary interests in the Owner; and in the event of a proposed sale or other disposition of a controlling interest in the Owner, Owner shall forthwith notify Operator in writing of such proposed sale or other disposition and of the names and addresses of the proposed transferees of such controlling interest.

(d) In the event Owner desires to offer shares of its stock or any shareholder desires to sell any stock of Owner to the public, then all or any portion of the stock of Owner may be sold through a public offering or offerings and any such shares so sold may be transferred from time to time without the consent of Operator. To the extent that any written materials prepared and made public in connection with any public offering (including, but not limited to, registration statement, prospectuses and advertising) make reference to the existence of this Agreement, such materials shall be subject to the prior written approval of Operator, which approval shall not be unreasonably withheld.

3. Subject to the foregoing, this Agreement shall inure to the benefit of and be binding upon the parties hereto, their respective heirs, legal representatives, successors, and assigns.

4. All continuing covenants herein contained shall survive the expiration or sooner termination of this Agreement.

ARTICLE X

CONDEMNATION

If the whole of the Property shall be taken or condemned in any eminent domain, condemnation, compulsory acquisition, or like proceeding by any competent authority for any public or quasi-public use or purpose, or if such a portion thereof shall be taken or condemned as to make it imprudent or unreasonable, in Operator's reasonable opinion, to use the remaining portion as a _____ _____ of the type and class immediately preceding such taking or condemnation, then in either of such events the term of this Agreement shall cease and terminate as of the date on which Owner shall be required to surrender possession of the Property as a consequence of such taking or condemnation, but, to the extent and only to the extent any award for such taking or condemnation includes compensation to Operator for any loss of income resulting from such taking or condemnation, such award shall be fairly and equitably apportioned between the Owner and Operator so as to compensate Operator for any such loss of income that it would have derived from its management fee for the remainder of the term of this Agreement. Operator shall continue to supervise and direct the management and operation of the Property until such time as Owner shall be required to surrender possession of the Property as a consequence of such taking or condemnation.

If only a part of the Property shall be taken or condemned and the taking or condemnation of such part does not make it unreasonable or imprudent, in Operator's reasonable opinion, to operate the remainder as a _____ of the same type and class as immediately preceding such taking or condemnation, this Agreement shall not terminate. In such event the entire award shall belong to the Owner, but out of the award to the Owner, so much thereof as shall be reasonably necessary to repair any damage to the Property, or any part thereof, or to alter or modify the Property, or any part thereof, so as to render the Property a complete and satisfactory architectural unit as a _____ _____ of the same type and class as immediately preceding the taking or condemnation, shall be used for that purpose.

ARTICLE XI

TERMINATION RIGHTS

This Agreement shall be terminated and, except as to liabilities or claims or either party hereto which shall have theretofore accrued or arisen, the obligations of the parties hereto with respect to this Agreement shall cease and terminate upon the happening of any of the following events:

1. Termination by Owner.

(a) If Operator shall apply for or consent to the appointment of a receiver, trustee, or liquidator of Operator or of all or a substantial part of its assets, file a voluntary petition in bankruptcy, or admit in writing its inability to pay its debts as they come due, make a general assignment for the benefit of creditors, file a petition or an answer seeking reorganization or arrangement with creditors or to take advantage of any insolvency law, or file an answer admitting the material allegations of a petition filed against Operator in any bankruptcy, reorganization, or insolvency proceedings, or if an order, judgment, or decree shall be entered by any court of competent jurisdiction, on the application of a creditor, adjudicating Operator a bankrupt or insolvent or approving a petition seeking reorganization of Operator or appointing a receiver, trustee, or liquidator of Operator or of all or a substantial part of its assets, and such order, judgment, or decree shall continue unstayed and in effect for any period of ninety (90) consecutive days; or

(b) If Operator shall fail to keep, observe, or perform any material covenant, agreement, term, or provision of this Agreement to be kept, observed, or performed by Operator, and such default shall continue for a period of thirty (30) days after notice thereof by Owner to Operator, or if such default cannot be cured within thirty (30) days then such additional period as shall be reasonable, provided that Operator has proceeded to cure such default,

then in case of such event and upon the expiration of the period of grace applicable thereto, the term of this Agreement shall expire, at the Owner's option, on ten (10) days' notice to Operator.

2. Termination by Operator. If at any time or from time to time during the term of this Agreement any of the following events shall occur and not be remedied within the applicable period of time herein specified, namely:

(a) The Owner shall fail to keep, observe, or perform any material covenant, agreement, term, or provision of this Agreement to be kept, observed or performed by Owner, and such default shall continue for a period of thirty (30) days after notice thereof by Operator to the Owner, or if such default cannot be cured within thirty (30) days, then such additional period as shall be reasonable, provided that Owner has proceeded to cure such default; or

(b) If the Property or any portion thereof shall be damaged by fire or other casualty and if the Owner fails to under-

take to repair, restore, rebuild, or replace any such damage or destruction within ninety (90) days after such fire or other casualty, or shall fail to complete such work diligently; or

(c) If the Owner shall apply for or consent to the appointment of a receiver, trustee, or liquidator of the Owner or of all or a substantial part of its assets, file a voluntary petition in bankruptcy or admit in writing its inability to pay its debts as they come due, make a general assignment for the benefit of creditors, file a petition or an answer seeking reorganization or arrangement with creditors or to take advantage of any insolvency law, or file an answer admitting the material allegations of a petition filed against the Owner in any bankruptcy, reorganization, or insolvency proceeding, or if an order, judgment, or decree shall be entered by any court of competent jurisdiction, on the application of a creditor, adjudicating the Owner a bankrupt or insolvent or approving a petition seeking reorganization of the Owner or appointing a receiver, trustee, or liquidator of the Owner or of all or a substantial part of the assets of the Owner, and such order, judgment, or decree shall continue unstayed and in effect for any period of ninety (90) consecutive days; or

(d) If the licenses for the sale of alcoholic beverages in the Property are at any time, without the fault of Operator, suspended, terminated, or revoked and such suspension, termination, or revocation shall continue unstayed and in effect for a period of sixty (60) consecutive days unless during such period Owner and Operator are able to negotiate a new fee structure and Budget taking into account the loss of liquor revenues,

then in the case of any such event and upon the expiration of the period of grace applicable thereto, the term of this Agreement shall expire, at Operator's option, on ten (10) days' notice to the Owner.

3. General. If, upon receipt of the aforesaid 10 day's notice, the defaulting party shall cure any default under subparagraph 1(a) or 2(c) of this Article XI within said ten-day period, or, as to any event of default under subparagraph 1(b), 2(a) or 2(b) of this Article XI which is not susceptible of being cured with all due diligence within such 10-day period, the defaulting party shall proceed promptly and with all due diligence to cure the same and thereafter to prosecute the curing of such default with all due diligence (it being intended that in connection with any default under said subparagraph 1(b), 2(a) or 2(b) not susceptible of being cured with all due diligence within such

10-day period, the time for the defaulting party to cure the same shall be extended for such period as may be necessary to cure the same with all due diligence), then such notice shall be of no force and effect and the rights of the parties shall be the same as existed prior to the giving of said ten-day notice.

If Operator shall have terminated this Agreement by reason of the occurrence of one or more of the events described in paragraph 2(b) of this Article XI and if the Owner shall commence to repair, restore, rebuild or replace the Property within one (1) year after the date of such termination by Operator, the Owner covenants and agrees that it will not enter into a management contract with any other _____ operator with respect to the Property without first offering the same to Operator for thirty (30) days on terms and conditions no less favorable to Operator than those which the Owner certifies it is willing to accept from another _____ operator as evidenced by a bona fide offer received by the Owner from such other _____ operator. Such offer shall be in writing and shall contain a certificate subscribed by the Owner setting forth the terms and conditions offered by such _____ operator which the Owner is willing to accept. Within thirty (30) days after the date of receipt by Operator of such written offer from the Owner, Operator may accept such offer in writing, and in such event Operator and Owner shall promptly thereafter enter into a management contract on the terms and conditions aforesaid. This provision shall be deemed to survive the expiration or sooner termination of this Agreement.

ARTICLE XII

MISCELLANEOUS PROVISIONS

1. No Partnership or Joint Venture. Nothing contained in this Agreement shall constitute or be construed to be or create a partnership or joint venture between the Owner, its successors or assigns, on the one part, and Operator, its successors and assigns, on the other part.

2. Agreement Not an Interest in Real Property; Subject and Subordinate. This Agreement shall not be deemed at any time to be an interest in real estate or a lien of any nature against the Property, or the land on which it is erected. This Agreement shall at all times be subject and subordinate to all mortgages on the Property, or the land on which it is erected which may now or hereafter be outstanding, to all renewals, modifications, consolidations, replacements, and extensions thereof. This clause shall be self operative and no further instrument of subordination shall be required by any mortgagee. However, Owner shall execute promptly any certificate or other document that any mortgagee may request as to the subordination of this Agreement.

3. Force Majeure. Neither party hereto shall be in default for failure to perform any of its obligations pursuant to this Agreement if and to the extent that it can establish that such failure was occasioned by any circumstances which were beyond its control and which by the exercise of due diligence and foresight it could not have prevented or overcome.

4. Modification and Changes. This Agreement cannot be changed or modified except by another agreement in writing signed by the party sought to be charged therewith or by its duly authorized agent.

5. Understandings and Agreements. This Agreement constitutes all of the understandings and agreements of whatsoever nature or kind existing between the parties with respect to Operator's managership of the Property. Operator makes no guarantee, warranty, or representation that there will be profits or that there will not be losses from the operation of the Property.

6. Headings. The article and paragraph headings contained herein are for convenience of reference only and are not intended to define, limit, or describe the scope or intent of any provision of this Agreement.

7. Approval and Consent. Whenever under any provision of this Agreement the approval or consent of either party is required, the decision thereon shall be promptly given and such approval or consent shall not be unreasonably withheld. It is further understood and agreed that whenever under any provisions of this Agreement approval or consent is required, the approval or consent shall be deemed to have been duly given if such approval or consent is given by the person executing this Agreement or any one of the persons, as the case may be, designated in a notification signed by or on behalf of the Owner. For all purposes under this Agreement, Operator shall determine solely from the latest such notification received by it the person or persons authorized to give such approval or consent. Operator may rely exclusively and conclusively on the designation set forth in such notification, notwithstanding any notice or knowledge to the contrary.

8. Governing Law. This Agreement shall be deemed to have been made and shall be construed and interpreted in accordance with the laws of the state of _____.

9. Binding Effect. This Agreement shall be binding upon and inure to the benefit of the parties hereto and their respective heirs, personal representatives, successors, and permitted assigns.

IN WITNESS WHEREOF, the parties hereto have executed, or caused to be executed, this Agreement all as of the day and year first above written.

_____

By _____

(Title)

ADDRESS:

_____

By _____

(Title)

ADDRESS:

_____

EXHIBIT A
(Site Description)

_____
_____
_____
_____
_____

APPENDIX D
MARRIOTT CORPORATION
HOTEL MANAGEMENT AGREEMENT

This Management Agreement ("Agreement") is executed as of the _____ day of _____, 19 ____ ("Effective Date"), by _____ ("Owner"), a _____ with a mailing address at _____
_____

and MARRIOTT CORPORATION ("Management Company"), a Delaware corporation, with a mailing address at ___
_____.

RECITALS:

A. Owner plans to construct and equip a modern, first-class Hotel (as defined and more fully described in Section 1.01 E) in
_____,

_____, and

B. Owner desires to have Management Company manage and operate the Hotel and Management Company is willing to perform such services for the account of Owner on the terms and conditions set forth herein.

NOW, THEREFORE, in consideration of the premises and the mutual covenants herein contained, the parties hereto agree as follows:

ARTICLE I
DEFINITION OF TERMS

1.01 *Definition of Terms*
The following terms when used in the Agreement shall have the meanings indicated:

A. *"Accounting Period"* shall mean the four (4) week accounting periods having the same beginning and ending dates as Management Company's four (4) week accounting periods, except that an Accounting Period may occasionally contain five (5) weeks when necessary to conform Management Company's accounting system to the calendar.

B. *"Fiscal Year"* shall mean Management Company's Fiscal Year which now ends at midnight on the Friday closest to December 31 in each calendar year; the new Fiscal Year begins on the Saturday immediately following said Friday. Any partial Fiscal Year between the Opening Date and the commencement of the first full Fiscal Year shall be included as part of the first full Fiscal Year. A partial Fiscal Year between the end of the last full Fiscal Year and the Termination of the Agreement shall, for purposes of the Agreement, constitute a separate Fiscal Year. If Management Company's Fiscal Year is changed in the future, appropriate adjustment to the Agreement's reporting and accounting procedures shall be made; provided, however, that no such change or adjustment shall alter the term of the Agreement or in any way reduce the distributions of Operating Profit or other payments due Owner hereunder.

C. *"Fixed Asset Supplies"* shall mean supply items included within "Property and Equipment" under the Uniform System of Accounts including linen, china, glassware, silver, uniforms, and similar items.

D. *"Gross Revenues"* shall mean all revenues and receipts of every kind derived from operating the Hotel and parts thereof, including, but not limited to: income (from both cash and credit transactions), before commissions and discounts for prompt or cash payments, from rental of rooms, stores, offices, exhibit or sales space of every kind; license, lease, and concession fees and rentals (not including gross receipts of licensees, lessees, and concessionaires); income from vending machines; health club membership fees; food and beverage sales; wholesale and retail sales of merchandise, service charges, and proceeds, if any, from business interruption or other loss of income insurance; provided, however, that Gross Revenues shall not include gratuities to Hotel employees or federal, state, or municipal excise, sales, or use taxes or similar Impositions collected directly from patrons or guests or included as part of the sales price of any goods or services.

E. *"Hotel"* shall mean the hotel building Owner is to develop in accordance with the provisions of Article III and shall include the Site (defined in Section 3.01), the improvements and all fixtures, furnishings, furniture, equipment and supplies installed therein.

F. *"Inventories"* shall mean "Inventories" as defined in the Uniform System of Accounts, such as provisions in storerooms, refrigerators, pantries and kitchens; beverages in wine cellars and bars; other merchandise intended for sale; fuel; mechanical supplies; stationery; and other expensed supplies and similar items.

G. *"Opening Date"* shall mean the formal opening date of the Hotel, which shall be established and certified by Management Company.

H. *"Operating Profit"* shall mean the excess of Gross Revenues over the following deductions ("Deductions") incurred by Management Company in operating the Hotel:

1. The cost of sales including salaries, wages, fringe benefits, payroll taxes and other costs related to Hotel employees;

2. Departmental expenses, administrative and general expenses and the cost of Hotel advertising and business promotion, heat, light and power, and routine repairs, maintenance, and minor alterations treated as Deductions under Section 8.01;

3. The cost of Inventories and Fixed Asset Supplies consumed in the operation of the Hotel;

4. A reasonable reserve for uncollectible accounts receivable as determined by Management Company;

5. All costs and fees of independent accountants or third parties who perform services required or permitted hereunder;

6. The cost and expense of technical consultants and operational experts for specialized services in connection with non-routine Hotel work;

7. An amount equal to three percent (3%) of Gross Revenues as reimbursement to Management Company for the Hotel's share of costs and expenses incurred by Management Company or its affiliated companies for services which benefit all Marriott hotels, are performed by personnel not normally located at the Hotel and are not Chain Services. Such services include executive supervision, consulting, planning, policy making, corporate finance, personnel and employee relations, in-house legal services, trademark protection, research and development, and the services of Management Company's technical, operational, and marketing experts making periodic inspection and consultation visits to the Hotel;

8. The Hotel's pro rata share of costs and expenses incurred by Management Company in providing Chain Services;

9. Operational insurance costs and expenses as provided in Sections 12.03 and 12.05;

10. Taxes, if any, payable by or assessed against Management Company related to the Agreement or to Management Company's operation of the Hotel (exclusive of Management Company's income taxes or personal or real property taxes assessed against the Hotel);

11. Such other costs and expenses as are specifically provided for elsewhere in the Agreement or are otherwise reasonably necessary for the proper and efficient operation of the Hotel.

I. *"Operating Loss"* shall mean a negative Operating Profit.

J. *"Termination"* shall mean the expiration or sooner cessation of the Agreement.

K. *"Uniform System of Accounts"* shall mean the *Uniform System of Accounts for Hotels,* Seventh Revised Edition, 1977, as published by the Hotel Association of New York City, Inc.

L. *"Working Capital"* shall mean funds which are reasonably necessary for the day-to-day operation of the Hotel's business, including, without limitation, amounts sufficient for the maintenance of change and petty cash funds, operating bank accounts, receivables, payrolls, prepaid expenses, and funds required to maintain Inventories, less accounts payable and accrued current liabilities.

1.02 *Terms Defined in Other Sections . . .*

ARTICLE II
APPOINTMENT OF MANAGEMENT COMPANY

2.01 *Appointment*

Owner hereby appoints and employs Management Company as Owner's exclusive agent to supervise, direct and control the management and operation of the Hotel for the term provided in Article IV. Management Company accepts said appointment and agrees to manage the Hotel during the term of the Agreement in accordance with the terms and conditions hereinafter set forth. The performance of all activities by Management Company hereunder shall be for the account of Owner.

2.02 *Delegation of Authority*

Hotel operations shall be under the exclusive supervision and control of Management Company which, except as otherwise specifically provided in the Agreement, shall be responsible for the proper and efficient operation of the Hotel. Management Company shall have discretion and control, free from interference, interruption or disturbance, in all matters relating to management and operation of the Hotel, including, without limitation,

charges for rooms and commercial space, credit policies, food and beverage services, employment policies, granting of concessions or leasing of shops and agencies within the Hotel, receipt, holding, and disbursement of funds, maintenance of bank accounts, procurement of inventories, supplies, and services, promotion and publicity and, generally, all activities necessary for operation of the Hotel.

2.03 *No Covenants or Restrictions*

Owner warrants that there will be on the Opening Date no covenants or restrictions which would prohibit or limit Management Company, after the necessary licenses and permits therefor have been obtained, from operating the Hotel, including cocktail lounges, restaurants, and other facilities customarily a part of or related to a first-class hotel. Owner agrees upon request by Management Company to sign promptly and without charge applications for licenses, permits or other instruments necessary for operation of the Hotel.

ARTICLE III
HOTEL

3.01 *Construction and Financing*

A. Owner shall, at its sole cost and expense, develop the Hotel on the Site ("Site") described in Exhibit __ under a financing plan mutually agreed upon by Owner and Management Company. The Hotel shall be designed, constructed, furnished, and fully equipped in accordance with a technical services agreement ("Technical Services Agreement") between Owner and Management Company (or one of its affiliated companies) and with time schedules, plans and specifications, all of which will be approved in writing by Owner and Management Company. The designs, plans, and specifications for the Hotel shall incorporate Management Company's fire and life safety standards and the standards set forth in Marriott Corporation's current edition of the "Hotel Design Guide," a copy of which has been supplied to Owner and incorporated herein by reference. Any changes in such time schedules, designs, plans, specifications, and fire and life safety standards shall be accomplished only pursuant to a written change order or other appropriate written evidence signed by Owner and Management Company.

B. Management Company will have the option of terminating the Agreement if:

1. Owner has not obtained a commitment for the long term debt financing of the Hotel within _____ ( ) days after the Effective Date, or

2. Construction on the Hotel has not commenced within _____ ( ) days after the Effective Date, or

3. Construction, furnishing and equipping of the Hotel has not been completed in accordance with Section 3.01 A within _____ ( ) months after construction has commenced.

3.02 *Ownership of Hotel*

A. Owner hereby covenants that it holds good and marketable fee title to the Site and that upon completion of the Hotel it will have, keep, and maintain good and marketable fee title interest therein free and clear of any and all liens, encumbrances, or other charges, except as follows:

1. Easements or other encumbrances (other than those described in subsection 2 and 3 hereof) which do not adversely affect the operation of the Hotel by Management Company;

2. Mortgages, deeds of trust, or similar security instruments which contain a provision that this Agreement will not be subject to forfeiture or Termination other than in accordance with the terms hereof, notwithstanding a default under such mortgage, deed of trust, or security instrument;

3. Liens for taxes, assessments, levies, or other public charges not yet due or which are being contested in good faith.

B. Owner shall pay and discharge, at or prior to the due date, any and all installments of principal and interest due and payable upon any mortgage, deed of trust, or like instrument described in this Section and shall indemnify Management Company from and against all claims, litigation, and damages arising from the failure to make such payments as and when required.

ARTICLE IV
TERM

4.01 *Term*

The initial term ("Initial Term") of the Agreement shall commence with the Effective Date and, unless sooner terminated as herein provided, shall continue for a period of twenty-five (25) Fiscal Years beginning with the first Fiscal Year commencing after the Opening Date. The term may thereafter be renewed by Management Company, at its option (on the same terms and conditions contained herein), for each of five (5) successive periods of ten (10) Fiscal Years ("Renewal Terms"), provided that Management Company is not then in default hereunder. If Management Company elects to exercise any such option to renew, it shall give Owner notice to that effect at least twelve (12) months prior to the expiration of the then current term.

ARTICLE V
COMPENSATION OF MANAGEMENT COMPANY

5.01 *Management Fee*

In consideration of services to be performed during the term of the Agreement, Management Company shall retain as its management fee a sum equal to _____ of Operating Profit. The balance of Operating Profit after deducting said amount and any amounts required to be paid by Owner shall be paid to Owner as provided in Section 5.02.

5.02 *Accounting and Interim Payment*

A. Within twenty (20) days after the close of each Accounting Period, Management Company shall submit an interim accounting to Owner showing Gross Revenues, Deductions, Operating Profit, and distributions thereof. Management Company shall transfer with each accounting any interim amounts due Owner and shall retain any interim management fee due Management Company.

B. Calculations and payments of the management fee and distributions of Operating Profit made with respect to each Accounting Period within a Fiscal Year shall be accounted for cumulatively. Within one hundred twenty (120) days after the close of each Fiscal Year, Management Company shall submit an accounting, as more fully described in Section 9.01, for such Fiscal Year to Owner, which accounting shall be controlling over the interim accountings. Any adjustments required by the Fiscal Year accounting shall be made promptly by the parties. No adjustment shall be made for any Operating Loss in a preceding or subsequent Fiscal Year.

ARTICLE VI
PRE-OPENING

6.01 *Description*

It is recognized that certain activities must be undertaken so that Hotel can function properly on the Opening Date and during the first Fiscal Year. Accordingly, Management Company shall:

A. Recruit, train, and employ the staff required for the Hotel;

B. Negotiate concession contracts for stores, office space, and lobby space;

C. Undertake pre-opening promotion and advertising, including opening celebrations;

D. Test the operations of the Hotel;

E. Provide, for a period to end not later than sixty (60) days from the Opening Date, a task force of experts and personnel to supervise and assist with certain pre-opening and opening operations;

F. Apply for the initial licenses and permits required for the operation of the Hotel as contemplated by the Agreement;

G. In general, render such other miscellaneous services incidental to the preparation and organization of the Hotel's operations as may be required for the Hotel to be adequately staffed and capable of operating on the Opening Date and during the first Fiscal Year.

The expenses relating to such activities ("Pre-Opening Expenses") shall include, but not be limited to, salaries and wages (including those of personnel of Management Company and its affiliated companies), costs of interim office space, professional fees, telephone expenses, staff hiring and training costs, travel and moving expenses, costs of opening celebrations, the cost of heat, light, and power not chargeable to the cost of constructing the Hotel, advertising and promotion expense, and miscellaneous expenses. Management Company shall from time to time as necessary prepare and submit estimates of Pre-Opening Expenses to Owner. In the event the Opening Date is delayed or postponed from the original date established therefor, such estimates shall be subject to revision to reflect any increases in Pre-Opening Expenses occasioned by such delay or postponement. Within one hundred twenty (120) days after the Opening Date, Management Company shall furnish Owner with an accounting describing and showing in reasonable detail the total amount of Pre-Opening Expenses.

6.02 *Responsibility for Pre-Opening Expenses*

Pre-Opening Expenses shall be borne by Owner and advanced to Management Company in accordance with the estimates described above, or as otherwise requested by Management Company. Pre-Opening Expenses incurred or paid by Management Company shall be promptly reimbursed by Owner upon receipt of a statement of account for such Pre-Opening Expenses. If, following the Opening Date, there are outstanding Pre-Opening Expenses which have been invoiced to Owner but have not been paid within thirty (30) days of receipt of said invoice(s), Management Company shall have the option to deduct such amounts from Owner's share of Operating Profit under Article V.

ARTICLE VII
WORKING CAPITAL AND FIXED ASSET SUPPLIES

7.01 *Working Capital and Inventories*

Prior to the Opening Date, Owner shall provide the funds necessary to supply the Hotel with Working Capital and Inventories and shall from time to time thereafter promptly advance, upon request of Management Company, any additional funds necessary to maintain Working Capital and Inventories at levels determined by Management Company to be necessary to satisfy the needs of the Hotel as its operation may from time to time require. Working Capital and Inventories so advanced shall remain the property of Owner throughout the term of the Agreement. Upon Termination, Owner shall retain any of its unused Working Capital and Inventories except for Inventories purchased by Management Company pursuant to Section 10.02.

7.02 *Fixed Asset Supplies*

Owner shall provide the funds necessary to supply the Hotel with Fixed Asset Supplies and shall from time to time thereafter promptly advance, upon request of Management Company, and additional funds necessary to maintain Fixed Asset Supplies at levels determined by Management Company to be necessary to satisfy the needs of the Hotel as its operation may from time to time require. Fixed Asset Supplies shall remain the property of Owner throughout the term of the Agreement except for Fixed Asset Supplies purchased by Management Company pursuant to Section 10.02.

ARTICLE VIII
REPAIRS, MAINTENANCE, AND REPLACEMENTS

8.01 *Routine Repairs and Maintenance*

Management Company shall maintain the Hotel in good repair and condition and in conformity with applicable laws and regulations and shall make or cause to be made such routine maintenance, repairs, and minor alterations, the cost of which can be expensed under generally accepted accounting principles, as it, from time to time, deems necessary for such purposes. The cost of such maintenance, repairs, and alterations shall be paid from Gross Revenues and shall be treated as a Deduction in determining Operating Profit. The cost of non-routine repairs and maintenance, either to the Hotel building or its fixtures, furniture, furnishings, and equipment ("FF&E") shall be paid for in the manner described in Sections 8.02 and 8.03.

8.02 *Repairs and Equipment Reserve*

A. Management Company shall establish an escrow reserve account ("Repairs and Equipment Reserve" or the "Reserve") in a bank designated by Management Company to cover the cost of:

1. Replacements and renewals to the

Hotel's FF&E and

2. Certain routine repairs and maintenance to the Hotel building which are normally capitalized under generally accepted accounting principles such as exterior and interior repainting, resurfacing building walls, floors, roofs, and parking areas, and replacing folding walls and the like, but which are not major repairs, alterations, improvements, renewals, or replacements to the Hotel building's structure or to its mechanical, electrical, heating, ventilating, air conditioning, plumbing, or vertical transportation systems, the cost of which are Owner's sole responsibility under Section 8.03.

B. During the period of time up to the expiration of the first Fiscal Year after the Opening Date, Management Company shall transfer into the Reserve an amount equal to one percent (1%) of Gross Revenues for such period of time; during the second Fiscal Year after the Opening Date, Management Company shall transfer into the Reserve an amount equal to two percent (2%) of Gross Revenues for such Fiscal Year; during the third, fourth and fifth Fiscal Years after the Opening Date, Management Company shall transfer into the Reserve an amount equal to three percent (3%) of Gross Revenues for each of such Fiscal Years; during the sixth through the tenth Fiscal Years after the Opening Date, Management Company shall transfer into the Reserve an amount equal to four percent (4%) of Gross Revenues for each of such Fiscal Years; commencing with the eleventh Fiscal Year after the Opening Date and for all Fiscal Years thereafter, subject to the provisions of subsection E, below, Management Company shall transfer into the Reserve an amount equal to five percent (5%) of Gross Revenues for each of such Fiscal Years. All amounts transferred into the Reserve shall be deducted from Owner's share of Operating Profit distributable to it under Article V.

C. Management Company shall from time to time make such (1) replacements and renewals to the Hotel's FF&E, and (2) repairs to the Hotel building of the nature described in Section 8.02(A)(2), as it deems necessary, up to the balance in the Repairs and Equipment Reserve. No expenditures will be made in excess of said balance without the approval of Owner. At the end of each Fiscal Year, any amounts remaining in the Repairs and Equipment Reserve shall be carried forward to the next Fiscal Year. Proceeds from the sale of FF&E no longer necessary to the operation of the Hotel shall be deposited in the escrow account and credited against the amount otherwise re-

quired to be deposited in the Reserve under Section 8.02(B), as shall any interest which accrues on amounts placed in the escrow account.

D. Management Company shall prepare an estimate ("Repairs and Equipment Estimate") of the expenditures necessary for (1) replacements and renewals to the Hotel's FF&E, and (2) repairs to the Hotel building of the nature described in Section 8.02 (A)(2), during the ensuing Fiscal Year and shall submit such Repairs and Equipment Estimate to Owner at the same time it submits the Annual Operating Projection described in Section 9.03.

E. The percentage contributions for the Repairs and Equipment Reserve described in Section 8.02(B) are estimates based upon Management Company's prior experience with new hotels. As the Hotel ages, these percentages may not be sufficient to keep the Reserve at the levels necessary to make the replacements and renewals to the Hotel's FF&E, or to make the repairs to the Hotel building of the nature described in Section 8.02 (A)(2), which are required to maintain the Hotel as a first-class facility. If the Repairs and Equipment Estimate prepared in good faith by Management Company excess the available funds in the Repairs and Equipment Reserve, Owner will:

1. Agree to increase the annual percentage in Section 8.02(B) to provide the additional funds required, or

2. Arrange to obtain outside financing for the additional funds required, in which event the principal and interest payments on such financing shall constitute Deductions in determining Operating Profit.

A failure or refusal by Owner to agree to either 1 or 2 above within a sixty (60) day period after Management Company's request therefor shall entitle Management Company to terminate the Agreement upon six (6) months' written notice to Owner.

8.03 *Building Alterations, Improvements, Renewals, and Replacements*

A. Management Company shall prepare an annual estimate of the expenses necessary for major repairs, alterations, improvements, renewals and replacements (which repairs, alterations, improvements, renewals and replacements are not among those referred to in Section 8.02(A)(2) to the structural, mechanical, electrical, heating, ventilating, air conditioning, plumbing, or vertical transportation elements of the Hotel building ("Building Estimate") and shall submit such Building Estimate to Owner for its approval at the same time the Annual Operating Projection is submitted. Management Company

shall not make any expenditures for such purposes without the prior written consent of Owner, which consent shall not be unreasonably withheld; provided that if major repairs, alterations, improvements, renewals, or replacements to the Hotel are required by reason of any law, ordinance, regulation, or order of a competent government authority, or are otherwise required for the continued safe and orderly operation of the Hotel, Management Company shall immediately give Owner notice thereof and shall be authorized to take appropriate remedial action without such approval if Owner does not act. The cost of all such repairs, alterations, improvements, renewals, or replacements shall be borne solely by Owner.

B. If Owner does not approve the Building Estimate as in good faith recommended by Management Company within sixty (60) days after it has been submitted, Management Company shall have the option of terminating the Agreement upon six (6) months' written notice.

8.04 *Liens*

Management Company and Owner shall use their best efforts to prevent any liens from being filed against the Hotel which arise from any maintenance, repairs, alterations, improvements, renewals, or replacements in or to the Hotel. They shall cooperate fully in obtaining the release of any such liens, and the cost thereof, if the lien was not occasioned by the fault of either party, shall be treated the same as the cost of the matter to which it relates. If the lien arises as a result of the fault of either party, then the party at fault shall bear the cost of obtaining the lien release.

8.05 *Ownership of Replacements*

All repairs, alterations, improvements, renewals or replacements made pursuant to Article VIII shall be the property of Owner.

ARTICLE IX
BOOKKEEPING AND BANK ACCOUNTS

9.01 *Books and Records*

Books of control and account shall be kept on the accrual basis and in material respects in accordance with the Uniform System of Accounts, with the exceptions provided in the Agreement. Owner may at reasonable intervals during Management Company's normal business hours examine such records. Within one hundred twenty (120) days following the close of each Fiscal Year, Management Company shall furnish Owner a statement in reasonable detail summarizing the Hotel operations for such Fiscal Year and a certificate of Management Company's chief accounting officer certifying that such year-end statement is true and correct. Owner shall have ninety (90 days after receipt to audit, examine, or review said statement. If Owner raises no objections within said ninety (90) day period, the statement shall be deemed to have been accepted by Owner as true and correct, and Owner shall have no further right to question its accuracy.

9.02 *Hotel Accounts, Expenditures*

A. All funds derived from operation of the Hotel shall be deposited by Management Company in Hotel bank accounts in a bank designated by Management Company and approved by Owner, which approval shall not be unreasonably withheld. Withdrawals from said accounts shall be made by representatives of Management Company whose signatures have been authorized. Reasonable petty cash funds shall be maintained at the Hotel.

B. All payments made by Management Company hereunder shall be made from authorized bank accounts, petty cash funds, or from Working Capital provided by Owner pursuant to Section 7.01. Management Company shall not be required to make any advance or payment to or for the account of Owner except out of such funds, and Management Company shall not be obligated to incur any liability or obligation for Owner's account without assurances that necessary funds for the discharge thereof will be provided by Owner. Debts and liabilities incurred by Management Company as a result of its operation and management of the Hotel pursuant to the terms hereof, whether asserted before or after the Termination of this Agreement, will be paid by Owner to the extent funds are not available for that purpose from the operation of the Hotel.

9.03 *Annual Operating Projection*

Management Company shall submit to Owner for its review thirty (30) days prior to the beginning of each Fiscal Year after the Opening Date an "Annual Operating Projection." Such projection shall project the estimated Gross Revenues, departmental profits, Deductions, and Operating Profit for the forthcoming Fiscal Year for the Hotel, taking into account the Hotel's market area and the integration of the Hotel into the Marriott hotel system. Management Company shall use its best efforts to adhere to the Annual Operating Projection. It is understood, however, that the Annual Operating Projection is an estimate only and that unforeseen circumstances such as, but not limited to, the costs of labor, material, services and supplies, casualty, operation of law, or eco-

nomic and market conditions may make adherence to the Annual Operating Projection impracticable, and Management Company shall be entitled to depart therefrom due to causes of the foregoing nature.

9.04 *Operating Losses: Credit*

A. To the extent there is an Operating Loss, additional funds in the amount of any such deficiency shall be provided by Owner within ten (10) days after Management Company has given written notice to Owner of such Operating Loss.

B. In no event shall either party borrow money in the name of or pledge the credit of the other.

ARTICLE X
TRADEMARK AND TRADE NAME

10.01 *Marriott Name*

During the term of the Agreement, the Hotel shall be known as a Marriott Hotel, with such additional identification as may be necessary to provide local identification. If the name of the Marriott hotel system is changed, Management Company shall have the right to change the name of the Hotel to conform thereto. The name "Marriott" when used alone or in connection with another word or words and the Marriott trademarks, trade names, symbols, logos, and designs shall in all events remain the exclusive property of Marriott Corporation, and nothing contained herein shall confer on Owner the right to use the Marriott name, trademarks, trade names, symbols, logos, or designs otherwise than in strict accordance with the terms of the Agreement. Except as provided in Section 10.02, upon Termination, any use of or right to use the Marriott name, trademarks, trade names, symbols, logos, or designs by Owner shall cease forthwith and Owner shall promptly remove from the Hotel any signs or similar items which contain the Marriott name, trademarks, trade names, symbols, logos, or designs.

10.02 *Purchase of Inventories and Fixed Asset Supplies*

Upon Termination, Management Company shall have the option, to be exercised within thirty (30) days after Termination, to purchase, at their then book value, any items of the Hotel's Inventories and Fixed Asset Supplies as may be marked with the Marriott name or any Marriott trademark, trade name, symbol, logo, or design. In the event Management Company does not exercise such option, Owner agrees that it will use any such items not so purchased exclusively in connection with the Hotel until they are consumed.

10.03 *Breach of Covenant*

Management Company and/or its affiliated companies shall be entitled, in case of any breach of the covenants of Article X by Owner or others claiming through it, to injunctive relief and to any other right or remedy available at law. Article X shall survive Termination.

ARTICLE XI
POSSESSION AND USE OF HOTEL

11.01 *Quiet Enjoyment*

Owner covenants that so long as Management Company is not in default under the Agreement, Management Company shall quietly hold, occupy and enjoy the Hotel throughout the term hereof free from hindrance, ejection, or molestation by Owner or other party claiming under, through, or by right of Owner. Owner agrees to pay and discharge any payments and charges and, at its expense, to prosecute all appropriate actions, judicial or otherwise, necessary to assure such free and quiet occupation.

11.02 *Use*

A. Management Company shall use the Hotel solely for the operation of a hotel under standards comparable to those prevailing in the Marriott hotel system and for all activities in connection therewith which are customary and usual to such an operation.

B. Management Company shall have the option to terminate the Agreement at any time upon sixty (60) days written notice to Owner in the event of a withdrawal or revocation, by any lawful governing body having jurisdiction thereof, of any material license or permit required for Management Company's performance hereunder where such withdrawal or revocation is due to circumstances beyond Management Company's control.

11.03 *Chain Services*

Management Company will, commencing with the Opening Date and thereafter during the term of this Agreement, cause to be furnished to the Hotel certain services ("Chain Services") which are furnished generally on a central or regional basis to other hotels in the Marriott chain and which benefit each hotel as a participant in the Marriott chain. Chain Services shall include (i) national sales office services, central training services, central advertising and promotion (including direct and image media and advertising administration), the Marriott national reservations system, and the Marriott computer payroll and accounting services, and (ii) such additional central or regional services as may from time to time be furnished for the benefit of hotels in the

Marriott chain or in substitution for services now performed at individual hotels which may be more efficiently performed on a group basis. Costs and expenses incurred in the providing of such services shall be allocated on a fair and equitable basis among all Marriott hotels owned, leased, or managed by Management Company in the United States receiving the same.

11.04 *Owner's Right to Inspect*

Owner or its agents shall have access to the Hotel at any and all reasonable times for the purpose of protecting the same against fire or other casualty, prevention of damage to the Hotel, inspection, making repairs, or showing the Hotel to prospective purchasers, tenants, or mortgagees.

ARTICLE XII
INSURANCE

12.01 *Interim Insurance*

Owner shall, at its expense, at all times during the period of constructing, furnishing, and equipping of the Hotel, procure and maintain adequate public liability and indemnity and property insurance (with limits and coverage to be mutually agreed upon) fully protecting Owner and Management Company against loss or damage arising in connection with preparing, constructing, furnishing, and equipping of the Hotel and pre-opening activities.

12.02 *Property Insurance*

A. Management Company shall, commencing with the Opening Date and during the term of the Agreement, procure and maintain, using funds deducted from Owner's share of Operating Profit distributable to it under Article V, with insurance companies reasonably acceptable to Owner and licensed to do business in the state where the Hotel is located, a minimum of the following insurance:

1. Insurance on the Hotel (including contents) against loss or damage by fire, lightning and all other risks covered by the usual standard extended coverage endorsements, with such deductible limits as are generally established by Management Company at the other hotels it leases or manages under the Marriott name in the United States, all in an amount not less than ninety percent (90%) of the replacement cost thereof;

2. Insurance against loss or damage from explosion of boilers, pressure vessels, pressure pipes, and sprinklers, to the extent applicable, installed in the Hotel;

3. Business interruption insurance covering loss of profits and necessary continuing expenses for interruptions caused by any occurrence covered by the insurance referred to in Section 12.02(A)(1) and (2), of a type and in amounts and with such deductible limits as are generally established by Management Company at the other hotels it leases or manages under the Marriott name in the United States.

B. All policies of insurance required under Section 12.02(A)(1), (2) and (3) shall be carried in the name of Owner, Management Company, and the holder of the first-lien permanent mortgage on teh Hotel; any losses thereunder shall be payable to the parties as their respective interests may appear.

C. Any mortgage on the Hotel shall contain provisions to the effect that proceeds of the insurance policies required to be carried under Section 12.02 shall be available for repair and restoration of the Hotel.

12.03 *Operational Insurance*

Management Company shall, commencing with the Opening Date and during the term of the Agreement, procure and maintain, using funds deducted from Gross Revenues, either with insurance companies reasonably acceptable to Owner and licensed to do business in the state where the Hotel is located, or by legally qualifying as a self insurer in that state, the following insurance:

A. Workers' compensation and employer's liability insurance as may be required under applicable laws covering all of Management Company's employees at the Hotel, with such deductible limits or self-insured retentions as are generally established by Management Company at the other hotels it leases or manages under the Marriott name in the United States;

B. Fidelity bonds, with reasonable limits and deductibles to be determined by Management Company, covering its employees in job classifications normally bonded in the other hotels it leases or manages under the Marriott name in the United States or as otherwise required by law, and comprehensive crime insurance to the extent Management Company and Owner mutually agree it is necessary for the Hotel;

C. Comprehensive general public liability insurance against claims for personal injury, death, or property damage occurring on, in, or about the Hotel, and automobile insurance on vehicles operated in conjunction with the Hotel, with a combined single limit of not less than Ten Million Dollars ($10,000,000) for each occurrence for personal injury, death and property damage, with such deductible limits or self-insured retentions as are generally established by Management Company at the other hotels it leases or manages under the Marriott name in the United States;

D. Such other insurance in amounts as Management Company in its reasonable judgment deems advisable for protection against claims, liabilities and losses arising out of or connected with the operation of the Hotel.

12.04 *Coverage*

All insurance described in Sections 12.02 and 12.03 may be obtained by Management Company by endorsement or equivalent means under its blanket insurance policies, provided that such blanket policies substantially fulfill the requirements specified herein. Deductible limits and self-insured retentions shall be as provided in the blanket policies covering the hotels leased or managed by Management Company under the Marriott name in the United States. In addition, Management Company may (if it has legally qualified to do so) self-insure or otherwise retain such risks or portions thereof as it does with respect to other hotels it leases or manages under the Marriott name in the United States.

12.05 *Cost and Expense*

Insurance premiums and any costs or expenses with respect to the insurance described in Section 12.03, including insurance reinsured by a subsidiary of Management Company, shall be Deductions in determining Operating Profit. Premiums on policies for more than one year shall be charged pro rata against Gross Revenues over the period of the policies. The expenses incurred in maintaining Management Company's self-insurance program shall be charged on an equitable basis to the hotels participating in such programs. Any reserves, losses, costs, damages, or expenses which are uninsured, or fall within deductible limits or self-insured retentions, shall be treated as a cost of insurance and shall be Deductions in determining Operating Profit. Upon Termination, an escrow fund in an amount acceptable to Management Company shall be established from Gross Revenues (or, if Gross Revenues are not sufficient, with funds provided by Owner) to cover the amount of any deductible limits or self-insured retentions and all other costs which will eventually have to be paid by either Owner or Management Company with respect to pending or contingent claims, including those which arise after Termination for causes arising during the term of the Agreement.

12.06 *Policies and Endorsements*

A. Where permitted, all insurance provided under Article XII shall name

Management Company and Owner as named insureds. The party procuring such insurance shall deliver to the other party certificates of insurance with respect to all policies so procured, including existing, additional and renewal policies and, in the case of insurance about to expire, shall deliver certificates of insurance with respect to the renewal policies not less than ten (10) days prior to the respective dates of expiration.

B. All policies of insurance provided for under Article XII shall, to the extent obtainable, have attached thereto an endorsement that such policy shall not be cancelled or materially changed without at least thirty (30) days prior written notice to Owner and Management Company.

ARTICLE XIII
TAXES

13.01 *Real Estate and Personal Property Taxes*

All real estate and personal property taxes, levies, assessments and similar charges on or relating to the Hotel ("Impositions") during the term of the Agreement shall be paid by Owner, at its sole expense, before any fine, penalty, or interest is added thereto or lien placed upon the Hotel or the Agreement, unless payment thereof is in good faith being contested and enforcement thereof is stayed. Owner shall, within the earlier of thirty (30) days of payment or three (3) days following written demand by Management Company, furnish Management Company with copies of official tax bills and assessments and evidence of payment or contest thereof.

ARTICLE XIV
HOTEL EMPLOYEES

14.01 *Employees*

A. All personnel employed at the Hotel shall at all times be the employees of Management Company. Management Company shall have absolute discretion to hire, promote, supervise, direct and train all employees at the Hotel, to fix their compensation and, generally, establish and maintain all policies relating to employment.

B. Management Company shall decide whom, if any, of the Hotel's employees shall reside at the Hotel, and shall be permitted to provide free accommodations and amenities to its employees and representatives living at or visiting the Hotel in connection with its management or operation. No person shall otherwise be given gratuitous accommodations or services without prior joint approval of

Owner and Management Company except in accordance with usual practices of the hotel and travel industry.

C. At Termination, other than by reason of a default of Management Company hereunder, an escrow fund shall be established from Gross Revenues (or, if Gross Revenues are not sufficient, with funds provided by Owner) to reimburse Management Company for all costs and expenses incurred by Management Company such as reasonable transfer costs, or severance pay, unemployment compensation, and other employee liability costs arising out of either the transfer or termination of employment of Management Company's employees at the Hotel, as the case may be.

ARTICLE XV
DAMAGE, CONDEMNATION, AND FORCE MAJEURE

15.01 *Damage and Repair*

A. If, during the term hereof, the Hotel is damaged or destroyed by fire, casualty, or other cause, Owner shall, at its cost and expense and with all reasonable diligence, repair or replace the damaged or destroyed portion of the Hotel to the same condition as existed previously. To the extent available, proceeds from the insurance described in Section 12.02 shall be applied to such repairs or replacements.

B. In the event damage or destruction to the Hotel from any cause materially and adversely affects the operation of the Hotel and Owner fails to promptly commence and complete the repairing, rebuilding or replacement of the same so that the Hotel shall be substantially the same as it was prior to such damage or destruction, Management Company may, at its option, elect to either undertake such work for the account of Owner or terminate the Agreement upon sixty (60) days written notice.

15.02 *Condemnation*

A. In the event all or substantially all of the Hotel shall be taken in any eminent domain, condemnation, compulsory acquisition, or similar proceeding by any competent authority for any public or quasi-public use or purpose, or in the event a portion of the Hotel shall be so taken, but the result is that it is unreasonable to continue to operate the Hotel, the Agreement shall terminate. Owner and Management Company shall each have the right to initiate such proceedings as they deem advisable to recover any damages to which they may be entitled.

B. In the event a portion of the Hotel shall be taken by the events described in Section 15.02(A), or the entire Hotel is

affected but on a temporary basis, and the result is not to make it unreasonable to continue to operate the Hotel, the Agreement shall not terminate. However, so much of any award for any such partial taking or condemnation as shall be necessary to render the Hotel equivalent to its condition prior to such event shall be used for such purpose; the balance of such award, if any, shall be fairly and equitably apportioned between Owner and Management Company in accordance with their respective interests.

15.03 *Force Majeure*

If acts of God, acts of war, civil disturbance, governmental action, including the revocation of any license or permit necessary for the operation contemplated in the Agreement where such revocation is not due to Management Company's fault, or any other causes beyond the control of Management Company shall, in Management Company's reasonable opinion, have a significant adverse effect upon operations of the Hotel, then Management Company shall be entitled to terminate the Agreement upon sixty (60) days written notice.

ARTICLE XVI
DEFAULTS

16.01 *Defaults*

The following shall constitute "events of default" to the extent permitted by applicable law:

A. The filing of a voluntary petition in bankruptcy or insolvency or a petition for reorganization under any bankruptcy law by either party, or the admission by either party that it is unable to pay its debts as they become due;

B. The consent to an involuntary petition in bankruptcy or the failure to vacate, within ninety (90) days from the date of entry thereof, any order approving an involuntary petition by either party;

C. The entering of an order, judgment, or decree by any court of competent jurisdiction, on the application of a creditor, adjudicating either party as bankrupt or insolvent or approving a petition seeking reorganization or appointing a receiver, trustee, or liquidator of all or a substantial part of such party's assets, and such order, judgment or decree's continuing unstayed and in effect for any period of ninety (90) days;

D. The failure of either party to make any payment required to be made in accordance with the terms hereof within ten (10) days after written notice that such payment has not been made; or

E. The failure of either party to perform, keep, or fulfill any of the other covenants, undertakings, obligations, or conditions set forth in the Agreement, and the continuance of such default for a period of thirty (30) days after notice of said failure.

Upon the occurrence of any of such events of default, the non-defaulting party may give to the defaulting party notice of its intention to terminate the Agreement for default after the expiration of a period of thirty (30) days from the date of such notice, and upon the expiration of such period, if the default has not been cured, the Agreement shall terminate. If, however, upon receipt of such notice, the defaulting party shall promptly (if such default is not susceptible of being cured within thirty (30) days) commence to cure the default, and shall thereafter diligently pursue such efforts to completion, then such notice shall be of no force and effect. The provisions of the immediately preceding sentence shall not apply to subsections A through D of Section 16.01, to Section 3.01(B), or to Section 20.01.

16.02 *Remedies*

A. In the event the Hotel has not been completed in the manner contemplated by Section 3.01(A) by the date set forth in the mutually agreed upon time schedules, Owner shall pay Management Company, as liquidated damages and not as a penalty, the sum of One Thousand Dollars ($1,000) per day for each day of delay in so completing the Hotel. If Management Company's operation of the Hotel precedes the date of such completion, Management Company shall be entitled to withhold such sum from that share of Operating Profit otherwise distributable to Owner pursuant to Section 5.01. The provisions of this Section 16.02(A) shall not apply where the delays in so completing the Hotel are due to action or inaction of governmental authorities having jurisdiction over the Hotel, strikes or like labor disturbances, casualty, weather, civil unrest, or shortages of critical materials and supplies, or other similar causes beyond the control of Owner.

B. Except as set forth in Section 16.02(A) above, the rights granted hereunder shall not be in substitution for, but shall be in addition to, any and all rights and remedies available to the non-defaulting party by reason of applicable provisions of law.

ARTICLE XVII
WAIVER AND PARTIAL INVALIDITY

17.01 *Waiver*

The failure of either party to insist upon a strict performance of any of the terms or provisions of the Agreement, or to exercise any option, right, or remedy herein contained, shall not be construed as a waiver or as a relinquishment for the future of such term, provision, option, right, or remedy, but the same shall continue and remain in full force and effect. No waiver by either party of any term or provision hereof shall be deemed to have been made unless expressed in writing and signed by such party.

17.02 *Partial Invalidity*

If any portion of the Agreement shall be declared invalid by order, decree, or judgment of a court, the Agreement shall be construed as if such portion had not been inserted herein except when such construction would operate as an undue hardship on Management Company or Owner or constitute a substantial deviation from the general intent and purpose of said parties as reflected in the Agreement.

ARTICLE XVIII
ASSIGNMENT

18.01 *Assignment*

A. Neither party shall assign or transfer or permit the assignment or transfer of the Agreement without the prior written consent of the other; provided, however, that Management Company shall have the right, without such consent, to (1) assign its interest in the Agreement to any of its affiliated companies, and any such assignee shall be deemed to be the Management Company for the purposes of the Agreement, and (2) sublease shops or grant concessions at the Hotel so long as the terms of any such subleases or concessions do not exceed the term of the Agreement. Nothing contained herein shall prevent (i) the conditional assignment of the Agreement as security for any mortgage which Management Company approves on the Hotel, (ii) the transfer of the Agreement in connection with a merger or consolidation or a sale of all or substantially all of the assets of either party or their respective affiliated companies; or (iii) an assignment of the Agreement in connection with an approved sale of the Hotel pursuant to Section 19.01(A)(2).

B. In the event either party consents to an assignment of the Agreement by the other, no further assignment shall be made without the express consent in writing of such party, unless such assignment may otherwise be made without such consent pursuant to the terms of the Agreement. An assignment by either Owner or Management Company of its interest in the Agreement shall not relieve Owner or Management Company, as the case may be, from their respective obligations under the Agreement, and shall inure to the benefit of, and be binding upon, their respective successors, heirs, legal representatives, or assigns.

ARTICLE XIX
SALE OF HOTEL

19.01 *Right of First Refusal*

A. If Owner receives a bona fide written offer to purchase or lease the Hotel and desires to accept such offer, Owner shall give written notice thereof to Management Company stating the name of the prospective purchaser or tenant, as the case may be, the price or rental and the terms and conditions of such proposed sale or lease, together with all other information requested by Management Company and reasonably available to Owner. Within ninety (90) days after the date of receipt of Owner's written notice and such other information, Management Company shall elect, by written notice to Owner, one of the following alternatives:

1. To purchase or lease the Hotel at the same price or rental and upon the same terms and conditions as those set forth in the written notice from Owner to Management Company or upon other terms acceptable to Owner, in which event Owner and Management Company shall promptly enter into an agreement for such sale or lease and shall finalize the same.

2. To consent to such sale or lease and to the assignment of the Agreement to such purchaser or tenant, provided that concurrently with the finalization thereof the purchaser or tenant, as the case may be, shall, by appropriate instrument in form satisfactory to Management Company, assume all of Owner's obligations hereunder. Such consent shall not relieve Owner from its obligations under the Agreement unless Management Company is satisfied that the purchaser or tenant is capable of performing such obligations. An executed copy of such assumption agreement shall be delivered to Management Company.

3. To terminate the Agreement by written notice to Owner, which notice will set an effective date for such Termination not earlier than thirty (30) days, nor more than one hundred twenty (120) days, following the date of the giving of such notice. Management Company shall have the right to change such effective date of Termination to coincide with the date of the finalization of the proposed sale or lease. Said notice of Termination shall not be effective if such sale or lease is not finalized.

B. If Management Company shall fail

to elect any of the above alternatives within said ninety (90) day period, the same shall be conclusively deemed to constitute an election and consent under subsection 2 above, and the provisions thereof shall prevail as if Management Company had consented in writing thereto. Any proposed sale or lease of which notice has been given by Owner to Management Company hereunder must be finalized within one hundred eighty (180) days following the giving of such notice, unless Management Company has exercised its option under subsection 1 above to purchase or lease the Hotel. Failing such finalization, such notice, and any response thereto given by Management Company, shall be null and void and all of the provisions of Section 19.01(A) must again be complied with before Owner shall have the right to finalize a sale or lease of the Hotel upon the terms contained in said notice, or otherwise.

C. Any sale, assignment, transfer, or other disposition, for value or otherwise, voluntary or involuntary, of the controlling interest in Owner (i.e., the possession directly or indirectly of the power to direct or cause the direction of the management and policies of Owner, whether through the ownership of voting securities, or by contract or otherwise) shall be deemed a sale or lease of the Hotel under Section 19.01(A) and shall be subject to the provisions thereof. Owner, from time to time, upon written request of Management Company, shall furnish Management Company with a list of the names and addresses of the owners of capital stock, partnership interest, or other proprietary interest in Owner.

ARTICLE XX
CONDITIONS

20.01 *Conditions to the Obligations of Management Company*

The obligations of Management Company hereunder shall be conditioned upon the following:

A. Timely completion of the Hotel in accordance with the terms of the Technical Services Agreement and the standards set forth in the Hotel Design Guide or in accordance with plans, specifications and time schedules otherwise agreed upon by Owner and Management Company.

B. Receipt at least ninety (90) prior to the projected Opening Date of all licenses, permits, decrees, acts, orders, or other approvals necessary for operation of the Hotel.

ARTICLE XXI
MISCELLANEOUS

21.01 *Right to Make Agreement*

Each party warrants, with respect to itself, that neither the execution of the Agreement nor the finalization of the transactions contemplated hereby shall violate any provision of law or judgment, writ, injunction, order, or decree of any court or governmental authority having jurisdiction over it; result in or constitute a breach or default under any indenture, contract, other commitment or restriction to which it is a party or by which it is bound; or require any consent, vote, or approval which has not been taken, or at the time of the transaction involved shall not have been given or taken. Each party covenants that it has and will continue to have throughout the term of the Agreement and any extensions thereof, the full right to enter into the Agreement and perform its obligations hereunder.

21.02 *Consents*

Wherever in the Agreement the consent or approval of Owner or Management Company is required, such consent or approval shall not be unreasonably withheld, shall be in writing and shall be executed by a duly authorized officer or agent of the party granting such consent or approval. If either Owner or Management Company fails to respond within thirty (30) days to a request by the other party for a consent or approval, such consent or approval shall be deemed to have been given.

21.03 *Agency*

The relationship of Owner and Management Company shall be that of principal and agent, and nothing contained in the Agreement shall be construed to create a partnership or joint venture between them or their successors in interest. Management Company's agency established by the Agreement is coupled with an interest and may not be terminated by Owner until the expiration of the term of the Agreement, except as provided in Articles XV or XVI.

21.04 *Confidentiality*

The parties hereto agree that the matters set forth in the Agreement are strictly confidential and each party will make every effort to ensure that the information is not disclosed to any outside person or entities (including the press) without the written consent of the other party.

21.05 *Applicable Law*

The Agreement shall be construed under and shall be governed by the laws of the state where the Hotel is located.

21.06 *Recordation*

The terms and provisions of the Agreement shall run with the land designated as the Site, and with Owner's interest therein, and shall be binding upon all successors to such interest. At the request of either party, the parties shall execute an appropriate memorandum of the Agreement in recordable form and cause the same to be recorded in the jurisdiction where the Hotel is located. Any cost of such recordation shall be initially borne by Owner, reimbursed to Owner from Gross Revenues, and treated as a Deduction.

21.07 *Headings*

Headings of Articles and Sections are inserted only for convenience and are in no way to be construed as a limitation on the scope of the particular Articles or Sections to which they refer.

21.08 *Notices*

Notices, statements and other communications to be given under the terms of the Agreement shall be in writing and delivered by hand against receipt or sent by certified or registered mail, postage prepaid, return receipt requested:

> *To Owner:*
>
> *with copies to:*
> (Owner's construction lender)
> and
> (Owner's permanent lender)
>
> *To Management Company:*
> Marriott Corporation

or at such other address as if from time to time designated by the party receiving the notice. Any such notice which is properly mailed shall be deemed to have been served as of five (5) days after said posting for purposes of establishing that the sending party complied with the applicable time limitations set forth herein, but shall not be binding on the addressee until actually received.

21.09 *Entire Agreement*

The Agreement, together with other writings signed by the parties expressly stated to be supplemental hereto and together with any instruments to be executed and delivered pursuant to the Agreement, constitutes the entire agreement between the parties and supersedes all prior understandings and writings, and may be changed only by a writing signed by the parties hereto.

IN WITNESS WHEREOF, the parties hereto have caused the Agreement to be executed as of the day and year first written above.